BEING ENGLISH IN SCOTLAND

BEING ENGLISH IN SCOTLAND

Murray Watson

EDINBURGH UNIVERSITY PRESS

Edinburgh University Press Ltd
22 George Square, Edinburgh

Reprinted 2004

Typeset in Goudy Old Style
by TechBooks, and
printed and bound in Great Britain
by Antony Rowe Ltd, Chippenham

A CIP record for this book is available from the British Library

ISBN 0 7486 1859 7 (paperback)

Contents

Figures and tables   vii
Acknowledgements   ix

1. A gentle wooing   1

2. Exposing an inexplicable gap in modern Scottish history   7

3. Scotland's largest minority group   26

4. 'There are more people of English birth than ever before'   45

    Introducing the oral testimonies   62

5. Taking the High Road   64

6. Structural 'invisibility'   83

7. Fitting in – the process of integration   104

8. Anglophobia   126

9. Sport, politics and the influence of the media   146

10. National identities   164

11. Conclusion   186

    Bibliography   190
    Index   203

Figures and tables

FIGURES

3.1	English-born in Scotland 1901–2001	27
3.2	Proportion English and all other migrants 1951–2001	28
3.3	Settlement patterns of English-born migrants 1951–2001	29
3.4	Origins of migrants from England 1971	32
3.5	Age comparison 1951–2001	40
3.6	Gender balance English-born 1951–2001	41
6.1	Determinants of visibility	85
8.1	Anti-English Behavioural Continuum	140

TABLES

3.1	Comparison, Scots-born in England and English-born in Scotland	28
3.2	Proportions of English-born in selected urban areas 2001	30
3.3	Proportions of English-born in selected rural and peripheral areas 2001	31
3.4	English-born by Standard Industrial Classification (SIC) 1961	34
3.5	Highlights – English-born by selected and detailed SIC 1961	35
3.6	Selected industry sectors – proportion of English-born	35
3.7	English-born by industry group 1991	36
3.8	English-born by occupation 1961	37
3.9	SOC sub major groups – English-born 1991	38
3.10	Economic activity	38
3.11	Employees – sector of employment	39
4.1	References to English-born residents in population or demographic sections	47
4.2	Parishes or areas with mentions of marriage and settlement of English-born service personnel	49
4.3	Employment patterns of English-born migrants	51

5.1	Influences on migratory decision-making	65
6.1	Ethnic groups in Scotland 1991	86
6.2	Church adherence in Scotland 1950–94	87
7.1	Participation rates of Scots and English migrants in local organisations and activities	117
7.2	Estimated perception of perceived national identity of migrants' children	122
10.1	Guide to testimony topics surrounding national identity	168
10.2	Expressed feelings about national identity	173

Acknowledgements

This book owes an enormous debt to so many people. At the top of the list are all the oral testimony contributors and my academic supervisor, Billy Kenefick. I am also appreciative of the encouragement I have received from other members of the history department at Dundee. Other members of the academic community, too, have provided invaluable guidance. These include John Dewhurst who assisted with the rigorous structure of the oral history sample, James Williams who provided the stimulation and encouragement to apply Foucauldian methodology, Chris Smout and Sir Bernard Crick who provided comment beyond their role as oral testimony contributors, Alan Findlay for his insight into the methodological approaches of human geographers, and Neil Rafeek, Arthur McIvor, Callum Brown, Hugo Manson, Graeme Smith and Wendy Ball who all shared their knowledge of oral history techniques. Al Thomson, Murdo MacLeod and David Gowland also provided invaluable editorial comments. The fact that some three quarters of the people mentioned above are English-born migrants in Scotland has no bearing on the outcome of this study.

I also owe a debt to a number of librarians and archivists, all of whom have been unfailingly helpful and patient, at the Universities of Dundee, St Andrews, Strathclyde and Stirling, the National Library of Scotland, St Mary's Mill Archives in Selkirk, The Isle of Mull Museum Trust, the Hawick Library, and the Central Library in Inverness. The staff at the General Register Office (Scotland) at Ladymead House are deserving of special recognition for their unstinting help at the outset of this research.

Having constructed a rigorous quota sample from which to gather oral testimonies, the problem was to identify potential contributors who matched the criteria in the model. This involved a considerable amount of detective work, and in this respect I received invaluable help from: Ian Landles, Nan Lyle, Malcolm Murray, Stuart Kenner, Mairi MacArthur, Ani Lhamo, Revd Fiona Douglas, Michael Northcott, Terry Neal, Gavin MacDonald,

Pat Cairney, Sonya Marshall, Hugo Manson, Alistair Allan, Kaukab Stuart, Morris Yeaman, Sally Brook, Kudlip Samra, Bill Gilby, Graham Law, Chris Whatley, Pat Barrett, Pam Fargie, and the shepherd who provided directions in isolated Waternish, on the Isle of Skye. Once the recordings had been made, there followed the mind-numbingly tedious process of transcribing the testimonies. Here my wife, Maggie, put in hundreds of hours of listening, typing, checking, and then double-checking the difficult-to-interpret bits, again and again. Her patience and thoroughness were exemplary. Following transcription I was especially grateful to a number of people who went out of their way to help me verify the testimonies. These included: Kenneth Silver, Carol Riddell, Mairi Macarthur, Councillor Drew Tulley, and Brian Wilson MP.

The research for this book was self-financed, so the grants I received from the Royal Historical Society and the Checkland Memorial Fund were much appreciated. Finally, thanks must go to Ron Smith and Liz Drummond for their fastidious proof-reading of this text. Any mistakes in it are mine.

The author acknowledges the use of Census data, source: General Register Office of Scotland, and the use of extracts of oral history interviews from the Scottish Borders Memory Bank project.

CHAPTER I

A gentle wooing

Being English in Scotland ventures into new territory. While the relationship between England and Scotland has been one of the dominant themes in Scottish and British history, from Bannockburn to the establishment of a devolved Scottish Parliament, historians have ignored the fact that English migrants have been settling in Scotland, in ever-increasing numbers. This is an extraordinary paradox, especially as there has been a profusion of historical interest in other migrant groups, such as the Irish, East European Jews, Italians, Lithuanians, Asians and Poles.

The arrival of English-born migrants in Scotland has often generated impassioned and irrational reactions from the native community, as well as from the migrants themselves. The language used to describe these settlers has been on occasion intemperate, and, at times, insulting. Amongst a lexicon of epithets discovered by this research were: white settlers, interloupers, bonglies, guffies, cash crofters, '87 Crash refugees, Sassenachs, dropouts, and FEBs (Fucking English Bastards). A Scottish Executive Minister, Ross Finnie, even accused the London-based head of the Confederation of British Industry of being an 'English prat'.[1] This traffic in insults was not one-way. A guidebook to the Highlands describing Fasnakyle House said, 'the bonglies (white settlers) in residence have put up a sign on the lawn saying, "Trespassers will be whipped and sent to the colonies"'.[2] These examples epitomise a prevailing undercurrent of Scots feelings, which some have suggested largely resulted from living in the cultural, political and economic shadow of England, since the thirteenth century.[3]

The research carried out for this book proves that the English have formed the largest, and arguably the most important, migrant group in Scotland in modern times. Using a range of different sources, and rigorously gathered life history testimonies, this study explores how this group of English-born migrants merged into, and contributed to, Scottish society in the second half of the twentieth century. In so doing many of the myths surrounding the English in Scotland have been dispelled. What emerges is that the migratory experience was extremely complex and multi-faceted in nature. The near invisible absorption of so many English-born migrants had far-reaching implications for the host communities at a local, regional and national level, as well as influencing Scotland's economy, its population, culture and society. At a political and constitutional level, after a number of false starts, Scotland gained some measure of devolved autonomy, and here English migrants showed a range of fascinating responses in the reconstruction of their own identities.

As will be seen, the English, other than as an invading army, have been coming to live and work in Scotland since before the Treaty of Union in 1707. Numbers began to rise in the middle of the nineteenth century, and increased by a massive 84 per cent in the second half of the twentieth century – the period of this study. This demographic growth, and pervasive spread of English-born migrants throughout Scotland, is evident from one of the most reliable of sources, the Censuses of Scotland.[4] This growth will be outlined and analysed in Chapter 3. Census data, however, conceals a range of contentious issues, and goes only part of the way to explain the multi-faceted complexity of the process of migration, both for the migrants themselves and the host communities that they came to live in. To begin to understand the implications for English-born migrants in Scotland, and the impact they have had on Scottish society, its culture, economy and politics, the analysis starts with an exploration of related academic studies. Remarkably, the historical work is essentially superficial, and where there are observations these are frequently misleading and inaccurate. Fortunately, there is a wide range of studies from anthropologists, sociologists, human geographers, political scientists and other academic disciplines. This work, along with the historiography, such as it is, will be considered in Chapter 2.

What emerges from the scholarship of these social scientists is that migration is an extremely complex, and fragmented, lifetime process. This poses many problems for interpretation and understanding, a procedure that is further hampered by a paucity of source material. It has been said that studying migration is 'a little like doing an unfamiliar jigsaw in the dark.'[5] A further difficulty is that many of the terms used to describe the process of migration are contested. For instance, what is migration and what does being English mean? In this book the term migration is used to refer to the phenomenon of relocation from one permanent residence to another, which involves an event, 'the move', and a participant, 'the migrant'.[6] English refers to people born in England, but even this is problematic. Should it just refer to place of birth or should it incorporate how people perceive their feelings of national identity? One correspondent to *The Scotsman*, who was born in England of Scots-born parents, considered himself a full-blooded Scot. He ended his letter by saying, 'Not everything born in a stable is a horse'.[7] On practical grounds the definition used here is 'born in England'. Even the term Scotland is potentially contentious. Writing about the *Making of Scotland* it was suggested:

> Scotland is in fundamental ways not like most other societies. It is, of course, a geographical area, a territory, partly defined by its climate, topography and natural resources, as well as economic factors deriving from considerations of geographical location. On a different level Scotland is an administrative unit, a sphere of jurisdiction within which certain administrative structures operate, based on geographical definition. As such, Scotland can be considered as a governed system, and as such, becomes politically meaningful. Most obviously the remit of the Scottish Office [this was written in 1989] helps to define Scotland politically and sociologically. Thirdly, Scotland exists at an ideological level: in the minds of the people, reflecting in part the historical residue as an erstwhile nation-state until 1707. At this level, Scotland survives as a taken-for-granted reference insofar as aspects of its culture (tartan, speech, anthem, flag) reinforce the sense of nationhood.[8]

To begin to make any sense of the phenomenon of English migration to Scotland, academic rigour is critical, especially in a post-modern world where not one single variable, but many, assume primacy in shaping social, political and economic behaviour.[9] Methodological approaches, however, rarely make for riveting reading and this is available for those wishing to critically assess the basis of this study elsewhere.[10] But for now a few words of explanation are called for. Many different sources were used. These included the Censuses of Scotland, *The Third Statistical Account of Scotland*, articles in the press, media broadcasts, a wide range of secondary literature, other academic research and a collection of oral history life stories.

One of the great benefits for studies of contemporary history is that many of the actors involved are still alive, and for this reason this study gathered nearly one million words of testimony from a statistically rigorous quota sample of English-born migrants living all over Scotland. (These are referred to as 'contributors' in the text.)[11] The sample was structured upon a socio-demographic model based on census analysis. The recorded testimonies reflect the geographical spread of English migrants, gender balance, the types of job they did and the industries they worked in. This means that reasonably reliable conclusions and generalisations can be made. Oral testimony, however, is not without its critics in historical circles. There are justifiable fears about the reliability of memory, of personal bias of both interviewer and interviewee, and of the influence of collective and retrospective versions of the past.[12] Techniques adapted from other social science disciplines were applied to minimise these problems. These included the use of open-ended questions to ensure that the contributors were relating what they wanted to tell and not what they thought the interviewer wanted to hear. Indeed the first part of the recordings, sometimes lasting an hour, had no interruptions from the interviewer. Only then would there be questions looking for clarification and challenges seeking verification or explanations about omissions. What emerged was a mass of complex detail, very often containing contradictions. Interpretation involved a four-stage process: (i) distinguishing between first-hand and secondary knowledge; (ii) seeking internal consistency within individual testimonies; (iii) verifying content against other sources; and (iv) looking for recurring themes throughout all the testimonies. Finally, interpretation entailed applying approaches recommended by Michel Foucault, one of the twentieth century's foremost thinkers and philosophers. Foucault insisted on objectivity. He rejected historical methods, which tended towards explaining historical events in a linear or hierarchical way, because 'the world as we know [it] is a tangled profusion of events'.[13] For these reasons this study employed Foucault's genealogical approach, seeking the appearance of recurrences, regularities, proximities and symmetries.[14] While recognising that Foucauldian genealogy is not a master-schema it does allow us to arrive at a 'principle of intelligibility',[15] the purpose being to make sense of the inherent complexities built into the fragmented source data.

Because of the structure of the sample of oral history contributors, and the difficulties associated with memory, one of the problems arising from the oral testimonies was the relative lack of data about the post-war years. Fortunately, the *Third Statistical Accounts of Scotland* provided a wealth of information about English migration in the 1940s, 50s and 60s, although much of this was hidden. Chapter 4 explores the reports of ministers, and other writers, in parishes throughout Scotland. This provides a revealing insight into why the English came, how they fitted in (or not), and what impact they had at a local community level.

The remaining chapters concentrate on the oral testimonies of the English-born migrants themselves. Analysis is heavily influenced by what the contributors perceived to be important in their lives in Scotland, in both private and public spheres. In the approach adopted for the life history testimonies, it was the contributors who set the agenda, and it was the topics, themes, and issues that they raised that became the priorities for analysis and interpretation. Overall the contributors raised some seventy different topics, many of which were interrelated. Chapters 5 to 7 explore the reasons why the English chose to come to Scotland, why most of them stayed, and what role they played in their local communities, as well as in society at large. Motivational and behavioural patterns proved to be complex, and, as will be seen, the English tended to integrate into Scottish society in a way that contributed to their lack of visibility. This has been intriguingly described as 'the gentle wooing', as opposed to 'the rough wooing' at the hands of Henry VIII in the sixteenth century.[16] During the course of analysis, many previously held myths and stereotypes about the English in Scotland, such as the (Glasgow) *Herald's* view that Scotland was an essentially anti-English society,[17] were dispelled. Chapter 8 looks at the issues surrounding Anglophobia, before moving on (in Chapters 9 and 10) to examine the occasions when these migrants were conscious of their Englishness and, in most cases, their construction of forms of Scottish, or surrogate British, identities.

However one looks at it, the English have formed the most significant migrant community in Scotland in modern times, if not of all time. The implications of this phenomenon are little understood, and this is certainly the case in British historiography. It is this omission that this book seeks to remedy. And inevitably, being the first in the field, there will be as many questions as answers.

– NOTES –

1. Martin, 'Anti-Englishness a Myth Says Study', *Herald*, 4/9/02, p. 1.
2. *Guide to the River Affric*, web site accessed 9/12/02.
3. Hearn, (2000), *Claiming Scotland: National Identity and Liberal Culture*, pp. 4–11.
4. Source: General Register Office of Scotland.
5. Pooley and Whyte, (1991), *Migrants, Emigrants and Immigrants: A Social History of Migration*, p. 4.
6. Stillwell, Rees and Boden, (1992), *Migration Processes and Patterns Vol. II: Population Redistribution in the UK*, p. 15.
7. Gray, 'Scots Ancestry', *Scotsman*, 5/3/03.
8. McCrone, Kendrick and Straw, (1989), *The Making of Scotland: Nation, Culture and Social Change*, p. 5.
9. Knox, (1999), *Industrial Nation: Work, Culture and Society in Scotland 1800–Present*, p. 2.
10. Watson, (2003), *The Invisible Diaspora: The English in Scotland 1945–2000*, unpublished Ph.D. thesis, University of Dundee.
11. Details of the recordings can be found in the Bibliography. Because people do not speak in the same way they write text there are certain difficulties in transcription. The strategy adopted in this study was to adopt a policy of open punctuation and to incorporate personal speech idiosyncrasies. This makes some of the extracts difficult to read. In a few cases minor editorial adjustments have been made to facilitate reading. Every effort was made to avoid altering the contributors' meanings.
12. Thomson, Frisch and Hamilton, 'The Memory and History Debates: Some International Perspectives', *Oral History*, Autumn 1994, p. 34.

13. Foucault, 'Nietzsche, Genealogy, History', in Rabinow, (1991), *The Foucault Reader: An Introduction to Foucault's Thought*, p. 89.
14. See especially, Rabinow, (1991), *The Foucault Reader: An Introduction to Foucault's Thought*; Foucault, (1980), *Power Knowledge*; and Foucault, (1972), *The Archaeology of Knowledge and the Discourse of Language*.
15. Gordon, 'Afterword', in Foucault, (1980), *Power Knowledge*, pp. 242–3.
16. The concept of 'the gentle wooing' was introduced by Liz Drummond, a Scot who has spent most of her life living and working in London.
17. See Chapter 8.

CHAPTER 2

Exposing an inexplicable gap in modern Scottish history

George Orwell writing in his *Tribune* column shortly after the Second World War suggested:

> In some areas, at any rate, Scotland is almost an occupied country. You have an English or anglicised upper class and a Scottish working class which speaks with a markedly different accent, or even part of the time, in a different language.[1]

Some fifty years later Siol nan Gaidheal (Seed of the Gael), an extremist political group, painted a similar picture of English settlers in Scotland:

> It must be made clear at the outset that those being considered under the heading 'white settler' are primarily those English advancing into the rural areas. However, the related movements of English decision-makers into the commercial centres, of English administrators into every area of our national life, and of English students into our universities also form elements of the same overwhelming colonialist thrust, and demand our attention.[2]

The idea that Scotland was a colonial outpost of a putative English empire was also discussed and debated in the arts and literature. One of the most influential plays in the second half of the twentieth century was *The Cheviot, the Stag and the Black, Black Oil*. Ironically, the play was written by an Englishman – John McGrath. In addition to repeated television performances, the work was performed all over the world, and significantly, before more than 30,000 people during several tours of the Highlands.[3] The play, performed by the 7:84 Theatre Company,[4] was a socialist and nationalist commentary on absentee landownership and capitalist exploitation. Writing in 1973, McGrath said 'theatre can never *cause* social change' but it 'can be a way people can find their voice, their solidarity and their collective determination'.[5] The stereotypical English white settler was portrayed throughout the play with the chorus of one song complaining:

Because English is the language of the ruling class.
Because English is the language of the people who own the highlands and
control the highlands and invest in the highlands . . . [6]

Before the 1973 performance in Lochinver, McGrath criticised the audience
as being full of white settlers 'trying to stomach' the production.[7] This
was, perhaps, an over-reaction. One of this study's English-born oral history
contributors, Liz Potts, who saw the play in Dornie, recalled:

> Going to see the play was very good . . . It made fun of all the right things . . . I
> think it did strike a chord with people . . . it didn't make them raving nationalists
> but it made them think. I think it was very good.[8]

The presence of English settlers also featured in novels. One of the
most widely recognised examples of a new genre of late-twentieth-century
Scottish fiction was Irvine Welsh's *Trainspotting*. Early in the novel the hero
Renton pondered in a bar:

> Ah hate cunts like that . . . Cunts that are intae baseball-batting every fucker that's
> different, pakis, poofs, n what huv ye. Fuckin failures in a country ay failures. It's
> nae good blaming it oan the English for colonising us. Ah don't hate the English.
> They're just wankers. We are colonised by wankers. We can't even pick a decent,
> vibrant, healthy culture to be colonised by. No. We're ruled by effete arseholes.
> What does that make us? . . . The most wretched, servile, miserable, pathetic trash
> that was ever shat intae creation.[9]

This colourful observation provides a rich commentary on the relationships between England and Scotland, and the Scots and English people. It
identifies important issues and themes, such as ambivalent racist attitudes
towards the English, colonialism, and inferiorism – all matters that will be
considered in later chapters. The theme of subservience was also raised by
the narrator in Ralph Glasser's *Scenes from a Highland Life*. He saw incomers
as 'new style colonialists sustaining their superior life on the backs of the
"natives"'.[10] Resentment percolated throughout Glasser's writing:

> Incomers the word is revealing. We . . . are inside, where we were born and where
> we *belong*, inside the mountain wall, our life. *They* are from beyond, from that
> other world.[11]

These are all powerful, resonant images. So, was Scotland therefore a
country occupied by the English? It is generally accepted that one of the

best starting places to prove, or disprove, hypotheses of this nature is to consult the relevant academic literature. What did this have to say about English migration to Scotland, and did it corroborate the views of Orwell and Siol nan Gaidheal? This chapter assesses what the literature has to say. We start by looking at the writing of historians, before moving on to explore the work of social scientists. This is a revealing exercise, illuminated as much by what is not said as by what is said.

— HISTORIANS —

Arguably, the dominant theme in Scottish history is the relationship between England and Scotland. Historiographer Royal T. C. Smout observed: 'what every child knows about Scottish history may be boiled down to half a dozen "mythic" episodes... All key myths involve clash with England or "English" values.'[12] These 'episodes' were Bannockburn, Flodden, Mary Queen of Scots, Bonnie Prince Charlie, the Clearances and the 'tragic defeat by an Anglicised set of employers' on Red Clydeside. Another important theme was the impact migrant groups had on Scottish society, her culture and economy. In his influential work *The Scottish Nation 1700–2000*, Tom Devine devoted his longest chapter to what he called *The New Scots*.[13] There were sections on the Catholic Irish, the Protestant Irish, Lithuanians, Italians, and the Jews in Glasgow. The English got only a passing mention.[14] Devine was by no means the only historian to have ignored, or underestimated, the significance and scale of English migration. The same accusation can be laid at the door of nearly everyone who has written about Scottish and modern British history. Intriguingly many historians of Scotland, including the above-mentioned Historiographer Royal for Scotland, are English-born.

While this book concentrates on the latter half of the twentieth century, the period of most impact, the English had been arriving in Scotland for a long time before that. According to Michael Flinn, English migration to Scotland had been growing since 1841.[15] There is also evidence that the English had been coming since before the Treaty of Union. In 1681 the Edinburgh-based New Mills Cloth Manufactory was set up under the control of Sir James Stanfield, an Englishman from London. This was the first framework knitting company in Scotland, and it employed workers from Yorkshire and the West of England.[16] Christopher Whatley writing about skill shortages in the eighteenth century wrote:

> Attempts had been made before 1707 to entice skilled workers to Scotland from elsewhere, even though... the costs of this strategy were high... There were language clashes and culture clashes which discouraged foreigners from staying

long. Englishmen bore the brunt of this xenophobia. Thus while they were used by the partners at Carron [one of the early iron foundries] to get the works off the ground, care was taken to keep their numbers at a minimum and to return them south as soon as was expedient.[17]

This trend continued throughout the nineteenth century. A typical example, in the 1860s, was when hosiery workers from the Midlands of England came to work in the knitwear mills in Hawick.[18] It was around this time that English migration began to make an impact on the Scottish demographic map. By 1921 the English had overtaken the Irish as the largest migrant group in Scotland.[19] Between 1951 and 2001 the number of English-born residents in Scotland increased by a massive 84 per cent. In 2001, for example, 8.1 per cent of the population were English-born.[20] (More detailed evidence can be found in Chapter 3.) By comparison, the Irish, at their height, formed 7.2 per cent of the population in 1851.[21] Such direct comparability makes Devine's contention that 'The Catholic Irish have been Scotland's main immigrant group of modern times'[22] hard to justify.

Until now there have been no serious historical studies about English migration to Scotland. It would be misleading, however, to suggest that the topic of English migration is totally absent from the historiography. It does feature, albeit superficially, when the English are mentioned in passing. Frustratingly, on occasions, historians have made interesting observations, which are not followed through.

James Kellas recognised that since the First World War the English had 'overtaken the Irish as the most substantial minority in Scotland'.[23] And even though he concluded that 'intermixing of Scots and English through marriage [and] migration had profound effects in the history of Britain'[24], substantive analysis was not forthcoming. Rosalind Mitchison in her *History of Scotland* similarly recognised that in the twentieth century 'the mainstream [of migrants] became English'.[25] She referred to the impact of Irish migration, but all she had to say about the English was that as a result of their settling into small communities they were more conspicuous, and they were often resented.[26] Analysis in later chapters will show these conclusions are open to question. Demographer Michael Anderson, writing about 'Population and Family Life' between 1914 and 1990, concentrated on net emigration. He failed to consider English migration to Scotland, although he concluded that there 'was significant cross-border migration from northernmost counties of England'.[27] This, as will be seen in Chapter 3, was something of an exaggeration.

A common feature of infrequent references to English migration is that analysis, at best, fails to recognise the complexity of this issue or, at worst, is entirely inaccurate. In Rab Houston and Bill Knox's *New Penguin History of Scotland* there was only one mention of English migration – in the introduction. Here the author(s) oversimplified by suggesting that modern English settlers went to the Highlands,[28] where they 'seem determined to be more Scottish than the Scots'.[29] This directly contradicted Mitchison, who wrote that the English came to Scotland as foreigners and that they treated Scots as 'honorary Englishmen'.[30] In *No Gods and Precious Few Heroes*, Christopher Harvie indicated that there had been an 'upward blip' in population figures in the 1970s as a result of in-migration of white settlers, 'who exchanged expensive south-eastern property for its cheaper Scottish equivalent'.[31] Ewan Cameron also referred to white settlers being responsible for repopulation of the Highlands,[32] but as will be seen in Chapter 3 this was an oversimplification. Harvie went on to say that these white settlers contributed towards increasing the Liberal vote in the general election of 1992,[33] but provided no evidence to support this. Again with no supporting proof he wrote that Liberal activists 'in major towns outside Greenock and Paisley, tended to be disproportionately English, remote from the working class'.[34] Here the implication was that English-born migrants were largely middle class. This flies in the face of the facts, as the data in Chapter 3 will prove.

The term 'white settlers' was used from the 1960s by the media, academics, political activists, and the public at large to describe so called 'urban refugees'[35] who migrated from urban to remote rural areas and the islands. The term meant different things to different people, and was commonly used to describe English incomers, though this was not always the case. There is evidence in the *Third Statistical Accounts of Scotland*,[36] from oral testimony and elsewhere that migrants from the Central Belt were also referred to as 'white settlers'. According to Jane Allen and Elizabeth Mooney the terms 'incomer' and 'white settler' were abused by the two extremist organisations 'Settler Watch' and 'Scottish Watch' in the 1990s. The term 'incomer' was:

> imbued with ethnic connotations: 'incomer' has been interpreted as meaning English. The use of 'White Settler', in particular, conveys feelings of colonisation where local culture is interpreted as being usurped by a more dominant 'English' culture. Even when incomers are not regarded as synonymously English the term is worryingly ethnocentric and xenophobic.[37]

Some so-called white settlers did not share this interpretation. In oral testimony, Mary MacLeod, who came from Worcestershire, proudly described herself as Skye's 'first white settler', and Fiona Langford, the editor of *Am Mulleach*, observed that one English incomer in Craignure (on Mull) had called his yacht *The White Settler*.[38] The concept of 'white settlers' contributed to creating a stereotype of English migrants, but careful reading of the historiography demonstrates that the nature of English settlement was much more complex. Furthermore, analysis of census records shows that only a small proportion of English migrants could be described in this way. (See Chapter 3.)

A note of controversy surrounding one aspect of English migration was introduced by William Ferguson. He wrote about the threat of admitting increasing numbers of English students to Scottish universities, and the damage they might bring to the 'democratic' tradition of Scottish higher education.[39] This was a theme that was taken to polemical, and frequently unsubstantiated, lengths by A. L. Walker.[40] His was a work that continued the debate started by George Davie[41] with the publication of *The Democratic Intellect*[42] in 1961, and continued by Davie in 1986 with his *Crisis of Democratic Intellect*.[43] This was not only a debate conducted in scholarly volumes. It also took place in the press, making it even more puzzling that historians failed to study English migration. Walker cited numerous examples, and in a letter to *The Scotsman*, in 1974, an academic from Stirling University wrote:

> Academic jobs [in Scotland] are already scarce. In the coming economic blizzard they will become even scarcer. Products of the over-inflated graduate schools of Oxford and Cambridge are likely to compete for what is available in Scotland in large numbers and, given the current appointment criteria, they are bound to reinforce the already excessive grip of the English universities on the whole structure of Scottish life.[44]

There were also hints in the historiography that suggested that English migrants were active in Scottish politics, in all the main parties. Unfortunately, comment was infrequent, and there was no quantitative analysis. Harvie in *No Gods and Precious Few Heroes* stressed the role English white settlers had played in the Liberal Party.[45] In *Travelling Scot* he referred to English-born residents working for the Scottish Labour Party during the 1979 referendum 'Yes' campaign.[46] Jonathan Hearn wrote about Middlesex-born Jackie Wilkes who participated in the Calton Hill rally in 1992 to recall the Scottish Parliament.[47] Another oral history contributor, Malcolm Dickson, a political scientist, emphasised such concerns after thirteen years of Tory rule. Christopher Harvie put this more colourfully:

> After the [1987] election results were out the term 'bloody English' was on a lot of lips in Scotland... Thatcher seemed to be hated so intensely north of the Border because she personified every quality we had always disliked in the English: snobbery, bossiness, selfishness... and stupidity.[48]

Intriguingly, this anti-Thatcher feeling and political diversity appeared throughout the oral testimonies. Four of the oral history contributors were Members of the Scottish Parliament (MSPs),[49] one from each of the four major parties. Indeed, English-born migrants were well represented in the new parliament with sixteen of the first batch of MSPs declaring that they were born in England.

Historians commented extensively about political relations between England and Scotland, and here care needs to be taken to make a distinction between 'England' when it refers to the nation, or is used as a synonym for Britain, and 'English', when it refers to people or migrants. This distinction is critical, particularly when one reads *Britain's Secret War: Tartan Terrorism and the Anglo-American State*.[50] In this publication Macleay and Scott described seventy-nine bombing incidents and forty 'political' bank raids between 1968 and 1990,[51] frequently muddling the terms 'England' and 'English'. But this work was less than rigorous, largely because reliable information was hard to come by, not least because the authors were working in the dark and secret world of terrorism and the security services. An illustration of inaccuracy,[52] for example, could be seen in a report of the fire-bombing of a Galashiels mill, causing some £900,000 of damage in 1982. According to Macleay and Scott, this was one of six acts of war claimed by Firinn Albanach. Shortly afterwards, a disgruntled employee, who was annoyed at not receiving sick pay, was arrested and convicted,[53] but Macleay and Scott failed to acknowledge this, or the reasons behind the fire-bombing. It was alleged that the attack on the Laidlaw and Fairgrieve Mill in Galashiels in 1982 was the result of Scottish workers being laid off while English workers were kept on. The management were also described as 'English oppressors'.[54] However questionable Macleay and Scott's narrative accounts may be, there can be no doubt about the existence of terrorist activity in Scotland. But organisations such as the Army for Freeing Scotland, the Scottish Citizens' Army, the Scottish Republican Army, Arm nan Gaidheal, the Scottish National Liberation Army, and the Tartan Army, tended to direct their angst at 'symbols of English rule',[55] rather than English settlers in Scotland. Most of the attacks and hoaxes were carried out on political parties, politicians and military bases in both England and Scotland. Significantly there were no reports of fire-bombing English settlers' homes as happened in Wales, although one of the oral history contributors talked about being threatened with a letter bomb (see Chapter 9).

From Firinn Albanach's claims about English management oppression it would be reasonable to assume that English management and control of Scottish-based business might be commonplace, and that economic historians would have something to say about this form of 'surrogate migration'.

Again the historiography disappoints, being more interested in the growth of American and Japanese multinational enterprises. In a detailed study, based on research into the share ownership of major Scottish-based companies, Scott and Hughes traced a breakdown of Scottish ownership through local kin networks between 1904 and 1974.[56] They concluded that by the 1950s English and American ownership was becoming increasingly important.[57] In the 1970s, and here they were talking about the first four years, thirteen out of the fifty-five largest firms in the non-financial sector had been taken over by English capital. This meant that the English-owned sector of the 'branch plant economy' accounted for 40 per cent of employment.[58]

Structural change and de-industrialisation in the second half of the twentieth century attracted the attention of economists and economic historians. A number of studies were conducted by the likes of Firn, Payne, Boyle, Burns, Watts, Hood, Reeves and Young,[59] amongst others. They were generally concerned with explaining industrial decline, and a period of substantial change – 'moving from ships to [micro] chips'.[60] Looking at ownership and control, this body of work tended to concentrate on multinational enterprises, especially those with American and Japanese origins. In spite of this, the work did suggest the scale of English ownership was important. Peter Payne wrote: 'the majority of larger enterprises are now units of national or multinational groupings, controlled not from Glasgow, Motherwell and Hawick, but from London, Houston and Tokyo.[61]

Firn's work clearly demonstrated the importance of English participation in the Scottish economy. In 1973, his research sample showed that of '318 branch plants operating in Scotland no less than 184 had headquarters in England'.[62] Firn's findings were corroborated by the Scottish Trade Union Congress who reported in 1989 that 'the biggest area of control [was] that represented by British [English] firms and conglomerates from the City of London'.[63] Although these studies concentrated on the manufacturing sector it is clear that capital, personnel, and decision-making from south of the Border had an impact on the Scottish economy, as well as a direct influence on migration. Analysis of the *Third Statistical Accounts of Scotland* showed the impact that the arrival of English firms had upon local communities.[64] Oral testimony too emphasised the importance of work in deciding whether to migrate or not.

On Tuesday 31 August 1999, a *Guardian* headline, 'Bad vibes up north',[65] announced the publication of the first history book about the English in Scotland. *Notes from the North: Incorporating a Brief History of the Scots and the English*[66] was written by Emma Wood, a Cambridge history graduate, and self-confessed white settler. Wood had come to live in Scotland in 1987 because she was completely 'besotted' by the beauty of the Highlands.[67] Within a year of arriving in Sutherland, however:

> Tiny doubts about the rightness of my being in Scotland at all started whispering in my ear and they wouldn't go away. Perhaps these doubts began with an unexpectedly powerful sense of how foreign a country Scotland is. All those comfortable similarities to England, with language at the top of the list, suddenly seemed superficial in comparison to the many concrete differences.[68]

This curiosity produced her book. Essentially her thesis was that throughout history Scotland had been dominated by England, 'you know hundreds and hundreds of years being at the wrong end of the pineapple', and that 'there were so many reasons (for the Scots) to blame things on the English'.[69] History, in other words, had created conditions where there was 'widespread distrust of English motives'.[70] The book doubled as a guide, explaining the historical relationship between England and Scotland, to help English migrants assimilate into northern society, as well as providing a contemporary account of the lives of English settlers in the Highlands. The historical treatment traced key historical events, from the 'decidedly unsubtle Edward I'[71] to the Treaty of Union, Culloden and the Clearances. The narrative and analysis was essentially simplistic, but this was a 'guide book' for English settlers themselves, rather than professional historians.

Wood's most original contribution was her collection and analysis of oral history data from which she argued that anti-English feeling was commonplace in the Highlands. The majority of her sample of interviewees related stories of bullying, being excluded from social networks, and other forms of racial prejudice. There were no examples of violence cited. As Wood reported in *The Guardian*: 'Many English people are shocked to find themselves in the despised position normally accorded to historically less fortunate races'.[72] There were some English incomers, however, with 'credible claims'[73] never to have been troubled by anti-English behaviour. They included a district nurse, a dyker, and an English-born Church of Scotland minister. Wood's methodology, however, is open to question. There was no statistical analysis, or rigorous attempt to match her sample in sociodemographic terms to the English-born population as a whole. On her own admission the sample was 'heavily weighted in favour of the middle class'.[74] Furthermore, there must be question marks about her interviewing technique. There is evidence to suggest that her questions and attitude were judgemental, perhaps steering the interviewees to provide the answers they thought the interviewer wanted to hear. Wood admitted her questions were 'powered [by] my own *angst*'.[75] Furthermore, she saw this oral history project as: 'the chance of asking all sorts of people how they lived with the contemptuous appellation of white colonialism branded on their foreheads.'[76] With such an approach a likely outcome would be life stories of unhappy experiences. Unfortunately there are no archived transcripts or tapes to establish whether this was the case. There is one area, however, where there can be no disputing Wood's views. She said in oral testimony that the history of English people in Scotland had not received 'any academic treatment.'

— SOME NATIONALIST PERSPECTIVES —

The preceding analyses demonstrate the paucity of historical debate surrounding the issue of English migration to Scotland. Ironically, the most challenging historiographical work on English migration, and this was far from comprehensive, came from a political scientist, and an anthropologist, in two studies on nationalism and national identity. Eric Zuelow advanced a new theory of *radical-ressentiment nationalism* in which: 'large-scale immigrations tend to create resentment amongst the native population'. He argued: 'Without a previously existing and electorally successful *ressentiment* nationalism, this resentment simply becomes racism.'[77] The large-scale immigration referred to here was that of the English in the second half of the twentieth century. Zuelow's hypothesis is largely based on the activities of two groups, Settler Watch and Scottish Watch, and what he described as 'immense press coverage'.[78] These groups emerged after the Conservative election victory in 1992. A German-born Ph.D. student researching Scottish history, Sonja Vathjunker, who later changed her name to Sonja Cameron, led Aberdeen-based Settler Watch. Activities largely consisted of a series of public meetings, poster and graffiti campaigns, which were predominantly anti-English. The press capitalised on the German origins of Vathjunker, the *Sun* running a typical headline: 'Kick English out of Scotland campaign led by a German'.[79] Scottish Watch was based in Dumfries, and according to Zuelow was more anti-English. Scottish Watch only had about 250 members.[80] Their publicity material included the sentiment that Scotland had suffered a 'holocaust of centuries-long persecution',[81] at the hands of the English. The Nazi metaphor was continued with leader Donald Sutherland referring to English immigration into Scotland as 'the Final Solution to the Scottish Question'.[82]

Zuelow's hypothesis was essentially flawed. His figures on English migration were wrong, as was his interpretation of the socio-economic make-up of these migrants. For example, Zuelow specified that the intercensal increase of English-born, between 1971 and 1981, was 47,389.[83] Analysis of census data reveals that the figure was only 18,444.[84] In his analysis he got only one intercensal increase correct. More importantly, Zuelow argued that the English migrants were 'largely disaffected city dwellers' of a higher social class and were 'in control', and that this served to 'increase the feeling that Scotland was an internal colony of England'.[85] Again, analysis of census data proves that this was a profoundly inaccurate assessment (see Chapter 3). Zuelow based much of his argument on Diana Forsythe's study of Stormay (pseud.), an island in the Orkneys.[86] Not only was this unrepresentative, it provided a sample only of around 100 people. In responding to this criticism Zuelow incorrectly claimed Forsythe's work was the only major study available and, while recognising such a small sample was problematic, nationalist perception was what he was concerned about, and not reality.[87]

Here lies the dilemma in interpretation. Zuelow argued that the outcome of *radical-ressentiment nationalism* was racism. Was Scotland a racist and anti-English society? Judging from the activities of the 'Watch' groups this could be answered in the affirmative, and certainly the media, with frequent references to 'racism' and 'xenophobia', would support such a proposition. But what were the experiences of the English living in Scotland? The vast majority of this study's oral history contributors denied experiencing anti-English racism. Many of those living in Scotland during the nineties had not heard of the 'Watch' groups, although some noticed roadside anti-English graffiti. Two, Emma Wood and T. C. Smout, recalled public meetings in Dingwall[88] and Anstruther, in which local people crammed village halls to protest about Scottish Watch public meetings. Emma Wood recalled:

> The media of course was obsessed with these people [Scottish Watch and Settler Watch] . . . But when it came down to it, my own experience of that was when they decided to come and hold public meetings in Dingwall . . . and in fact people who turned up, not English people, Scottish people, who turned up to swamp the meeting just because of free speech and anti-racism, you know the whole thing was a shambles and came to nothing . . . they [Scottish Watch] were just overwhelmed by negative reaction and by anti-racist people who broke up the meeting.

The experiences in Dingwall and Anstruther, as well as those of the majority of oral history contributors, cast serious doubt on Zuelow's theory. His thesis, and especially his assertions about 'ethnic' nationalism and the inevitability of anti-English racism, must certainly be laid to rest when looking at the findings of the Commission for Racial Equality (CRE). In 1999, *The Guardian* reported that over the previous five years the CRE 'has received

22 complaints of anti-English racism, 5 per cent of its Scottish case load'.[89] Given that the English outnumbered all other migrant groups and ethnic minorities by a factor of two to one,[90] this was an insignificant number, questioning further Zuelow's theory of *radical-ressentiment nationalism* and its outcome of racism.

Anthropologist Jonathan Hearn recognised, from the outset, the difficulties involved in generating a comprehensive theory of nationalism, and saw it 'as a term best used to designate a complex and little understood web of social processes'.[91] His study *Claiming Scotland* is an eclectic collection of discourses, considering the dynamics of social organisation, the development of institutional forms, and the creation of linkages between Scottish history and the cultural construction of nationalism. Hearn found that English migrants held similar views to Scots on the egalitarian myths of history. This according to Hearn 'seemed to indicate a process of "going native" acquiring the perspective of one's adopted country'.[92] This was mirrored, to a degree, in the oral testimonies gathered for this study,[93] when contributors were seeking to explain their attitudes towards their feelings of Scottishness and Englishness, both in terms of internalisation and how they interacted with other people. Like Zuelow, Hearn saw the Scots living with a legacy of resentment, created as a result of being used to living in the cultural, linguistic and historical shadow of England.[94] He argued that identities were 'often constructed in opposition to a particularly significant other', and that in this context 'Englishness undoubtedly plays that role in relation to Scottishness, a role arising out of a long and complex history of rivalry and interdependence'.[95] The idea of the English or England as that 'significant other' is not unique to Hearn. Authorities like T. C. Smout,[96] and organisations such as Siol nan Gaidheal,[97] have used it in different ways to explain nationalism in Scotland. In the context of this research it is a useful tool to try to explain acculturation and assimilation of English-born migrants when *they* begin to see the English or England as the 'significant other'.

– SOCIAL SCIENTISTS –

English migration to Scotland attracted more attention from other academic disciplines, including geographers, economists, sociologists, anthropologists, ethnographers and political scientists. According to geographer Huw Jones, two factors were responsible for this interest: 'oil developments and peripheral counterurbanisation.'[98] There is an extensive literature on counterurbanisation featuring the role of English-born migrants. According to Diana Forsythe, from the 1970s peripheral rural areas encountered a new type of resident, 'urban refugees', who were disaffected with urban life.[99] Her study was limited to a small Orkney island, but other studies of Scotland emerged. Looking at long-distance migration to the Highlands and Islands, Jones, Ford, Caird and Berry described 'counter-urbanization' or 'population turnaround' as the 'net flow of migrants from major conurbations, primarily to their hinterlands but also to remoter, peripheral . . . rural regions'.[100] Jones et al. advanced two theories to explain this form of migration. The first was Fielding's Marxist explanation, where non-metropolitan areas experienced structural improvements and low wage levels that were attractive to employers. The second was Wardwell's model of rural-urban convergence, where city dwellers were prepared to exchange material wealth for a better quality of life.[101]

Short and Stockdale's study of six rural areas in the Highlands and Islands found that the dominant reason behind English-born migration was quality of life, of which the most important factors were access to scenic areas, low levels of crime and a good place to bring up children.[102] They also found that employment, housing and personal reasons were other influences behind the decision to migrate. Another study listed no less than seventeen separate forces responsible for the urban to rural shifts in population distributions.[103]

Many researchers commented on the socio-economic impact of counterurbanisation and the hostility it engendered. Shucksmith et al. argued that the English incomer had been the focus of all that was perceived to be wrong with rural communities, and had become the target for Settler Watch campaigns.[104] Related to this was the perception that the English were largely middle class, destroying local lifestyles and benefiting from moving from expensive housing areas, making it difficult for locals to afford housing.[105] Efforts to measure the impact of English counterurbanisation on the employment and housing markets were carried out in a number of small-scale studies.[106] Generally, survey results found that the English had a positive effect on the local economy, creating jobs and improving housing provision. Stockdale et al. concluded: 'in-migration to rural Scotland has brought numerous opportunities . . . rural job creation and net investment in the rural housing stock.'[107] Studies also showed that hostility towards the English, although it existed, was exaggerated. Jones found 'little evidence in our field areas that English in-migration has provoked cultural conflict'.[108] According to Lumb, when there were difficulties, especially in small communities, the personalities of those involved tended to be a critical factor.[109]

Interestingly, a number of studies found that in economic and social terms English and Scottish incomers were similar.[110] Furthermore, incomers from the Central Belt of Scotland were often 'incorrectly designated "English" by other rural residents'. Shucksmith et al. found that a North Ayrshire housing estate was allegedly 'full of The English', when it was predominantly occupied by lowland Scots. English was not a term exclusively used to refer to ethnicity, but also to middle-class ways of behaviour.[111] Anthropologists Jedrej and Nuttall in their important work on white settlers argued that, 'the vocabulary of "locals" and "incomers" is a complex and deeply embedded metaphor providing the terms through which people express and give meaning to the experiences which constitute their lives.'[112] Therefore:

> The use of the expression 'white settlers' to describe usurping incomers is also an ironic but pointed self reference by those who deliberately identify themselves not just as 'locals' but particularly as 'black natives', all of which is part of the imaging of a Scotland whose traditions are threatened by a colonial relationship to a metropolitan England.[113]

A further complicating factor was that after generations of depopulation, incomers to rural areas, regardless of their origins, tended to be as numerous as locals. In their 1989 study of Coigach, MacLeod and Payne recorded that there were only ten 'born and bred locals' compared to 156 incomers.[114] At the south end of Loch Awe, ethnographer J. B. Stephenson, in his study of Ford in 1981, found that most of the declining population were incomers, a number of whom were English.[115]

It is important to remember that studies about counterurbanisation failed to reflect the scale and heterogeneity of English migration. As will be seen in Chapter 3, the majority of English migrants settled in urban areas. While counterurbanisation was an important phenomenon it involved only a relatively small proportion of English migrants. It was widely written about, however, and it is surprising that historians failed to notice it. Jedrej and Nuttall referred to the process in terms of 'The Englishing' of Scotland.[116] Furthermore, they cited a 'vigorous public debate' in the Scottish media.[117] Their views were corroborated by David McCrone, who referred to this as a 'stushie' – the Scots for uproar or commotion.[118]

The discovery of oil in the North Sea brought significant social and economic change throughout northern Scotland, the Western Isles, Orkney, Shetland, and in particular the Grampian region. It also generated a significant output of sociological and economic research, 'largely driven by public policy issues'.[119] Studies ranged from the theory and practice of migrant workers, through industrial relations, to local authority accommodation of oil-related developments, and cultural change.[120]

While recognising the scale of inward migration and its social and economic impact on host communities, these studies paid little attention to the nationality, country of origin or place of birth of the new oil workers and managers. Only a few referred to the impact of English-born oil workers. In one, J. D. House observed that few locals had the skills for working in the oil industry, and that it was mainly the Americans who filled the top jobs and technical roles, with the English occupying middle management positions. The Scots tended to work in clerical, semiskilled and unskilled jobs.[121] Social class also featured as a variable, explaining relationships between migrant workers and locals. Judith Ennew pointed out, in her study about the impact of oil on Lewis, that the English were seen as middle class. Additionally, referring to SNP rhetoric about the English, she wrote: 'conceptually the English have become the middle class and the class struggle has been subverted by the nationalist struggle'.[122]

The concepts of social class and colonialisation were frequently used by social scientists to explain the phenomenon of migration to northern Scotland, whether it was oil-related or through counterurbanisation. In many cases the English were seen as middle-class colonisers by locals, and by some academics, like Beveridge and Turnbull.[123] This was a dangerously simplistic construction. As David McCrone observed: ' "English" is undoubtedly a shorthand for some complex and contradictory terms'.[124] McCrone went on to ask why nationality had been used to make sense of social change rather than say 'townspeople/rural dwellers, lowlanders/highlanders or working class/middle class?'[125] He responded as follows:

> The answer is that these social categories are probably included in the Scottish/English shorthand, but they are deemed of lesser significance. In other words we have decided to use one discourse rather than others which might do just as well as these explanations. We have chosen to use the language of ethnicity and nationality because that is especially salient in our current political and economic situation.[126]

What McCrone is saying here is that care needs to be taken when interpreting the terms 'English' and 'Scottish'. Similarly, caution needs to be applied when interpreting social scientists' findings about English-born migrants in Scotland. Their studies were largely rural-based, and are not representative of an essentially urban-based migration.

— Conclusion —

So what does this overview of the academic literature tell us? There is certainly insufficient empirical data to prove the colonising theories of Orwell, McGrath, Welsh, Glasser, and Siol nan Gaidheal. A number of social scientists hinted at a colonialist thrust from south of the Border, but the fact that their work tended to disregard mainstream English migration devalues these conclusions. When it comes to the work of historians, the current historiography almost totally ignores the topic of English migration to Scotland. When English migration is discussed, debate is superficial, and all too often misleading or inaccurate. Why historians, who constantly analyse the relationship between England and Scotland, have ignored Scotland's largest migrant group is a mystery. This book aims to fill this gap, by providing the first rigorous and historically meaningful study of the English diaspora in Scotland. This particular history is, after all, long overdue.

– NOTES –

1. Orwell and Angus, (1968), *The Collected Essays, Journalism and Letters of George Orwell, Vol. IV, In Front of Your Nose*, p. 285.
2. Siol nan Gaidheal, *Demography: The White Settler Phenomenon*, web site accessed 27/4/00.
3. McGrath, (1994), *The Cheviot, the Stag and the Black, Black Oil*, pp. vi and xxvii.
4. The 7:84 Theatre Company was so named following an article in the *Economist* that claimed 84 per cent of the wealth was owned by 7 per cent of the people.
5. McGrath, (1994), *The Cheviot*, p. xxvii.
6. Ibid., p. 52.
7. Ibid., p. xx.
8. Liz Potts is a pseudonym. Contributors to the oral history research are referred to by pseudonyms, unless they are public figures. Oral history contributors will not be cited each time they appear in the text unless it is not obvious they are oral history contributors. See Bibliography for details.
9. Welsh, (1994), *Trainspotting*, p. 78.
10. Glasser, (1981), *Scenes from a Highland Life*, p. 21.
11. Ibid., p. 13.
12. Smout, (1994), 'Perspectives on the Scottish Identity', p. 108.
13. Devine, (1999), *The Scottish Nation 1700–2000*, pp. 486–522.
14. Ibid., p. 486.
15. Flinn et al., (1977), *Scottish Population History from the 17th Century to 1930s*, p. 20.
16. Wells, (1972), *The British Hosiery and Knitwear Industry: Its History and Organisation*, pp. 24–5.
17. Whatley, (2000), *Scottish Society 1707–1830: Beyond Jacobitism Towards Industrialisation*, p. 81.
18. Bogle and Smith, (1998), *The Green Machine: 125 Years of Hawick Rugby*, p. 4.
19. Kenefick, 'Demography,' in Cooke et al., (1998), *Modern Scottish History 1707 to the Present Vol 2: The Modernisation of Scotland 1850 to the Present*, p. 115.
20. The Census of Scotland, 2001.
21. Devine, (1999), *The Scottish Nation*, p. 487.
22. Ibid., pp. 486–7.
23. Kellas, (1968), *Modern Scotland: The Nation Since 1870*, p. 23.
24. Ibid., p. 234.
25. Mitchison, (1993), *A History of Scotland: Second Edition*, p. 400.
26. Ibid., p. 424.
27. Anderson, (1992), 'Population and Family Life', p. 14.
28. In absolute and relative terms more English migrants settled elsewhere in Scotland. See Chapters 4 and 5.

29. Houston and Knox, (2001), *The New Penguin History of Scotland: From the Earliest Times to the Present Day*, p. xxv.
30. Mitchison, (1993), *A History of Scotland*, p. 424.
31. Harvie, (1993), *No Gods and Precious Few Heroes: Scotland Since 1914*, p. 167.
32. Cameron, 'The Scottish Highlands: From Congested Districts to Objective One', in Cooke et al., (1998), *Modern Scottish History 1707 to the Present Vol 2: The Modernisation of Scotland 1850 to the Present*, p. 154.
33. Harvie, (1993), *No Gods and Precious Few Heroes*, p. 171.
34. Ibid., p. 147.
35. Boyle, (1995), 'Modelling Population Movement into the Scottish Highlands and Islands from the Remainder of Britain, 1990–1991', p. 5.
36. See Chapter 4.
37. Allan and Mooney, 'Migration into Rural Communities: Questioning the Language of Counterurbanisation', in Boyle and Halfacree (eds), (1998), *Migration into Rural Areas: Theories and Issues*, chap. 15.
38. Langford, (2001), Oral Contributor.
39. Ferguson, (1994), *Scotland 1689 to Present*, p. 408.
40. Walker, (1994), *The Revival of the Democratic Intellect*.
41. Davie's work, which is altogether more scholarly than Walker's, was concerned with the Anglicisation of Scottish universities in terms of the undermining of the Scots geometrical tradition and that of generalist education and not with numbers of English students or academics.
42. Davie, (1961), *The Democratic Intellect*.
43. Davie, (1986), *The Crisis of the Democratic Intellect: The Problem of Generalism and Specialisation in Twentieth Century Scotland*.
44. *Scotsman*, 20/9/74.
45. Harvie, (1993), *No Gods*, p. 147.
46. Harvie, (1999), *Travelling Scot: Essays on the History, Politics and Future of the Scots*, p. 167.
47. Hearn, (2000), *Claiming Scotland*, pp. 31–2.
48. Harvie, (1999), *Travelling Scot*, p. 209.
49. Mary Mulligan MSP (Labour). Nick Johnston MSP (Conservative). Euan Robson MSP (LibDem.). Mike Russell MSP (SNP).
50. Scott and Macleay, (1990), *Britain's Secret War: Tartan Terrorism and the Anglo-American State*.
51. Ibid., p. 201.
52. Ibid., p. 113.
53. *Southern Reporter*, 27/1/83, p. 1 and p. 5; 3/2/83, p. 1; 24/2/83, p. 1; 3/3/83, p. 1; *Border Telegraph*, 25/1/83, p. 1; 1/3/83, p. 1.
54. Scott and Macleay, (1990), *Britain's Secret War*, p. 113.
55. Ibid., p. 201.
56. Scott and Hughes, (1980), *The Anatomy of Scottish Capital*.
57. Ibid., p. 136.
58. Ibid., pp. 189–200.
59. See: Firn, (1975), 'External Control and Regional Development: the Case of Scotland'; Payne, (1992), *Growth and Contraction: Scottish Industry c1860–1990*; Boyle et al., (1989), *Scotland's Economy: Claiming the Future*; Watts, (1981), *The Branch Plant Economy: A Study of External Control*; Hood et al., (1981), 'Foreign Direct Investment in Scotland: The European Dimension'.
60. Knox, (1999), *Industrial Nation: Work Culture and Society in Scotland, 1880–Present*, pp. 254–64.
61. Payne, (1992), *Growth and Contraction*, pp. 48–9.
62. Firn, (1975), 'External Control and Regional Development', p. 403.
63. Cited by: Boyle et al., (1989), *Scotland's Economy: Claiming the Future*, p. 15.

64. See Chapter 4.
65. Wood, (1999), 'Bad Vibes Up North', *Guardian Unlimited, Special Reports*, web site accessed 15/9/00.
66. Wood, (1998), *Notes from the North: Incorporating a Brief History of the Scots and English*.
67. Emma Wood, Tape MW0029, 20/6/01.
68. Wood, (1998), *Notes from the North*, p. 24.
69. Emma Wood, Tape MW0029, 20/6/01.
70. Wood, (1999), 'Bad Vibes Up North', p. 1.
71. Ibid., p. 1.
72. Ibid., p. 1.
73. Ibid., p. 2.
74. Wood, (1998), *Notes from the North*, p. 118.
75. Ibid., p. 116.
76. Ibid., p. 114.
77. Zuelow, (1995), *Nationalism in a Global Age: The Case for Scotland's Three Nationalisms*, web site accessed 1/3/01, p. 1.
78. Ibid., p. 9. Zuelow cited that 160 articles and letters appeared in *The Aberdeen Press and Journal* and that 52 articles appeared in *The Scotsman* on the topic of Settler Watch in the eleven months after May 1993.
79. *Sun*, 11/9/93, p. 1.
80. *Scotsman*, 13/10/95. Cited by Zuelow, *Nationalism in a Global Age*, p. 10.
81. Cited by Zuelow, (1995), *Nationalism in a Global Age*, p. 10.
82. Cited by Zuelow, (1995), *Nationalism in a Global Age*, p. 11.
83. Ibid., p. 5.
84. The Censuses of Scotland, 1971 and 1981. Also see Chapter 4.
85. Zuelow, (1995), *Nationalism in a Global Age*, p. 6.
86. Ibid., pp. 5–6.
87. Email correspondence between the author and Eric Zuelow in August 2001.
88. Emma Wood's testimony was confirmed by an article in the *Ross-shire Journal*, 'Stormy Passage for Scottish Watch at Dingwall Meeting', *Ross-shire Journal*, 8/4/94, p. 2.
89. Seenan, 'Attacks blamed on Scot's Racism', *Guardian Unlimited Special Reports*, 24/3/99, web site accessed 22/2/01.
90. The Census of Scotland, 1991.
91. Hearn, (2000), *Claiming Scotland*, p. 2.
92. Ibid., p. 153
93. See Chapter 10.
94. Hearn, (2000), *Claiming Scotland*, p. 3.
95. Ibid., p. 11.
96. Smout, (1994), 'Perspectives on the Scottish Identity', pp. 108–12.
97. Siol nan Gaidheal, *Devolution in Scotland and Nationalism in England*, web site accessed 3/4/01.
98. Jones, 'Migration Trends in Scotland: Central Losses and Peripheral Gains', in Stillwell, Rees and Boden (eds), (1992), *Migration: Processes and Patterns Vol. II: Population Redistribution in the UK*, p. 114.
99. Forsythe, (1980), 'Urban Incomers and Rural Change', pp. 287–307.
100. Jones et al., (1984) 'Counter-urbanization in Societal Context: Long-distance Migration to the Highlands and Islands of Scotland', pp. 437–44.
101. Ibid., pp. 437–8.
102. Short and Stockdale, (1999), 'English Migrants in the Scottish Countryside: Opportunities for Rural Scotland?', pp. 177–92.
103. Findlay et al., (2000), 'The Labour-market Impact of Migration to Rural Areas', p. 333.
104. Cited by Stockdale et al., (2000), 'The Repopulation of Rural Scotland: Opportunity and Threat', p. 245.

105. See, amongst others: Boyle, (1994), 'Modelling Population Movement into the Scottish Highlands and Islands', pp. 5–12; Shucksmith et al., (1996), *Rural Scotland Today: The Best of Both Worlds?*, p. 113; Short and Stockdale, *English Migrants in the Scottish Countryside*, pp. 177–92.

106. See, amongst others: Lumb, (1980), 'A Community-based Approach to the Analysis of Migration in the Highlands', pp. 611–27; Findlay, et al., (2000), 'The Labour-market Impact of Migration to Rural Areas', pp. 333–48; Shucksmith et al., (1996), *Rural Scotland Today*, chap. 6; Stockdale, et al., (2000), 'The Repopulation of Rural Scotland', pp. 243–57.

107. Stockdale et al., (2000), p. 255.

108. Jones et al., (1984), 'Counter-urbanization in Societal Context', p. 443.

109. Lumb, (1980), 'Integration and Immigration: Some Demographic Aspects of Highland Communities', p. 57.

110. See, amongst others: Short and Stockdale, (1999), 'English Migrants in the Scottish Countryside', p. 191; Dickson, (1994), 'Should Auld Acquaintance Be Forgot? A Comparison of the Scots and English in Scotland', pp. 112–34.

111. Shucksmith et al., (1996), *Rural Scotland Today*, p. 472–3.

112. Jedrej and Nuttall, (1995), 'Incomers and Locals: Metaphors and Reality in the Repopulation of Rural Scotland', p. 116.

113. Ibid., p. 118.

114. Macleod and Payne, (1994), ' "Locals" and "Incomers" ', in Baldwin (ed.), (1994), *Peoples and Settlement in North-West Ross*, p. 396.

115. Stephenson, (1984), *Ford: A Village in the West Highlands of Scotland*.

116. Jedrej and Nuttall, (1996), *White Settlers*, pp. 52–8.

117. Ibid., p. 3.

118. McCrone, (1994), 'Who Do We Think We Are?', p. 1.

119. Moore (ed.), (1980), *Labour Migration and Oil*, Introduction.

120. See amongst others, Moore (ed.), (1980), *Labour Migration and Oil*; Parsler and Shapiro (eds), (1980), *The Social Impact of Oil in Scotland: A Contribution to the Sociology of Oil*.

121. House, (1980), 'Oil Companies in Aberdeen', pp. 87–104.

122. Ennew, (1980), 'Gaelic as the Language of Industrial Relations', chap. 4.

123. Beveridge and Turnbull, (1989), *The Eclipse of Scottish Culture: Inferiorism and the Intellectuals*.

124. McCrone, (1994), 'Who Do We Think We Are?', p. 1.

125. Ibid., pp. 1–2.

126. Ibid., p. 2.

CHAPTER 3

Scotland's largest minority group

The clearest quantitative picture about the extent and nature of English migration into Scotland comes from the Censuses of Scotland. These provide a wealth of detail, telling us how many people came, when they came, where they came from, where they settled, what jobs they did and a lot more besides. The censuses are one of the most reliable sources of data, although some problems arise when studying migration.[1] There are two main difficulties. The first is that country of birth data, which permits identification of English-born residents, does not appear in all the data tables. Furthermore, census-by-census this critical variable often appears in different tables. This is related to the second difficulty where comparisons over time can be problematic; for example, census definitions of social class and occupational groups vary. In 1951, the variable of Socio Economic Group (SEG) was introduced. This was immediately changed in the next census. In 1991, this data was classified under Standard Occupational Classification (SOC) and in 2001 occupation was classified under the new SOC coding conventions, agreed in 2000. In spite of this, and provided reasonable care is taken in interpreting the data, a reasonably reliable demographic model can be created. This chapter will first consider the magnitude of English migration before moving on to explore patterns of regional settlement, socio-economic and occupational backgrounds, and, finally, age and gender distribution. This chapter inevitably contains a number of statistical tables and graphs. As such it is not necessarily the most absorbing of narratives. For readers who are averse to figures I hesitate before offering apologies as this is the only way to present some fascinating and revealing conclusions.

— Background trends —

What is clear is that the growth in the number of English-born residents accelerated throughout the twentieth century, with the exception of 1931 when it fell absolutely compared to 1921.

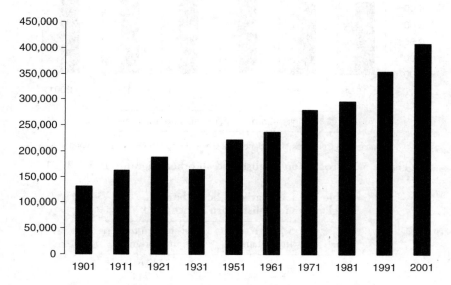

Source: The Censuses of Scotland. The General Register Office for Scotland. There was no census in 1941 because of the Second World War.

Figure 3.1 English-born in Scotland 1901–2001

The likely explanation for this fall was the general economic recession in Scotland in the 1920s and 1930s. Turning to the second half of the century, however, there was absolute growth in the number of English-born in each decade. There was an increase from 222,161 in 1951 to 408,948 in 2001, representing an overall growth of 84 per cent.

Looking at all of Scotland's migrant groups together, while growth of the English-born group was exceptional, in comparison with that of all other migrants, the proportion of all other migrants grew much more slowly. In the second half of the twentieth century, the English grew from almost equal numbers to nearly twice the size of all other groups.

There was one area where the English came lower down a notional league table of migrants (see table 3.1) and this is when they are compared with Scots migrating south of the Border.

Here we see there were usually around twice the number of Scots living in England than vice versa. Given that the English population base was

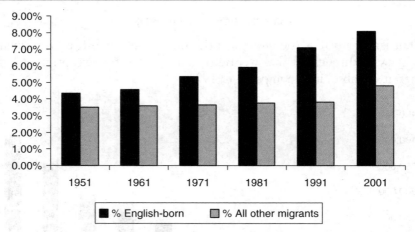

Figure 3.2 Proportion English and all other migrants 1951–2001

Table 3.1 Comparison, Scots-born in
England and English-born in Scotland

Year	Scots-born resident in England	English-born resident in Scotland
1951	565,828	222,161
1961	634,144	236,744
1971	755,790	279,340
1981	731,472	297,784
1991	743,856	354,268
2001	796,049	408,948

Source: The Censuses of England and Scotland.

around ten times the size of Scotland this meant that the population loss of
Scots to England was considerably greater than the loss of English people
to Scotland.

– REGIONAL VARIATION –

There are a number of myths and stereotypes surrounding English migration
to Scotland. Foremost of these were that the English were largely middle
class taking top jobs, or were mainly retired people exchanging more expensive property in the south east for a rural idyll in the Highlands or Islands.
The censuses provide the perfect test bed to establish whether this is fact
or misconception. Figure 3.3 demonstrates that the English settled all over
Scotland.

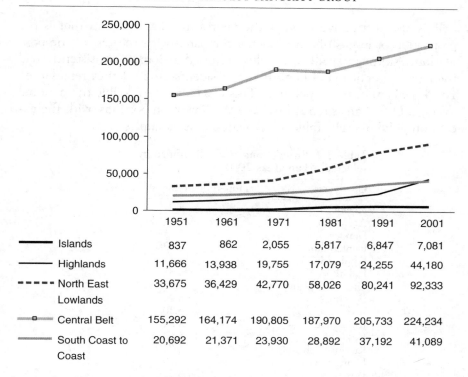

	1951	1961	1971	1981	1991	2001
Islands	837	862	2,055	5,817	6,847	7,081
Highlands	11,666	13,938	19,755	17,079	24,255	44,180
North East Lowlands	33,675	36,429	42,770	58,026	80,241	92,333
Central Belt	155,292	164,174	190,805	187,970	205,733	224,234
South Coast to Coast	20,692	21,371	23,930	28,892	37,192	41,089

Source: The Censuses of Scotland. The General Register Office for Scotland.

Figure 3.3 Settlement patterns of English-born migrants 1951–2001

Some caution is required when interpreting these figures as there are a number of inherent weaknesses, largely arising from differences in the way census data were presented.[2] For instance, some of the data does not differentiate between the mainland and some islands. Skye was incorporated in the Highlands, Mull in Argyll and Bute, and before 1981 the Western Isles, now Eilean Siar, was included in the Highlands. Taking appropriate care a number of reliable conclusions can be drawn.

The first stereotype to bite the dust is that the English were counter-urbanising 'white settlers'. Figure 3.3 clearly shows that the English settled all over Scotland and in absolute terms the vast majority lived in the urban Central Belt. It also shows that there was relatively consistent growth in all geographical areas. There is an optical illusion, however, in the graph. This arises because of the lower numbers of English in the Islands and Highlands. The figures show that the biggest proportional growth was in the Islands (by a factor of 8) and in the Highlands (by a factor of 4), compared to the Central Belt where the increase was less than a half.

It is also instructive to view the figures in relative terms, that is the proportion of English-born residents compared with the rest of the population. Although small in absolute terms the Borders consistently had the largest proportion of English-born residents. In 2001 they represented 16.84 per cent of the population. This was more than double the national average. Urban areas tended to have the lowest proportions, with the exception of Edinburgh. Table 3.2 provides some examples.

Table 3.2 Proportions of English-born in selected urban areas 2001

Urban area	Proportion of English-born %
Aberdeen	8.04
Ardrossan	3.77
Dundee	5.85
Dunfermline	9.00
Edinburgh	12.15
Falkirk	4.81
Greater Glasgow	3.83
Greenock	3.04
Inverness	8.30
Kilmarnock	4.31
Kirkcaldy	5.68
Kirkintilloch	4.74
Livingston	8.09
Paisley	3.50
Perth	7.84
Stirling	9.46

Source: The Census of Scotland 2001. The General Register Office for Scotland.
The national average was 8.08 per cent.

There was a different pattern in rural and peripheral areas where there tended to be greater concentrations of English-born residents. Arguably this created conditions where these migrants, or incomers, were more likely to stand out and where there was more potential for tensions to arise. This was covered briefly in the previous chapter and will be the subject of further analysis in later chapters. Table 3.3 provides some examples with larger than average English-born concentrations.

These figures appear to support counterurbanisation theories and when you drill down into census data to postcode level you find there are areas where there are greater concentrations of English-born residents; for example in 1991, in one postcode area on the south of Mull, English-born residents outnumbered Mulleachs and Scots.[3] It would be a mistake to conclude that these figures suggest that people were purely trying to escape the stresses and strains of urban life down south. For example, the large

Table 3.3 Proportions of English-born in selected rural and peripheral areas 2001

Rural/peripheral area	Proportion of English-born %
Aboyne	19.35
Aviemore	16.56
Banchory	19.22
Braco	21.75
Brodick	15.30
Chirnside	26.83
Coldingham	29.00
Drumnadrochit	22.76
Findhorn	34.92
Gatehouse of Fleet	21.40
Gretna	43.77
Kilcreggan	27.58
Kinloss	47.54
Portpatrick	21.54
Tobermory	23.06

Source: The Census of Scotland 2001. The General Register Office for Scotland.
The national average was 8.08 per cent.

percentage in Kinloss can be explained by the RAF station there, and two of the oral history contributors observed that Banchory had grown as a commuter town serving the North Sea oil industry.[4] Furthermore, as will be seen in Chapter 5, the motivations of migrants were more complex. The most important conclusion from this regional analysis is that migration affected the whole of Scotland and that it was predominantly urban-based.

Much of what is observed here suggests occupationally motivated migration. There appears to be a correlation between migratory volumes and the areas offering the greatest employment opportunities. Indeed, this hypothesis will be supported in the socio-economic and age group analyses. Further possible corroboration can be found from oral testimony: over half the contributors cited a job move as one of the main reasons for moving to Scotland. In most cases, however, there was a mix of factors influencing the decision to move north. This was not obvious from census analysis, and more detailed discussion about migratory motivation will be found in Chapter 5.

Turning to the origins of migrants, work from a number of studies has shown that the Irish, Lithuanians, Jews, Italians, and Asians tended to come from close-knit communities within relatively confined geographic areas. The English were different, although a number of assumptions need to be made when interpreting census data. In the censuses after 1971, where questions were asked about previous location of residence there were no published tables showing country of birth, and of course there will have been people of other nationalities, including returning Scots, moving from England to Scotland. Bashir Maan highlighted this complexity in his study of *The New Scots: The Story of Asians in Scotland*.[5] He reported that in the 1960s and 1970s, Asians who had originally emigrated to the textile districts of northern England moved on into Scotland, bringing with them English-born children of Asian origin. The censuses did not make this distinction.[6]

The 1971 census incorporated the most extensive questioning to date about migration, seeking data about places of residence one year and five years before census day. Unfortunately none of the published tables include place of birth data, making any investigation about English-born migrants difficult, if not impossible. There are numerous tables about migrants from England and Wales but as these will include returning Scots-born as well as migrants from all other countries, any interpretation is hazardous.

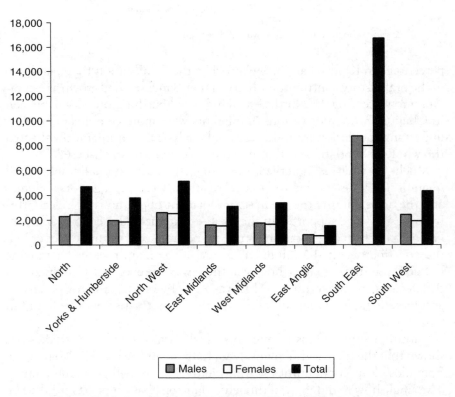

Source: The Census of Scotland 1971. The General Register Office for Scotland.

Figure 3.4 Origins of migrants from England 1971

There is one table, however, from which it is possible to draw reasonable conclusions.[7] This specifies the English area of origin of migrants from England. Although the table included migrants from all countries of birth, it is reasonable to assume that a significant proportion were English-born migrants.

This suggests that English-born migrants came from all over England. Erring on the side of caution, the preponderance of migrants from the south east reflects the demographic balance and the economic and political significance of the region. It is also well known that it was a magnet for Scottish migration to England, and, as such, return migration could be expected. Unfortunately this level of detail about the origins of English-born migrants is not available from earlier censuses. Looking at other factors, however, it would not be unreasonable to assume that English-born migrants came from all over England throughout the second half of the twentieth century. This conclusion is also supported by data gathered from the oral testimony and survey research, as well as research carried out by geographer Paul Boyle.[8] These studies provide further evidence to support the contention that the English differed from other migrant communities that tended to come from more tightly knit geographic areas.

— SOCIO-ECONOMIC AND OCCUPATIONAL BACKGROUNDS —

What did these English-born migrants, who came to live all over Scotland, do once they settled here? A common stereotype[9] of English migrants was of an essentially middle-class group, benefiting from house price differences between the south east of England and Scotland. The media, and groups such as Scottish Watch and Settler Watch, consistently painted this picture. Sandy Mathers described 'the movement of large numbers of English middle classes into Scotland' in terms of 'wealthy halfwits' and 'wealthy idlers' bringing a 'loadsamoney' culture.[10] Siol nan Gaidheal also propagandised that there was a colonialist conspiracy.[11] Unfortunately, the variables of socio-economic group, occupation and industry related to country of birth receive scant coverage in the published tables in the censuses. Data extracted from the 1961 and 1991 censuses makes it possible to assess both the industrial participation and occupational (putative class) structure of English-born residents. This comparison conveniently covers a time of distinct structural change in the Scottish economy and as such provides a revealing insight into the changing role played by English-born migrants. In 1961 Scotland's economy was still based in its industrial and manufacturing past, whereas in 1991 the branch plant economy and service industries had become established. The key question is: did this data reflect the commonly held stereotype, or show a different picture? The following analysis will first assess the sectors in which the English worked before looking at the types of jobs they did.

In 1961, when, unlike later in the twentieth century, there were still more people employed in manufacturing than service industries, the English showed a bias towards the service sector and the public sector. This can be seen in table 3.4.

Table 3.4 English-born by Standard Industrial Classification (SIC) 1961

Sector	Males	Females	TOTAL
Public administration and defence	13,260	1,230	14,490
Professional and scientific services	6,940	7,520	14,460
Distributive trades	6,420	5,360	11,780
Miscellaneous services	5,400	5,670	11,070
Transport and communication	6,160	780	6,940
Engineering and electrical goods	5,460	830	6,290
Construction	4,790	350	5,140
Agriculture, forestry, fishing	4,000	560	4,560
Textiles	1,740	1,480	3,220
Shipbuilding and marine engineering	2,770	90	2,860
Food, drink and tobacco	2,030	620	2,650
Insurance, banking and finance	1,530	580	2,110
Chemicals and allied industries	1,920	150	2,070
Paper, printing and publishing	1,580	430	2,010
Mining and quarrying	1,700	50	1,750
Metal manufacture	1,510	120	1,630
Gas, electricity and water	1,340	60	1,400
Vehicles	1,080	30	1,110
Other manufacturing industries	820	210	1,030
Clothing and footwear	330	540	870
Bricks, pottery, glass, cement, etc.	720	50	770
Timber, furniture, etc.	640	110	750
Metal goods n.e.s.[a]	620	120	740
Leather, leather goods and fur	100	60	160

Source: Census of Scotland 1961. The General Register Office for Scotland.
a. n.e.s. means not elsewhere specified.

More detailed analysis of these Standard Industrial Classifications shows which industry sectors were most heavily populated by English-born residents (see table 3.5).

Again this shows a public sector bias with national government service, educational services, medical and dental services, and local government services featuring strongly.

Another way of looking at these figures is to review sector-by-sector participation in relative terms. In 1961, the proportion of English-born amounted

Table 3.5 Highlights – English-born by selected and detailed SIC 1961

Sector	Males	Females	TOTAL
National government service	11,500	940	12,440
Retail distribution	4,080	4,640	8,720
Educational services	2,640	2,730	5,370
Medical and dental services	1,410	3,680	5,090
Catering, hotels, etc.	1,720	2,230	3,950
Agriculture and horticulture	3,030	500	3,530
Local government service	1,760	290	2,050
Wholesale distribution	1,480	490	1,970
Railways	1,830	70	1,900
Private domestic service	300	1,430	1,730
Motor repairers, distributors, garages and filling stations	1,210	270	1,480
Road passenger transport	1,000	190	1,190
Hairdressing and manicure	170	350	520

Source: Census of Scotland 1961. The General Register Office for Scotland.

to 4.57 per cent of the population. The sectors where there were proportionally the largest concentration of English-born workers were as follows:

Table 3.6 Selected industry sectors – proportion of English-born

Sector	Proportion of English-born %
Public administration and defence	11.98
Professional and scientific services	6.77
Chemicals and allied industries	5.85
Miscellaneous services	5.40
Other manufacturing industries	5.36
Insurance, banking and finance	4.98
Gas, electricity and water	4.69

Source: Census of Scotland 1961. The General Register Office for Scotland.

Thirty years later, in 1991, the census employed different methods for analysing industry groups, providing only ten categories for analysis.[12] This makes comparison difficult. At a broad level, however, it is possible to see some interesting changes. Reflecting shifts in employment patterns generally, there was a near threefold increase in the numbers of English-born females working. In 1961, they formed 27.04 per cent of the English-born working population. This increased to 40.03 per cent in 1991. A more detailed breakdown of the industry groups can be seen in table 3.7. Reflecting structural changes in the economy, between 1961 and 1991 there were distinct changes in the employment patterns of English-born residents. In

1961, 33 per cent were employed in all manufacturing sectors, but this had decreased to 21 per cent in 1991. Employment trends reversed in the service sector with the proportion increasing from 61 per cent in 1961 to 74 per cent in 1991. Going marginally against the national trend in 1961, 6 per cent were employed in agriculture, forestry, fishing and mining. This had increased to 9 per cent in 1991.

Table 3.7 English-born by industry group 1991

Sector	Males	Females	TOTAL
Agriculture, forestry and fishing	4,160	1,310	5,470
Energy and water	7,000	950	7,950
Mining	2,500	570	3,070
Manufacturing metal	9,470	1,990	11,460
Other manufacturing	6,910	4,080	10,990
Construction	7,720	1,060	8,780
Distribution and catering	15,950	17,830	33,780
Transport	7,630	1,680	9,310
Banking and finance	12,310	8,310	20,620
Other services	35,760	37,720	73,480

Source: Custom analysis from General Register Office for Scotland.

This leads logically to occupational status. A commonly held perception is that the English took only managerial or white-collar jobs. Looking first at 1961, a larger proportion of the English-born, compared with the rest, took white-collar jobs. The figures in table 3.8 show 47.57 per cent of the English-born were in non-manual occupations[13] (31.92 per cent for the population as whole). More significantly, what this also means is that more than half of English-born residents were in manual occupations at 52.43 per cent (68.08 per cent in the whole population). This certainly dispels the perception that English migrants were largely middle class, in 1961 at least.

The 1991 census painted a slightly different picture, and on a different canvas. The ever-changing nature of the employment market led the Registrar to use a different means of recording occupational status. In 1991, he used the Standard Occupational Classification (SOC) sub major groups means of measurement. This, along with the totals by gender, can be seen in table 3.9.

Compared with thirty years earlier, there was a significant shift of English-born residents towards non-manual occupations, in which some two-thirds of them worked – in 1961 under half were in non-manual jobs. This, in part, reflected structural changes in the economy. In 1961, 12.11 per cent were administrators and managers. This had increased to 19.81 per cent in 1991. These figures might give some credence to Siol nan Gaidheal's fears about the spread of English decision-makers and administrators, but

Table 3.8 English-born by occupation 1961

Occupational category	Males	Females	TOTAL
Farmers, foresters, fishermen	4,470	540	5,010
Miners and quarrymen	1,130	0	1,130
Gas, coke and chemicals makers	550	10	560
Glass and ceramics makers	250	30	280
Furnace, forge, foundry, rolling mill workers	410	30	440
Electrical and electronic workers	2,020	60	2,080
Engineering and allied trades workers n.e.s.[a]	7,790	350	8,140
Woodworkers	1,190	40	1,230
Leather workers	210	50	260
Textile workers	790	950	1,740
Clothing workers	250	870	1,120
Food, drink and tobacco workers	820	290	1,110
Paper and printing workers	690	190	880
Makers of other products	460	140	600
Construction workers	1,500	0	1,500
Painters and decorators	730	40	770
Drivers of stationary engines, cranes, etc.	920	0	920
Labourers n.e.s.[a]	3,530	80	3,610
Transport and communications workers	5,480	510	5,990
Warehousemen, storekeepers, packers, bottlers	1,840	640	2,480
Clerical workers	5,270	6,420	11,690
Sales workers	6,300	3,970	10,270
Service, sport and recreation workers	4,800	6,290	11,720
Administrators and managers	4,880	200	5,080
Professional, technical workers, artists	10,530	5,760	16,290
Armed forces	7,970	300	8,270
Inadequately described occupations	460	90	550
Total economically active	75,240	27,850	103,090
Total economically inactive (aged 15 and over)	12,830	74,390	87,220

Source: Census of Scotland 1961. The General Register Office for Scotland.
a. n.e.s. means not elsewhere specified.

the figures do show that, in 1961, every other English worker was employed in a manual occupation, and that in 1991, four out of five were employed in jobs that were not in management or administration. In a study carried out in 1993, political scientist Malcolm Dickson found similarities between English-born residents and Scots-born living in Scotland (see tables 3.10 and 3.11).

These figures show a diversity of activity, shared in similar proportions between the English and native-born population. In terms of employment and economic activity, the English were a heterogeneous group. This could go some way towards accounting for the invisibility of the English, especially when compared with other, and earlier, migrants, who tended to be homogeneous. The Irish and the Lithuanians were associated with manual

Table 3.9 SOC sub major groups – English-born 1991

SOC category	Males	Females	TOTAL
Corporate managers and administrators	16,760	5,460	22,220
Managers/proprietors in agriculture and services	8,770	5,640	14,410
Science and engineering professionals	8,680	940	9,620
Health professionals	1,940	1,430	3,370
Teaching professionals	6,250	5,530	11,780
Other professional occupations	4,210	2,190	6,400
Science and engineering associate professionals	4,340	980	5,320
Health associate professionals	840	6,390	7,230
Other associate professional occupations	6,480	3,870	10,350
Clerical occupations	4,790	10,120	14,910
Secretarial occupations	410	6,590	7,000
Skilled construction trades	2,070	60	2,130
Skilled engineering trades	5,340	140	5,480
Other skilled trades	6,490	1,680	8,170
Protective services occupations	9,280	890	10,170
Personal service occupations	3,640	8,650	12,290
Buyers, brokers and sales representatives	2,470	960	3,430
Other sales occupations	1,660	6,200	7,860
Industrial plant and machine operators, assemblers	5,420	1,700	7,120
Drivers and mobile machinery operators	4,260	190	4,450
Other occupations in agriculture, forestry and fishing	1,500	540	2,040
Other elementary occupations	3,920	5,200	9,120
Occupation not stated or inadequately described	1,650	830	2,480
TOTAL	111,170	76,180	187,350

Source: Custom analysis from General Register Office for Scotland.

Table 3.10 Economic activity

Status	English-born living in Scotland %	Scottish-born living in Scotland %
Self-employed	13.1	10.4
Full time	46.4	42.4
Part time	6.5	10.9
At home	5.4	6.7
Retired	14.9	14.3
Unemployed	4.8	6.0
Student	5.4	5.1
Unable to work	1.8	3.5
Other	1.8	0.8

Source: M. Dickson, 'Should Auld Acquaintance Be Forgot? A Comparison of the Scots and English in Scotland', *Scottish Affairs*, no. 7, Spring 1994, p. 118.

labour; early Indian migrants were, almost exclusively, itinerant pedlars, and the Italians, after selling figurines, were associated with ice cream and catering. Dickson's data also showed that the proportion of employees in 'influential positions is only marginally higher amongst English people than

Table 3.11 Employees – sector of employment

Sector	English-born living in Scotland %	Scottish-born living in Scotland %
Private	44.9	53.5
Education	15.7	11.8
Health	12.4	10.8
Social services	2.2	3.3
Civil service	5.6	4.6
Local government	9.0	8.1
Nationalised industry/public corps	3.4	4.6
Other	5.6	3.1

Source: M. Dickson, 'Should Auld Acquaintance Be Forgot?'

Scots'. With 31.5 per cent of the English in management, compared with 25.4 per cent of the Scots, this arguably dismisses the stereotype that the English held the 'top jobs'.

– Age and gender distribution –

Another stereotypical view of English migration was that it was dominated by retired people coming to Scotland for a better quality of life and cheaper housing. This perception was emphasised in the media and by writers like Emma Wood, a Yorkshire-born migrant living in Easter Ross. She referred to white settlers as 'grey settlers'.[14] Do the census data support this view? Again data are incomplete. There are only two published tables showing ages and England as the country of birth, in 1951 and 2001. The 1961 census showed ages but only for England and Wales as country of birth, but by calculating the English-born as 96 per cent of the total it is possible to make some comparisons.[15] Taking three age groups – young people, from birth to age nineteen; working age, from twenty to sixty-four; and old age, sixty-five and over[16] – one can see a number of differences between the English-born and the whole population, as illustrated in figure 3.5.

The first thing to be seen is that, proportionately, there were fewer young English-born than the population as a whole. Given the proportion of English-born in the working age, or child rearing, group, this is hardly surprising. People in this age group would have had children in Scotland and the children would have been recorded in the censuses as such. This explanation is confirmed by oral testimony and survey data. The largest proportion was in the working age category, where it was higher than that of the population as a whole. This is further evidence supporting the argument that economic and occupationally driven migration was an important motivation for coming to Scotland. The grey settler stereotype is finally

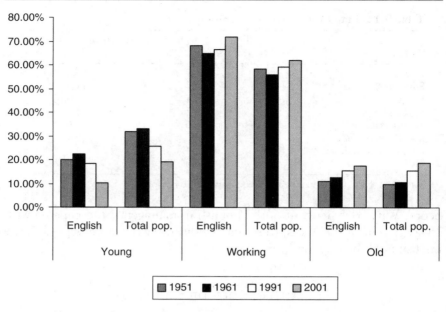

Source: Census of Scotland 1951, 1961, 1991 and 2001. The General Register Office for Scotland.

Figure 3.5 Age comparison 1951–2001

laid to rest when looking at the old age category, where the proportions of English-born and the rest of the population are much the same. Considering the age distribution overall, undoubtedly the most significant finding is that around two thirds of the English-born were in the working age category, compared with three fifths for the whole population.

One of the features of Scots migration to England was that males outnumbered females. This might suggest economic migration. In the case of English migration to Scotland were there similar patterns? By contrast there were always more English-born females than males living in Scotland, as can be seen in figure 3.6. This shows a gender balance proportionally in line with Scotland as a whole, as well as the country norm of more females than males. (In 1961 the proportion of females in Scotland stood at 51.99 per cent; in 1991 it was 52.14 per cent.[17]) Looking at migration, however, evidence generally suggests there are usually more male migrants than female, so in this respect the English-born in Scotland were unusual.

There were regional variations, however, where males outnumbered females, though only marginally. In the censuses of 1971, 1981 and 1991, English-born males outnumbered English-born females in Fife, Grampian, Orkney, Shetland and the Western Isles. Here job opportunities arising from

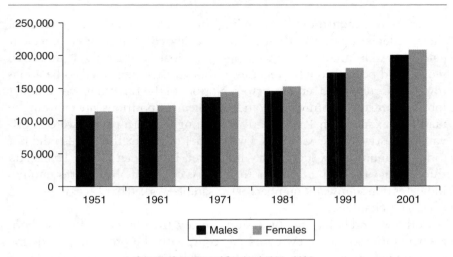

Source: Censuses of Scotland 1951– 2001.

Figure 3.6 Gender balance English-born 1951–2001

North Sea oil would have attracted males. In 1961, there were more English males than females in Angus, Caithness, Fife, Inverness, Moray, Ross and Cromarty, West Lothian, and Shetland. In 1971, there were more English males in the Highland and Lothian regions. The most likely explanation for these trends is a correlation with male employment opportunities, especially the pull of North Sea oil.

– CONCLUSION –

What does all this data tell us? Without doubt the English were the most significant group of migrants in this period. Their capacity to remain invisible from historical scrutiny is indeed a mystery. As noted in Chapter 2, however, other academic disciplines studied the English in Scotland. There is a wide collection of work from geographers, sociologists, anthropologists, ethnographers, and political scientists. These academics have tended to concentrate on the phenomena of counterurbanisation, and the migration of retired people to rural areas. There has been disproportionate attention drawn to these so-called 'white settlers', but, as this demographic analysis shows, 'white settlers', who often included ex-urban Scots in their number, represented only a small proportion of English-born residents in Scotland. There is perhaps less mystery surrounding the reasons why the English were invisible within society as a whole. The English did not arrive or migrate *en masse*. There was a steady growth over almost two centuries. Furthermore, this analysis demonstrates that the English were heterogeneous, in terms of their settlement patterns, their origins, and above all in their employment patterns. Additionally, there was wide participation throughout industrial sectors and occupational categories, although there appeared to be a bias toward the public and service sectors. Notions of the English in white-collar jobs, holding top administrative and management positions, are far from the mark; for example, in 1961, nearly 2,000 English-born people were in private domestic service. Compared with other migrants, the English did not form communities as such. They integrated into society at all levels and throughout Scotland. Furthermore, analysis of the life history testimonies indicates that significant numbers of the sample worked hard at assimilation. (See later chapters.)

In the second half of the twentieth century, the number of English-born residents in Scotland grew by 84 per cent, with the proportion doubling from around one in twenty-four of the population to one in twelve. These national figures mask significant regional variations, perhaps explaining the prevalence of studies on peripheral areas. In some pockets of the country, for instance in the Borders and Dumfries and Galloway, there were around twice the national average of English-born. Further north, analysis of the 1991 Samples of Anonymised Records showed that in one postcode area on Mull, around half of the population were English-born. The average proportion of English-born residents on Mull in 1991 was nearly one in four, compared to less than one in ten in 1961.

In developed economies with stagnant population growth, net migration tends to be a more important demographic factor than birth and death rates.[18] In Scotland there was generally positive net migration from English-born migrants, though the numbers (in the low thousands) had only a marginal impact. The main exception to this was in some rural and peripheral communities where population density was low, and where there had been a history of depopulation through out-migration. In these areas English-born migrants played an important role in restoring the demographic balance. Two examples were Mull – known locally as 'the Officers' Club'[19] – and Kincardineshire, where there were significant inward flows of English migration. Mull is a good example of counterurbanisation migration, while Kincardineshire is mixed, with a significant element of commuters settling in places such as Banchory and travelling to work in Aberdeen. There were net population gains of English-born residents throughout the country generally, with the exception of twelve areas in Strathclyde,[20] Dundee City, and Clackmannan, where there were small net losses of English-born during the period being reviewed. These losses mirrored population decline in these areas. The explanation, according to Huw Jones, was the depressed nature of the economy, especially in Strathclyde.[21]

A degree of caution needs to be applied when interpreting the census data. Information is comparatively restricted. There are limitations in data provision, as well as gaps that will require further research, and imaginative analysis of other source material. Notwithstanding, the censuses are an extremely valuable, reliable and relatively comprehensive source, one that allows us to gain a sound insight into the socio-demographic position of the English in Scotland. However one looks at it, the English diaspora is clearly under-researched. The English are evidently one of the most significant migrant communities in Scotland, without doubt the largest in modern times. As such, this is a migrant group that surely merits greater recognition in the Scottish history.

– NOTES –

1. For a detailed analysis and an explanation of methods to work round the problems, please see Watson, 'The English Diaspora: Discovering Scotland's Invisible Migrants – 1945 to 2000', *Scottish Economic and Social History*, vol. 22 (pt 1), 2002. This paper also fleshes out demographic detail contained in this chapter.
2. For a detailed analysis of the methodology applied here, please see Watson, (2003), *The Invisible Diaspora: The English in Scotland 1945–2000*, (unpublished Ph.D. thesis, University of Dundee).
3. Census of Great Britain 1991, Small Area and Local Based Statistics, Zone ID 6332BX, accessed through MIMAS database at the University of Manchester. The postcode area referred to was PA706.
4. Neil Bayfield and Ronnie Mitchell. Their observations were corroborated by the author's analysis of the censuses of Scotland.
5. Maan, (1992), *The New Scots: The Story of Asians in Scotland*, chap. 5.
6. In the 1991 census, in keeping with Maan's findings, data indicated that 3,993 of the English-born residents had ethnic origins from India, Pakistan and Bangladesh. Overall 1.77 per cent of English-born residents were non-white.
7. Census of Scotland, 1971, table 2, *Migration Tables*, 100%.
8. P. Boyle, 'Modelling Population Movement into the Scottish Highlands and Islands from the Remainder of Britain, 1990–1991', *Scottish Geographical Magazine*, vol. 111, no. 1, 1995, pp. 5–12.
9. Analysis of perceptions and concepts of national stereotypes is notoriously difficult and prone to subjectivity. However, work carried out by Budge and Urwin, (1966), *Scottish Political Behaviour: A Case Study in British Homogeneity*, pp. 120–5; and I. Lindsay, 'The Uses and Abuses of National Stereotypes', *Scottish Affairs*, 20, Summer 1997, pp. 133–48, provides sufficient evidence to justify this argument.
10. S. Mathers, *The Settler Problem; Cause & Effect*, web site accessed 29/1/02.
11. Siol nan Gaidheal, *Demography: The White Settler Phenomenon*, web site accessed 27/4/00. Also see Chapter 2.
12. These were: Agriculture, forestry & fishing; Energy & water; Mining; Manufacturing metal; Other manufacturing; Construction; Distribution & catering; Transport; Banking & finance; Other services.

13. This calculation does not take people employed in the armed forces into consideration.
14. Wood, *Notes from the North*, p. 142.
15. This is a reasonable calculation based on data from other tables.
16. Data extracted from the 2001 census is calculated on the basis that the young are aged between 0 and 15; the working age is from 16 to pensionable age, which was 60 for females and 65 for males. This has a knock-on effect for the old category. Overall these differences only have a marginal impact on the data presented and the conclusions we can draw.
17. The Censuses of Scotland, 1961 and 1991.
18. See Coleman and Salt, (1992), *The British Population: Patterns, Trends and Processes*, p. 10.
19. Finlay, (1987), *Mull the Isle of the Fairest*, p. 54. Campbell Finlay, himself a Scot, was a colonel. Research indicates that many of the colonels were also Scots, although the term was used to describe the Anglicisation of the island in the 1970s and 80s.
20. These were Bearsden and Milngavie, Clydebank, Cunninghame and Doon, Dumbarton, East Kilbride, Eastwood, Glasgow City, Inverclyde, Kilmarnock and Loudon, Lanark, Monklands, and Renfrew.
21. Jones, 'Migration Trends for Scotland: Central Losses and Peripheral Gains', in Stillwell, Rees, and Boden, (1992), *Migration: Processes and Patterns Vol. II: Population Redistribution in the UK*, p. 106.

CHAPTER 4

'There are more people of English birth than ever before'

In the last chapter the censuses provided a quantitative and statistical picture of the growth of English migration. It is now time to turn to the qualitative evidence. For the early post-war years one of the most comprehensive sources was *The Third Statistical Account of Scotland*. And, in spite of the designation 'statistical', the thirty-three volumes, covering every parish, burgh and city, are essentially qualitative and not quantitative. The Accounts followed a 200-year-old tradition. The first, or old, *Statistical Account of Scotland* was published between 1791 and 1799, and edited by Sir John Sinclair. The second, or *New Statistical Account of Scotland*, was mainly produced in the 1840s. The *Third Statistical Account of Scotland* was published between the 1950s and the 1980s. As with its predecessors, parish ministers and lay people were invited to produce essay-style accounts of their parishes. Under the guidance of editorial teams, which brought a degree of consistency, the writers were invited to follow a set approach and structure. They covered issues such as history, antiquities, famous people, population, geography, topography, climate, communications, public services, industry, commerce, religion, and the way of life.

Of real value to this study was the fact that the *Third Statistical Account of Scotland* was created primarily as a contemporary historical record. It is comprehensive both in its geographical coverage and in covering a wide range of themes and issues deemed to be important at the time. It is, however, partial. The authors are mostly male and Presbyterian, so potential for bias must be borne in mind, especially when reviewing comments about relationships between incomers and resident Scots. It is also true to say that the reportage and analyses are mainly qualitative, and fall short of more modern social scientific precision. This is largely a function of the background of the authors, and the period in which the Accounts were written. Because of this, they provide a valuable insight into contemporary perceptions. The material contained in *The Third Statistical Account* was produced between

1950 and the early 1980s. Some of the earlier material was written before the publication of the 1951 census results. Of these Accounts, most were revised up to ten years later. The majority were written in the 1950s and, looking specifically at references to English-born residents, it is interesting to note changes in attitudes, and observations, apparent in the later Accounts.

Analysis of the thirty-three volumes throws up five distinct themes. These are: (i) population change; (ii) the marriage of service personnel; (iii) industry and employment-pull factors; (iv) the case of language and the English; and (v) attitudes towards the English. The last two distinctions overlap and will be analysed as one coherent theme. Each of these main factors will now be covered in turn.

— POPULATION CHANGE —

The most common place where English-born residents were mentioned was in the sections devoted to population. References tended to be to numbers of English-born residents in each parish (see table 4.1). Some of this data was extracted from the census tables, while other Accounts clearly rely on local knowledge and observation.

There was wide variation in the way this population data was presented. Some Accounts gave precise figures, like the one from Gairloch, where it was noted: 'of a total of 1,884...44 are English'.[1] In the introduction to the Argyll volume the editor wrote: 'Of the immigrants furth [outside] of Scotland the English-born recorded a substantial rise between 1931 and 1951 (1,752 or 2.9 per cent in 1931; 2,859 or 4.4 per cent in 1951).'[2] The Account for the County of Perth and Kinross clearly indicates the scale of English-born residents: 'In 1961 nearly 10,000 people had come to Perthshire from the rest of the British Isles, chiefly England'.[3] The description 'nearly 10,000' is not precise. But it is more precise than many of the Accounts, which, like the one for Glassford in Lanarkshire, provided no quantitative material whatsoever. This was clear in the observations of The Revd Donald MacDonald, who wrote: 'Living in the parish are some of English or Dominion extraction and there is also the inevitable leavening of the Irish'.[4] This could have meant either a large proportion or a small proportion of his parishioners were English-born. In this case it matters little to this analysis. What it does show, along with all the other references in table 4.1, is that there existed a substantial body of evidence, albeit difficult to find, that suggested the English were a significant migrant community in Scotland. This corroborates the earlier census analysis.

Furthermore, in relative terms compared with other migrant communities, the censuses also demonstrated that the English were the dominant

Table 4.1 References to English-born residents in population or demographic sections

Area or parish	Area or parish	Area or parish
Outskerries	Harray	Stronsay
Kildonan	Tongue	Gairloch
Kilmore	Kilchoman	Marnoch
Duffus	Inverness and Brora	Kilmorack
Abernelty	Kilmonivaig	Strath
Coull	Forfar	Alloa
Menstrie	Saltoun	Ratho
Newbattle	Cockpen	Stirling
Baldernock	Dunipace	Lanark
Cambuslang	Glassford	East Kilbride
Carnwath	Dunsyre	Dolphinton
Pettinain	Biggar	Dunbartonshire
Luss	Garelochhead	Renfrew
Greenock	Port Glasgow	Neilston
Paisley	West Kilbride	Fife
Perth	Dall	Weem
Alyth	Rattray	Kilspindie
Methven	Crieff	Fowlis Wester
Glendevon	Strowan	Aberfoyle
Dunblane	Kinross	Eyemouth
Newlands	West Linton	Selkirk
Minto	Yetholm	Morebattle
Roxburgh	Anworth	Kirkbean
Wigtown	Stranraer	Dumfries
Mouswald	Lockerbie	St Mungo
Aberdeen	Edinburgh	Glasgow

Source: The Third Statistical Account of Scotland.

group. In the Statistical Accounts reference was made to migrants from other countries, especially Ireland. And in the Accounts written shortly after the Second World War, there were occasional references to Polish soldiers, displaced persons, and former prisoners of war. Even so, the most common references were about the English. Many of these observations, in the population sections of the Accounts, contained explanations about the causes of migration, as well as other comments about the English. These, in combination with references in other sections, provide invaluable insight into contemporary perception. It is to these that we now turn.

— SERVICE PERSONNEL AND MARRIAGE —

One of the most regular references was to migration through marriage of service personnel. This involved both Scots servicemen returning with English brides and Scots girls marrying locally billeted English servicemen. To a lesser extent English female service personnel married local husbands, as well as Scots female service personnel bringing back Englishmen. Unfortunately there are no quantitative records.[5] In terms of service personnel marriages, the impact of the Second World War and its legacy in the post-war years cannot be underestimated. Sue Bruley, in her work on *Women in Britain since 1900*, concluded:

> Never before or since has British society been so massively affected by warfare. The enormous mobilization of resources, scale of government intervention and the extent of civilian involvement made this even more of a 'total war' than the First World War.[6]

This level of dislocation was reported in a number of Accounts. According to M. C. Arnott, in Wigtonshire alone, 'one million men passed through Stranraer camps'.[7] After commenting on the attractions of Stranraer girls, Arnott wrote: 'After the war a proportion of the erstwhile sailors, soldiers and airmen who had left their wives in Stranraer returned to take up residence in the town'. Further up the coast, E. L. Menzies recalled that 'The Second World War made the greatest changes in modern times as servicemen from all parts of Great Britain were stationed in Tobermory and chose to make it their home when they were demobilised'.[8] And according to former BBC newsreader Richard Baker, between 1940 and 1945 Tobermory Bay was the scene of intensive naval training involving some 200,000 men.[9]

This level of disruption, and mobility, undoubtedly created opportunities to find marriage partners. In addition, moral standards changed significantly during the war. This helped to create a climate that led to more marriages. According to John Costello, 'sex and sexuality in all its guises and complexities played an extensive role in the war experience'. By way of explanation[10] Costello cited Sigmund Freud, from *Reflections on War and Death* (1917), when he wrote, 'the connection between violence and eroticism was evident in the tendency of society in wartime to throw off repressions which civilisation has imposed on the human sex drive'.[11] Explanations of this nature are, however, not forthcoming in the clerically dominated Statistical Accounts. Nonetheless, the change in sexual *mores*, and a climate in which members of the ATS attracted the disparaging epithet 'Officers' Groundsheets', or where members of the WAAF were referred to as 'Pilots' Cockpits',[12] possibly provided an environment encouraging marriage among service personnel.

The impact of service marriages continued in the post-war years. Conscription and national service moved Scots to England and English people to Scotland until the early 1960s. The Account for Inverness, written in 1951 and revised in 1970, commented that 'as a centre for military training... some of the military personnel have stayed on and made their homes here on being discharged'.[13] Furthermore, changing military strategies created new bases, such as the expansion of the RAF airfield at Kinloss. This ensured the continued flow of service personnel north of the Border. Corroborative evidence can be found from analysis of census data in 1951 and 1961, which confirms the presence of English-born people, predominantly males, in areas where there were military bases. In this respect, in the introduction to the *1951 Birthplaces Volume of the Census of Scotland*, the Registrar General considered it important enough to write: 'Outside the southern counties [of Scotland] the percentage [of English-born] was highest... where service personnel in considerable numbers were stationed and enumerated – many of whom were English-born'.[14] Table 4.2 clearly shows that migration through military marriage was experienced across the length and breadth of Scotland.

Table 4.2 Parishes or areas with mentions of marriage and settlement of English-born service personnel

County	Parish
Orkney	Sanday
Sutherland	Kildonan
Moray and Nairn	Duffus
Inverness-shire	Inverness and Brora
Argyllshire	Tobermory
Angus	Forfar
Perth and Kinross	Kilspindie
Perth and Kinross	Kinross
Renfrewshire	Paisley
Ayrshire	West Kilbride
Lanarkshire	Coatbridge
Lanarkshire	Cambuslang
Kirkcudbright and Wigtown	Wigtown
Kirkcudbright and Wigtown	Stranraer
Dumfriesshire	Langholm
Peebles and Selkirkshire	West Linton

Source: The Third Statistical Account of Scotland.

There is further corroborative evidence that marriages of English-born service personnel took place in locations not recorded in the Statistical Accounts. Oral testimony revealed that from a battalion of (c. 500) Royal Marines based at Stobs camp near Hawick in Roxburghshire in 1941, some 30 English-born troops married local girls. The majority of these returned to Hawick after the war and two were known to be still living there in 2000.[15]

Returning to the Statistical Accounts, author after author implied that this type of marriage, and the presence of English troops, had an impact on local communities, especially small ones. John Mackay writing about the Orkney island of Sanday observed:

> Generally speaking, relationships between troops and the isle folks were excellent and one or two of the officers married girls belonging to Sanday. The servicemen who got on best with the islanders were those who were most sympathetic to the classless structure of Sanday society and who did not try to impress people with their own sense of importance.[16]

In Forfar, The Revd D. M. Bell and W. S. McCulloch noted that this type of marriage 'led to an infusion of blood in this somewhat close knit community',[17] while in West Linton the minister claimed that it was the 'widely known charm'[18] of the place that attracted English service personnel.

It was not only English service personnel who contributed to the phenomenon of military or wartime marriages. In Kilspindie there was mention of English migration as a result of marriages to Landgirls.[19] In West Kilbride, the Account acknowledged that other types of 'war influences' brought English people north through marriage:

> A valuable element in the village is the group of English families who came from the south to work in the ICI [explosives] or the services or to escape the bombing and have remained. They take their share of work in the Masonic lodges and on the committees of the bowling and golf clubs and one has become secretary of the recently formed Burns Club. On the Parent–Teacher Association, they help to temper the Scottish ideas about education, with the freer and more social English attitude.[20]

The Statistical Accounts give other examples of marriage bringing English-born migrants north. This is illustrated in Abernelty and Kincardine[21] where English servants on sporting estates married local people. The editor of the Edinburgh volume commented that: 'in recent years [the late 1940s and early 1950s] there has been intermarrying between Edinburgh people and European immigrants and naturally between the Scots and the English'.[22] Further along the coast, in oral history research amongst residents in Eyemouth, Netta Rae, a schoolteacher, commented that Eyemouth fishermen going down to Lowestoft in Suffolk for the herring often netted English brides[23] as well as their usual catch.

— INDUSTRY AND EMPLOYMENT-PULL FACTORS —

The war, its aftermath and the effect of marriage clearly brought migrants north, but there were other influences too. Another, identified in the Statistical Accounts, was industry-specific employment-pull. There are a number of references to English-born migrants filling roles requiring specialist skills and expertise. This can be seen in table 4.3.

Table 4.3 Employment patterns of English-born migrants

Employment field	Area
Oil	Shetland
Doctors	Sanday
Nurses	Sanday
Maids on sporting estates	Abernelty
British Aluminium Company	Fort William
Hydroelectricity	Kilmonivaig
Forestry	Kilmonivaig
Atomic energy	Reay
Business	Aberdeen
Civil Service	Aberdeen
Cotton finishing and silk printing	Dunblane
Sporting industry	Dall
New industries	Lanarkshire
Male mental nurses	Carnwath
Research	East Kilbride
Planners and civil servants	East Kilbride
Woollen mills	Alloa
Distillers Company	Menstrie
Rolls-Royce	Paisley
BEA Maintenance	Renfrew
ICI	West Kilbride
Dockwork	Dunfermline
Professionals	St Mungo
Nationalised industries	Stewartry
New industries	Edinburgh
Academics	Edinburgh

Source: The Third Statistical Account of Scotland.

The Statistical Accounts do not provide a comprehensive or quantitative picture of employment and English-born migrants. Nonetheless, table 4.3 clearly demonstrates the diversity and geographical dispersal of employment attracting English people. Although there were only twenty-six references it would not be unreasonable to assume that this pattern was spread throughout Scotland. Analysis of the 1961 census confirms this (see Chapter 3).

Turning again to the Statistical Accounts, a common outcome of English employment, judging from the authors' comments, was a tendency for these newcomers to have a significant impact on local economies and communities. This is most evident in the western Central Belt, and certain peripheral areas. G. Thomson, in his introduction to the Lanarkshire volume, explained there were two causes for the increase in English migration: 'Scots servicemen bringing home English brides and English firms sending skilled workers to occupy key positions in branch factories in the new industrial estates'.[24] Rolls-Royce, for example, brought technologists to Paisley,[25] and in nearby Renfrew the relocation of 'the British European Airways depot to Renfrew from Liverpool' led to some migration there in 1949.[26] Perhaps the most surprising observation came from C. F. Hoy writing about East Kilbride:

> The New Town Project has provided many opportunities for local people; but, for the vast amount of building and other constructional work, large numbers of workers travel daily from other areas. The directive staff and technical planners were almost all appointed from beyond the parish, many of them from England and are now part of the permanent population. This was also true of other staffs of the research establishments, so that the New Town had at first a substantial English community. Indeed of the new families settled by 1952, one-fifth were from across the border... But by 1958 the English community numbered only 4 per cent of the population.[27]

Peripheral areas, too, experienced the impact of the employment-driven English migration: Fort William with its bauxite plant,[28] nearby Kilmonivaig with hydroelectricity and forestry,[29] oil in Shetland,[30] and nuclear energy at Dounreay[31] and Thurso.[32] The arrival of oil and nuclear power in small, close-knit communities had a major impact with extensive reportage from different authors. This will be covered in more detail below. One of the difficulties in using the Statistical Accounts, however, is that they were written over a thirty-year period. For instance, the Aberdeenshire Account was written more than twenty years before the North Sea oil boom, the only reference: 'through the ramifications of business and the civil service there are more people of English birth than ever before'.[33] By comparison, the Account for neighbouring Kincardine was written in the 1980s. It talks about an accelerated rate of change brought about by the North Sea oil boom: 'House prices have risen sharply and are in line with Aberdeen's and are now amongst the highest in the country'.[34] There was no mention of the English in the Kincardine volume. Interestingly, data from the censuses, covering the period of the North Sea oil boom, indicates that the number of English-born residents in Kincardineshire increased from 880 in 1951 to 7,772 in 1991.[35]

A common thread was the pull that industrial and economic development created for specialist skills, not available locally or elsewhere in Scotland. There are frequent references to professionals, technologists, administrators, specialist workers, researchers, academics, and so on. Another factor that had an impact was the growth and development of English-owned companies. We have seen how BEA, ICI, Rolls-Royce, the British Aluminium Co., as well as the new industries in Lanarkshire and around Edinburgh, brought workers north. Evidently, relocation or expansion of English companies brought English staff and management to Scotland. Analysis of the industry and commerce sections in the Statistical Accounts should have provided confirmatory evidence. There were, however, very few references to location of ownership and/or country of birth of workers. Exceptionally, in the account for Inverness, Dixons, the postcard manufacturer from the Isle of Wight, and the Leicestershire engineering firm of Partridge, Wilson & Co., were attributed with bringing English migrants with them.[36] Undoubtedly, English-owned companies would have been a source of migration. There is evidence in the Statistical Accounts, but this is scant.

One interesting group of observations concerns earlier [pre-1945] migration and the relatively seamless integration of English workers. Christopher Whatley, in his work on Scottish society, outlined the tradition of English workers coming north throughout the previous three hundred years.[37] The Statistical Accounts provide further evidence. The Revd I. S. C. Knox from Menstrie, in Clackmannanshire, wrote about how the English had integrated into the community:

> In this village a large proportion of the people are descended from local stock, for, while old families with their complicated relationships, make up the core of inhabitants, to these have been added several families of English origin. During the nineteenth century many workers in wood came from England in connection with the 'charrier' and settled where their work was.[38]

In Renfrewshire we learn that Lancastrian workers arrived in Neilston in the nineteenth century, when an English firm took over Orr's Thread Mill. Apparently, many families 'are still traceable by their family names, for example Hodgson, Haydock and Eckersley'.[39] One of the most eloquent accounts was from Coatbridge. The minister, the Revd W. Hamilton, referred to the sometimes troublesome integration of the English, mentioning both long-term employment-pull and service personnel marriages:

The iron trade was comparatively new to Scotland [eighteenth and nineteenth centuries] and therefore help had to be sought from England . . . The workers, who came principally from Staffordshire, did not at first commend themselves. Miller [in the *Second Statistical Account of Scotland*] says 'The majority were very illiterate, purse-proud and arrogant, quarrelsome and overbearing'. But they soon settled down, and, on the whole, made a valuable contribution to the growth of the new community. The houses that had to be built for them were much more commodious than those occupied by other working folk, and their dwellings 'were often patterns of cleanliness and order'. The origins of a number of prominent families in Coatbridge lie over the Border . . . The fellowship of war [Second World War] had permanent results on the life of the town. Many soldiers married Coatbridge girls, just as many Coatbridge men married girls in England and elsewhere. Generally it is girls from other quarters who have come with their husbands to make their homes in the town, though not a few strangers who married Coatbridge girls have also settled in Coatbridge. Some indication of possible transfer of population through this marriage exchange can be given by one side of the story, the marriages in Coatbridge in the years 1940–46. In that period 2,607 marriages took place in Coatbridge and of these 359 or 13.8 per cent had one or other of the contracting parties furth of [outside] Scotland. [A table shows 230 English males and 20 English females].[40]

To readers in the early years of the twenty-first century, the language of the last extract, and indeed the language of many of the Accounts, is obviously from a different era. What can the use of language tell us about contemporary attitudes?

LANGUAGE AND MEANING AND ATTITUDES TOWARDS THE ENGLISH

The English are described or referred to in the Statistical Accounts in a variety of ways. The terms used include migrants, immigrants, incomers, people from over the Border, newcomers, contingent, strangers, influx of, invasion of, Atomics (workers at Dounreay), interloupers, Sassenachs, and white settlers. Analysis of these terms can tell us something about attitudes towards the English, at least from the perspective of the writer. Analysis shows a range from the non-judgemental and neutral to prejudiced and hostile. For instance, The Revd J. C. Steen referred to the 'slow infiltration' of English into Lockerbie before expressing his fears about possible transformation into an English town:

While a good part of the population comes from all over Scotland, especially Ayrshire, the strange feature of this century has been the slow infiltration of

English into the town, their numbers now go into the hundreds [the population, according to Steen, at the time of writing in 1951, was 3,376], and in time Lockerbie may become a town more English than Scottish.[41]

In the majority of the Accounts, most of the terms used to describe the English are neutral and objectively descriptive. The few authors using the terms 'influx of' and 'invasion of' could be accused of some form of anti-English bias, but careful examination of the texts discounts such an interpretation. The terms 'white settlers' and 'interloupers', however, could reflect negative attitudes. 'Interlouper' is used once, in the Eyemouth account. 'Loup' or 'lowp' is an Orkney or Shetland verb, meaning dance or jump.[42] Orkney and Shetland are a long way physically and linguistically from Eyemouth, although there is likely to have been contact between fishing communities. Local residents have not been able to explain the meaning of the term, but one English-born resident, living in the Borders, saw the word 'interlouper' as 'interloper', and therefore a derogatory term.[43] Coincidentally, the term 'ferry louper' was used to describe incomers to the Western Isles during the war, although this term was not used in the Statistical Accounts. The Eyemouth Account was less circumspect. Migrants came from:

The north east of England and to a lesser extent from the West of Scotland. The latter tend to be retired people who spent holidays in Eyemouth in the pre and post war periods. At times a minority may express some antipathy towards the incomers or 'interloupers'.[44]

The term 'white settlers' is more widely used. The Sutherland parish reports included frequent references: 'Assynt has become more cosmopolitan over the past thirty years...The term "white settler" is used without rancour.'[45] In Kinlochbervie: 'Perhaps a decade ago, the phrase [white settler] was used by a vociferous few, but it is not part of the current parlance. People from all over have integrated into this society. The people here are not xenophobic'.[46] In Tongue it was reported:

Roughly 50 per cent are incomers, described by some locally as 'white settlers'. Their presence is regarded with mixed feelings, while Scottish Highland people are shy in coming forward, the Sassenach being of a more outgoing nature is inclined to 'take over' and attempts to enforce his or her preferences on the local population. Our way of life was attractive to them until they came to live here, then some endeavour to convert us to theirs.[47]

The term 'white settler' was used only in the Sutherland Accounts, and significantly these were written in the 1980s. Other peripheral rural areas that experienced population growth from counterurban migration, namely Orkney, Shetland, Ross and Cromarty, Argyll and Bute, had no references to 'white settlers' in their Accounts. Significantly all these accounts were written in the 1950s. This tends to suggest that the phrase 'white settler' became a term of abuse/description only from the 1970s. The Statistical Accounts provide no clue as to the precise origins of the term 'white settler', only a suggestion as to the timing of its introduction into the language. One of the oral history contributors[48] suggested that it was the invention of the editor of the *West Highland Free Press*, Brian Wilson. Wilson was approached in 2001, when he was Minister of State for Industry and Energy, to see if he would confirm this attribution. He replied:

> I can assure you that I do not have the dubious honour of having introduced the phrase 'white settler' in a Scottish context. Indeed, I have never liked, or I hope, used the phrase – wittingly or unwittingly – it often carries a racist connotation. The first time I was aware of the term was in the early days of the *West Highland Free Press* when there was a campaign in Skye against a particularly obnoxious landlord ... At one point, there was a demonstration against his activities and I recall the posters carried references to him as a 'white settler'.[49]

The term 'white settler' has been, and is still, used in the press and broadcast media to mean 'English'. This is also the case in some of the Accounts, but it was used also to describe incomers from elsewhere in Scotland, as well as from England. This is entirely consistent with the conclusions of anthropologists Jedrej and Nuttall in their study of rural repopulation in Scotland.[50]

Another linguistic theme identifying English-born migrants was the issue of accents and dialect, as well as the demise of Gaelic. In the Account for the Shetland parish of Detling, the authors observed that: 'Local children surrounded by mainland accents [not only English] are tending to lose the dialect'.[51] In Duffus, in Moray and Nairn, it was not uncommon to hear a Cockney accent.[52] Similarly, Cockney accents were heard in Forfar,[53] and Hampshire ones in Menstrie.[54] In Thurso, with its proximity to the Dounreay Atomic Energy plant, a wide variety of accents were noted 'to mix happily with the Caithness dialect'.[55] In the north, north west and in the islands there was widespread comment about the decline of Gaelic. Typical of the comments was the one from the Small Isles parish:

> The children tend to drop Gaelic as soon as they go to school. One reason may be that some of the pupils are 'incomers' from the English-speaking mainland and, as it appears to be easier for Gaelic-speaking children to pick up English than for English to learn Gaelic, English soon becomes the language of the playground.

Another reason why children drop their native tongue is that it is not the every day language of their teacher.[56]

The decline of Gaelic is attributed to the use of English, as practised throughout Scotland. English-born residents were not singled out as those responsible. The reasons tend to be attributed to general Anglicisation and the use of English in schools and on radio and television. Radio and television were also accused of contributing to the decline of local dialects in Orkney. Professor Miller, in his introduction, commented: 'This invasion [of English and Welsh population] together with radio, and to a far greater extent television, has greatly eroded the Orkney form of speech which was current in the 1950s'.[57] In a later study of Stormay (pseud.), an Orkney island, Diana Forsythe found the playground had a surprising impact on attitudes to accent and dialect: 'Because of the preponderance of English children at the school, some of the Stormay children no longer sound Orcadian at all; they sound English. This apparently was a sore point with some Orcadian parents.'[58]

Accent, according to sociologist David McCrone[59] and author George Orwell,[60] was a differentiator of class, as well as contributing towards the confusion of associating English-born residents with the middle class. The Statistical Accounts, generally, do not provide evidence to support these theories. There is one interesting exception from Muckairn in Argyllshire. The 'Way of Life' section describes the two main social groups in the district:

> There are two main social groups in the district. The very small landowning or 'county' group, comprising those of independent means, is largely Conservative in politics; to it belong the dozen or so Episcopalians among us. This group, English in origin and identifiable by a distinctive cultured English accent largely consists of incomers, though some of them having settled here for a generation or two, are accepted as an integral and influential part of the community. The other main group, including artisans, crofters, tradesmen and labourers, tends to be Labour or Socialist in sympathy... This group, though mainly indigenous, also has some incomers, mostly from other parts of the Highlands and Islands. The one group is never set against the other; politics and class do not obtrude themselves in the inter-relations of daily life.[61]

This extract says as much about attitudes as it does about relationships between social class and language.

Descriptions and comments about attitudes between resident Scots and English incomers occur throughout the Accounts. This can be seen from extracts already shown in this chapter. There are other Accounts which provide insights into attitudes, as well as information about the impact of English-born residents in local communities. Kenneth Silver, an English-born teacher in Jedburgh, wrote about the English in the introduction to the Roxburghshire volume: 'through their quite disproportional representation on local committees of voluntary and charitable organisations, many such "incomers" contribute valuably to community life'.[62] This type of observation mirrors those, as previously illustrated, from the parishes of West Kilbride[63] and Tongue.[64] It also corroborates the findings of a number of the social science studies discussed in Chapter 2. There was a hint of resentment in Silver's account, but he recognised a valuable contribution, unlike that in Tongue where the Sassenach was recorded as inclined to 'take over' and enforce his or her preferences on the local population.[65] There was clear resentment in other Accounts, as seen in Orkney, where incomers seemed to threaten old customs and conventions:

> The traditional ways of life, too, have changed and have become distinctly less Orcadian in all sorts of ways. For example, a time was when Orcadians kept a small boat so that they could go to the cuithes [young coalfish] with a view to supplementing their diet: now racing dinghies and yachts are more characteristic.[66]

John Drever wrote similarly about Sanday: 'Englishmen who talked arrogantly of ignorant country people, and who tried to impress the local farmers with their superior wisdom did not enjoy their exile on this island but fortunately this type was rare'.[67] Diana Forsythe confirmed the existence of these attitudes. In her long-term study she found that in Stormay (pseud.) there was conflict in the selection of officers for local clubs and organisations, especially over the more assertive styles of the incomers. There was much resentment in evidence in a very politicised campaign to remove the head of a hostel on mainland Orkney. One local was to comment: 'When they come here they think us delightfully old-fashioned, but no sooner are they established than they want everything that is part of the rat race'.[68] Meanwhile, a few miles across the Pentland Firth, social upheaval was predicted, and planned for. The Account for the Parish of Reay, the home of Dounreay Nuclear Power Station, outlined, at length, how the local community prepared for the 'invasion' of incomers – including technologists, scientists and managers from England. D. M. Carmichael recounted how good two-way communication and planning by the 'Authority' were 'the readily discernable factors which contributed to the smooth and rapid expansion of the community'. The success of this process is perhaps best summed up by the choice of section headings by the author. After sections on 'Nuclear Fission' and 'Nuclear Propulsion' there is a section on 'Social Fusion'[69] – the text does not allude to explosive relationships!

In some places, it was the different values of the incomers that caused difficulties for the locals. In Lochbroom the minister was worried about the decline in churchgoing: 'There is no doubt that their [incomers, some of whom would have been Scots] influence has been harmful to the local community, most of whom have been brought up to go to church'.[70] While along the coast at Gairloch:

> Suspicion of the incomer and his motives are natural enough. There is, however, abundant sign that most locals welcome the infusion of new blood and ideas, while quietly and politely declining any values considered inappropriate to their way of life.[71]

In many respects these views on Gairloch provided a representative summary of most writers' attitudes to English migrants throughout Scotland. Similar sentiments were expressed in the Account for Town and Kirk Yetholm, at the other end of the country, where incomers were mostly from the north east of England. Here this attitude was somewhat differently expressed: '[They] tend to make a sense of community interdependence harder to focus, but on the other hand it undoubtedly brings a width of experience and ability, which can lead to a richness of community experience'.[72]

– CONCLUSION –

While the Accounts do illustrate differences between locals and incomers, in the main there is a relative absence of comment about social tensions between English-born residents and local Scots. Most of the observations about language and attitudes are found in rural and peripheral parishes. This is not altogether surprising. In these types of community newcomers tend to stand out. In urban areas, by comparison, unless they are concentrated geographically in communities, like the Jews in the Gorbals (Glasgow), or the Irish in Lochee (Dundee), they are less likely to stand out. When the English are referred to in the urban Accounts it tends to be in relation to industry or employment. Interestingly in the Edinburgh volume there are sections on the French, Norwegians, Americans, Danes, Italians, Poles, Ukrainians, Belgians, Dutch, Swedes, Finns, Icelanders, Spaniards, Portuguese, Austrians, Swiss, Hungarians, Germans, Greeks, Nigerians, Indians, and Pakistanis – but no section on the English!

So what can we have gained from this analysis? Clearly the censuses and the *Third Statistical Account of Scotland* are distinctly different types of source.

The censuses provide a rigorous, quantitative snapshot of the population every tenth year. They cover a wide range of demographic variables, but the relative scarcity of published 'country of birth tables' restricts analysis of English-born residents. *The Third Statistical Accounts*, to a degree, help to fill these gaps. They are quantitatively less rigorous, but, being mainly qualitative, provide a different perspective. They are particularly useful for the immediate post-war years, although it should be recognised that collectively they were written and published over a thirty-year time span. Bearing this in mind, they do indicate the significance of service personnel marriages, the impact of specialist employment-pull, and how language and attitudes towards the English tend to generate, and project, a picture that is one of quiet integration, and a largely unobtrusive process of assimilation. What is evident is that the observation in the 1960 Aberdeenshire Account that 'there are more people of English birth than ever before' applied throughout Scotland.

– NOTES –

1. Mather (ed.), (1987), *The Third Statistical Account of Scotland* [hereafter referred to as S.A.], *Ross and Cromarty*, p. 307.
2. MacDonald (ed.), (1961), S.A., *Argyll*, p. 81.
3. Taylor (ed.), (1979), S.A., *Perth and Kinross*, p. 29.
4. Thomson (ed.), (1960), S.A., *Lanark*, p. 385.
5. Letter to the author, dated 7/11/00. The Ministry of Defence, Defence Records 2b, wrote: 'Unfortunately we cannot help you with your enquiry concerning English Army personnel and inter-marriage with Scotish [sic] partners'.
6. Bruley, (1999), *Women in Britain Since 1900*, p. 92.
7. Laird and Ramsay (eds), (1965), S.A., *Kirkcudbright*, p. 458.
8. MacDonald (ed.), (1961), S.A., *Argyll*, p. 107.
9. Baker, (1999), *The Terror of Tobermory: Vice-Admiral Sir Gilbert Stephenson KBE, CB, CMG*, p. vii, and p. 155.
10. See Costello, (1985), *Love, Sex and War: Changing Values 1939–45*.
11. Ibid., p. 10.
12. Ibid., p. 79.
13. Barron (ed.), (1985), S.A., *Inverness*, pp. 70–1.
14. Census of Scotland, 1951, *Vol, III, Birthplaces*, p. xliii.
15. J. Smith (pseud.), Tape MW0006, 10/12/99.
16. Miller (ed.), (1985), S.A., *Orkney*, p. 129.
17. Illsley (ed.), (1977), S.A., *Angus*, p. 361.
18. Bulloch and Urquhart (eds), (1964), S.A., *Peebles and Selkirkshire*, p. 210.
19. Taylor (ed.), (1979), S.A., *Perth and Kinross*, p. 390.
20. Strawhorn and Boyd (eds), (1951), S.A., *Ayrshire*, p. 362.
21. Barron (ed.), (1985), S.A., *Inverness*, p. 309.
22. Keir (ed.), (1966), S.A., *Edinburgh*, p. 135.
23. N. Rae, in discussion with author, Melrose 27/10/00.
24. Thomson (ed.), (1960), S.A., *Lanark*, p. 123.
25. Moisley and Thain (eds), (1962), S.A., *Renfrew*, p. 315.

26. Ibid., p. 367.
27. Thomson (ed.), (1960), S.A., *Lanark*, p. 433.
28. Barron (ed.), (1985), S.A., *Inverness*, p. 385.
29. Ibid., pp. 417–8.
30. Coull (ed.), (1985), S.A., *Shetland*, p. xix.
31. Smith (ed.), (1986), S.A., *Caithness*, pp. 155–60.
32. Ibid., p. 181.
33. Hamilton (ed.), (1960), S.A., *Aberdeen*, p. 43.
34. Smith (ed.), (1988), S.A., *Kincardine*.
35. The Censuses of Scotland, 1951 and 1991. The area of measure in 1951 was Kincardine-shire. In 1991 it was Kincardine and Deeside. This only makes a marginal difference when looking at this rate of population growth.
36. Barron (ed.), (1985), S.A., *Inverness*, p. 95.
37. Whatley, (2000), *Scottish Society 1707–1830*, p. 81, p. 83, p. 114 and p. 151.
38. Crouther (ed.), (1966), S.A., *Clackmannan*, pp. 544–5.
39. Moisley and Thain, (eds), (1962), S.A., *Renfrew*, p. 266.
40. Thomson (ed.), (1960), S.A., *Lanark*, p. 216.
41. Houston (ed.), (1962), S.A., *Dumfries*, p. 320.
42. Macleod et al. (eds), (1988), *The Pocket Scots Dictionary*, p. 154.
43. Conversations conducted by the author in October 2000.
44. Herdman (ed.), (1992), S.A., *Berwick*, p. 223.
45. Smith (ed.), (1988), S.A., *Sutherland*, p. 58.
46. Ibid., p. 163.
47. Ibid., p. 270.
48. Liz Potts (pseud.), Tape MW0026, 18/6/01.
49. Correspondence from Brian Wilson MP, 30/8/01.
50. See Chapter 1.
51. Coull (ed.), (1985), S.A., *Shetland*, p. 26.
52. Hamilton (ed.), (1965), S.A., *Moray and Nairn*, p. 297.
53. Illsley (ed.), (1977), S.A., *Angus*, p. 361.
54. Crouther (ed.), (1966), S.A., *Clackmannan*, pp. 544–5.
55. Smith (ed.), (1988), S.A., *Caithness*, p. 184.
56. Barron (ed.), (1985), S.A., *Inverness*, p. 440.
57. Miller (ed.), (1985), S.A., *Orkney*, p. xi.
58. Forsythe, (1980), 'Urban-Rural Migration and the Pastoral Ideal', p. 38.
59. McCrone, (1992), *Understanding Scotland*, p. 128.
60. Orwell and Angus, (1968), *The Collected Essays, Journalism and Letters of George Orwell, Vol. IV*, p. 285.
61. MacDonald, (1961), S.A., *Argyll*, p. 189.
62. Herdman (ed.), (1992), S.A., *Roxburgh*, p. 14.
63. Strawhorn and Boyd (eds), (1951), S.A., *Ayrshire*, p. 362.
64. Smith (ed.), (1988), S.A., *Caithness*, p. 184.
65. Smith (ed.), (1988) S.A., *Sutherland*, p. 270.
66. Miller (ed.), (1985), S.A., *Orkney*, p. xi.
67. Ibid., p. 129.
68. Forsythe, (1980), 'Urban-Rural Migration and the Pastoral Ideal', p. 41.
69. Smith (ed.), (1988), S.A., *Caithness*, pp. 155–62.
70. Mather (ed.), (1987), S.A., *Ross and Cromarty*, p. 287.
71. Ibid., p. 314.
72. Herdman (ed.), (1992), S.A., *Roxburgh*, p. 386.

Introducing the oral testimonies

The remaining chapters are informed by the testimonies of this study's sample of English-born oral history contributors. It is their life stories, their experiences, their perceptions and their discourses that form the basis of analysis and narrative. The life history approach provides a platform for rigorous analysis on two principal grounds. First, the contributors themselves set the agenda. They identified the issues and themes that they considered important in light of their migration and life experiences in Scotland. In terms of Foucault's guidelines, these can be considered the genealogies, or events of significance, from which to seek connections, recurrences, regularities, proximities and symmetries. Secondly, the basis of the quota sampling provides reasonable grounds from which to draw conclusions and make generalisations in line with Gordon's principle of intelligibility.

The data that emerged from the contributors' testimonies provided a migrant-centric view, in which it needs to be recognised that 'reality' has a different appearance to different individuals.[1] This created potential hazards in interpretation. First, Daniel Schacter cautioned that contributors often had different memories of the same event.[2] The testimonies in this study provided frequent illustrations of this phenomenon, for example where anti-English comments were perceived by most contributors as banter or teasing, but as racist by others. This is entirely consistent with Foucault's explanations of discursive formations,[3] and the 'rich uncertainty of disorder.'[4] Secondly, the data represents the testimony of English-born migrants only. In this situation 'memory is a social process, embedded in a specific cultural context',[5] that of migration to Scotland. And as Anne Ollila argued: 'People remember those things that their culture expects them to remember; there are communal mechanisms which control our modes of memory, and which suggest what is important and worthy of remembering.'[6] That the testimony is restricted to this single group is not a major problem. After all, this is a study of English migrants. Nevertheless, to gain a rounded understanding of their position in Scotland it was necessary to verify and compare their testimonies alongside data from a wide range of other primary and secondary sources, many of these being from a Scottish perspective.

CHAPTER 5

Taking the High Road

OVERCOMING PROBLEMS IN ANALYSING CAUSALITY IN MIGRATION

This chapter starts at the beginning, exploring the reasons why English-born people migrated to Scotland. When studying migration, historians have traditionally relied on two analytical models. These are: push and pull, and cause and effect. These are useful tools, but they risk over-simplifying complex reality. This may be an outcome of the incomplete and fragmentary nature of available source data. Without access to detailed life histories of individual migrants, analysis has relied on aggregate statistical information such as that found in censuses, passenger lists and other official records. These are essentially quantitative and impersonal. As such they do not explain the dynamics of migration, and reveal little about causality. Migration is a significant life event with complex ramifications for the individuals concerned, as well as for the communities they join and leave behind. The reasons why individuals and families migrate are extremely complex, and pre-twentieth century sources about personal experiences are frequently limited to diaries and letters home. These too have limitations. They are restricted to the literate and communicative, and fail to represent the whole social spectrum of migrants. In comparison with oral life history testimonies, they do not provide such rich insight into the fears, aspirations and experiences of individual migrants.

Models of push and pull typically identify the interaction of economic factors, forms of persecution in the place of origin, personal crises, and the effects of family/social networks on chain migration. All of these have been used at one time or another to explain why different groups have migrated to Scotland. For instance, Devine argued that economic factors were signif-icant causes of the second phase of Irish immigration. In the middle of the nineteenth century, the potato famine and land shortages pushed the Irish into Scotland and elsewhere. At the same time there was economic pull from rapid industrial growth, which created employment opportunities.[7] According to Devine the 'abundant supply of unskilled and semi-skilled [Irish] labour was crucial to Scottish industrial success'.[8] Religious and political persecution has also been used to explain migration to Scotland. Examples of this include twenty-first-century asylum seekers, and earlier East European Jews and Lithuanians.[9] Examples of family and social networks and chain migration were particularly important for Italian migrants where the *padrone* (a father-like figure-cum-entrepreneur who organised business structures and travel to and from Scotland and Italy) played an influential role in organising movement to and from Scotland.[10]

How does this form of analysis help explain English migration to Scotland? In the second half of the twentieth century the English economy was generally in a healthier state than the Scottish, so economic push and pull were unlikely to be influential. Similarly, religious and political persecution was non-existent. And, as English migrants tended to come individually, or as single family units, chain migration and networking did not apply. So what brought the English to Scotland in such numbers? Geographers have cited seventeen reasons, from the expansion of commuting distances, through the restructuring of industrial locations in the countryside, to the acceleration of retirement migration to residential locations offering a higher quality of life. But these were explanations of counterurbanisation, and, as illustrated in Chapter 3, this accounts only for a small proportion of English migrants.

Close inspection of the life histories found that there were many different reasons for coming to Scotland. Of the full sample, nearly nine out of ten contributors cited multiple, interrelated reasons for making the move north. Table 5.1 sets out the most common explanations.

Table 5.1 Influences on migratory decision-making

Reasons cited	% of sample
Employment	55.17
Promotion or a better job	15.52
Became a student	8.62
Redundancy	3.45
Retirement	6.90
Semi-retirement	5.17
Came as a child	17.24
Lifestyle choice	31.03
To be with spouse or partner	27.59
Returning to Scotland	17.24
Personal crisis	3.45

Source: Oral testimonies collected for this study.

The complex nature of and inter-relationships that exist between these factors, therefore, must be addressed, and in the remainder of this chapter they will be closely analysed and tested.

— THE INFLUENCE OF EMPLOYMENT —

In Chapter 3, census analyses indicated that the prime motivation for English migration was employment pull. Yet only 13.79 per cent of the life history contributors cited job move as the *only* reason for coming to Scotland. Of those, half were taking up their first jobs at the start of their careers, and all of them were to remain in Scotland. For example, Rob Nicholson started his career in 1972, in the Berwick, Roxburgh and Selkirk constabulary, largely because he could not get a job with the Northumbrian force. Mary Mulligan, who subsequently became an MSP, secured her first job as a graduate trainee in Glasgow in 1983. Of the others, one was a professional footballer, Trevor Steven, who was transferred to Rangers FC in 1989. He too settled permanently in Scotland, returning after a short spell playing for Marseille in France. Martin Robson worked for a year on an oil rig to pay for two years' backpacking round the world in the mid-1970s. He returned to England to take up a career in financial services, later acquiring a timeshare in Deeside. Two were reluctant migrants who were transferred to Scotland by their employers. In 1951, Tim Underwood was a trainee sales representative for the Lancashire-based textile firm Tootal-Broadhurst-Lee. He recalled:

> This is how I came to Scotland because they sent me here. At the time I was not terribly happy about coming all the way up here. I didn't particularly want to. I would have much rather been in the Midlands or in the south but it was not to be.

Jim Grant, a Liverpudlian, worked for Scottish Life in Liverpool, but was transferred to the company's head office in Edinburgh in 1981. He was very reluctant to bring his family to Scotland:

> I tried as hard as I could to get a job in Liverpool because obviously we had a family of three children, one still at school and two that had just left school and nobody wanted to leave where we were. But I couldn't get a job, Liverpool was very depressed at the time...so I had to take the option of coming up to Edinburgh.

Both these reluctant migrants, however, settled down in their new homes, and subsequently retired in Scotland.

The majority of the testimonies, however, cited multiple reasons for migrating to Scotland. This further contradicts the conclusions drawn from census analysis, which suggested that English migration was occupationally driven. Indeed, 44.83 per cent of the contributors moved for reasons other than employment. And, of the 55.17 per cent who mentioned that employment was a factor, three quarters noted that there were other factors involved in the decision to migrate. Here, gender was a complicating factor. Three quarters of those contributors who mentioned employment were male. This did not mean that females were not drawn by employment pull, taking into consideration the females who came as a part of a family group, either as wives/partners or daughters.

− THE INFLUENCE OF AMBITION −

One of the more common reasons behind employment-led migration was to take a promotion or to set up a new business, or to change employer to move to a better job. But in all these cases other factors and influences came into play – for example, in the cases of Ron Curran, Christine Kirkton and Tom Bond.[11]

Ron Curran was a trade union official, who was promoted from regional officer in Tyneside to the position of Scottish national officer of the National Union of Public Employees (NUPE). He also cited other reasons, such as a liking for Scotland gained as a mature student at Newbattle Abbey College in Midlothian. In addition he wanted to return to his roots:

> I really felt I was back to my roots in Scotland. My father was a Scotsman. His father was a Scotsman. My grandfather came over from Ireland in 1837 . . . He told us that the family had been blacked after the strike in Lanarkshire and I felt I've got a score to settle.

Christine Kirkton left England as child in 1956. Her father, in partnership with three other Englishmen, bought a small estate on Mull: 'My father had decided that living in England was becoming slightly claustrophobic and he really wanted what we all now term probably 'the good life' and the space round about him.'

Tom Bond, after graduating in chemical engineering from the University of Manchester, started his career in the oil industry with Esso at the Fawley Refinery near Southampton. Bond was ambitious, and after a spell with Esso Europe in London he became an operations manager with Occidental who were building a new refinery on Canvey Island in Essex. This coincided with the 1970s' oil crisis and forced him to reappraise his career plans, bringing him to Aberdeen in 1979. He recalled:[12]

> So having spent all my time, rather all my working life in the south of England after a short trip to the States I came to Aberdeen for what I thought was going to be a two-year assignment before I went elsewhere with Occidental and that two-year assignment then turned into twenty-two years and I'm still here, having come here in '79. My career with Occidental took a few turns. I went up to the Flotta oil terminal so I spent three years in the Orkney Islands. At that time my kids were at school, I've got three kids; my kids were at school in Aberdeen. I had to really put them into boarding school. They had actually been to a lot of different schools because of my moves down south between Esso and then actually moving to Occidental and over to the States with Oxy so my eldest daughter by the time she was twelve had been to seven different schools, my next, six different schools and my youngest five different schools, so when I had this move to Flotta I really didn't want to move them again, especially since my eldest was going on into secondary education, so we left them but they boarded at Albyn and at Gordon [in Aberdeen]. I did that for three years and then came back here to look after the Dutch Operations for Occidental, based in Aberdeen but I spent quite a lot of time travelling off shore as I had done when I first came up here.

Bond's experience is quite revealing, demonstrating a number of forces influencing personal life choice. He was clearly an ambitious career executive, and this determined where he would live and work. Global economic pressure on oil prices threatened his and his family's livelihood in England. His company's discovery of the Piper and Claymore fields in the North Sea provided a timely opportunity for career advancement. Significantly, at the time, Bond saw this only as a temporary move. He was just as likely to have moved to the USA, South America, the Middle East or elsewhere.[13] Bond chose to come to Scotland, and arguably economic factors in the push-pull model were influential here. The extract also reveals how important family considerations were in the decision to remain in Scotland, in particular educational stability for his three children. Family considerations were evidently very important in influencing Bond to pursue his career ambitions in Scotland, and to retire there. There were other considerations too in making this migration permanent. Elsewhere in the testimony there was evidence about the importance of social networks and lifestyle considerations. The family were members of the Petroleum Club in Aberdeen and participated in a wide variety of activities in the wider community as well as building up a network of friends. The family also grew to appreciate the lifestyle in the north east of Scotland.

When we first came up here granite was grey and dismal on a dismal day but on a sunny day it's great, it's the silver city. Now I find it difficult now that if you go back to England, seeing all the red-bricked buildings, they look ugly to me, which is the reverse to how it was when I first came up here . . . The weather. On the one hand it's not as cold here as everyone in England imagines in the winter, in fact probably the better time to be here is in the winter when you have nice clear skies. When you go down there [England] you get far more misty type, in the winter anyway, it's as if there's a slight fog or smog around especially in some of the inner cities . . . that's one thing you notice up here, you talk about traffic jams in the rush hour but it's nothing compared with down there . . . The quality of life is far better up here.

The examples of Curran, Kirkton,[14] and Bond highlight the significance of a range of factors in migratory decision-making. In their cases improving employment opportunities was an important consideration, but it was by no means the only one. Furthermore, they did not need to migrate to Scotland to improve their circumstances. They could have remained in England, or gone elsewhere. Notwithstanding, in all but retirement migration, and perhaps in the case of refugee migration, employment will be an important consideration, with the need to create an income to live.

In the examples given in the foregoing testimonies, was the push-pull model wholly appropriate or accurate? In macro-economic terms the push-pull model seeks to explain migration *push* in terms of unemployment, poor economic opportunities or the sense of relative deprivation in the country of origin, and *pull* in terms of demand for labour in the country of destination. Since the Second World War, using comparative measures such as unemployment rates and gross domestic product, the Scottish economy lagged behind that of England.[15] There were few compelling economic reasons to be pushed out of England to Scotland and, equally, relatively unattractive prospects to pull English migrants to Scotland. If anything, economic considerations provided a disincentive for migration. Indeed, as seen in Chapter 3, there was a much larger migratory movement, in absolute and relative terms, of Scots to England.

An interview with political scientist Malcolm Dickson raised the issue of Scots migration to England. He sought to explain migration between England and Scotland, and vice versa, in structural terms, and as far as the economy was concerned he argued that the border between England and Scotland did not exist:

I think perhaps what we're talking about here is very different structural reasons for migration. Certainly if we are talking about [the] kind of Irish migration in the nineteenth and early twentieth centuries there were very firm economic structural reasons for migration of that nature. I think in relation to English migration, you . . . also . . . have to look at the reverse as well because Scots flow out of Scotland . . . But if we look at, for example, economic integration between Scotland and England there is a high degree of crossover of economic activity. England is Scotland's single largest economic market and therefore there is a sense in which the nature of the late-twentieth-century/early-twenty-first-century economic interests lead for that natural kind of crossover, which ignores the boundary and the Border effect, and as a consequence will lead to this kind of cross-migration, . . . unlike the migration [of] the Irish in the late nineteenth/early twentieth century.

And it is clear that Dickson has a case here. The studies carried out by Firn, Scott, Hughes and others (see Chapter 2) demonstrated the close economic and business links between England and Scotland. In addition, the testimonies of Armstrong, Bond, Curran and Grant, in this chapter, confirmed how economic integration stimulated their personal migrations. In each of these examples, the Border was, arguably, an irrelevance. Perhaps the diffuse nature of economic interests in England and Scotland could be one factor in explaining the invisibility of English-born migrants in Scotland. It could be argued that, in the cases where movement was for reasons of employment transfer, it was migration within the United Kingdom economy rather than between England and Scotland. What weakens this hypothesis was the recognition, by the majority of English-born migrants in their oral evidence, that Scotland was, and is, a different country. The issue of difference will be looked at in more detail in Chapter 10.

— THE INFLUENCE OF MARRIAGE AND PARTNERS —

A further noteworthy factor in migration decision-making concerned the role of spouses or common-law partners. This can be categorised in four ways. First, there were people accompanying partners. These were normally wives and included Lucy Dowling, Pat Waters and Amanda Adams. Second, there were people who married Scots and came to live in Scotland as a direct result. These included Jimmy Smith and Eileen MacDonald, both of them as the result of wartime weddings. Analysis of the contributors' questionnaires indicated that of those married, 24.44 per cent were married to a Scot, 6.67 per cent were married to someone born outwith England and Scotland, and 68.89 per cent had English-born spouses. Third, there were people, like the recently qualified Peter Crown and Neil Bayfield, whose employment location was influenced by their desire to be near their partners. Crown took a job in Hawick to be near his girlfriend at Newcastle University.

Bayfield turned down a job in New Zealand and took one in Banchory to be nearer his girlfriend in North Wales. Fourth, there were people who came with their partners to change their way of life. This group forms a significant proportion of the 31.07 per cent who talked about lifestyle. These included Emma Wood, Isobel Murray, Sarah Brown and Amanda Green. Most of these migrants planned a permanent move but in the case of Brown and Green they originally came for a couple of experimental years – to Shetland and Lewis respectively. Both of these women were married and had young children. The new lifestyles were financed by their husbands taking local authority jobs. Initially the wives did not have paid employment. In both cases the families quickly assimilated into remote island life and their migration became permanent. A common feature of these 'lifestyle' migrants was that they tended to move to peripheral rural areas – conforming, to a degree, to the counterurbanisation model. This was not always the case, however, as seen with Sarah Andrews and her husband:

> In Harrogate where I was living at the time [1976] and coincidentally met a girl from Peterhead who obviously still had family up there and we talked about Peterhead, the oil industry and what was going on up there and so on. And my husband being a bit of an adventurous character and looking for, after twenty years on his part, sort of in the Air Force man and boy, felt he wanted to do something a little bit different. So the oil field quite appealed to him, the oil industry, so the girl that I met recommended that em we give it a try and that if we wanted a contact in the area she would give us details of her brother- and sister-in-law who were living up there, who would be more than pleased to welcome us into the area. So it was all a bit sort of not necessarily planned, I suppose. But at that time we were young we didn't have any children. It appealed to the adventurous side of my husband and I was quite happy to try somewhere and something new. So we moved up to Scotland on that basis.

Clearly, in this instance, the decision to relocate, after a career in the RAF, was to industrial/urban Scotland, and not the rural peripheries.

— The influence of lifestyle choice —

In 31.03 per cent of the testimonies, contributors mentioned 'quality of life'. Care needed to be taken in interpretation, however, in two respects. First, there is a need to differentiate between quality-of-life factors that were a pre-migration consideration and those that were post-migration rationalisation. The following quote, applied with hindsight, helps to illustrate this point: 'a traffic jam in Dundee is five cars. A traffic jam in Yorkshire is, you know, five miles. It's just so much more relaxed however stressful it gets up here, it's never as bad as it was down there'.[16] Secondly, quality of life is an imprecise term, and contributors used it in different ways to mean different things. Examples of that are apparent in some of the testimony quoted above. In the case of Emma Wood who migrated with her partner, quality of life largely meant the environmental attraction of the Sutherland landscape. In the case of the Brown and Green families they too sought environmental attractions, but in their cases they sought the isolation and community of island life. Peter Crown, who wanted to remain near his girlfriend in New- castle and his English-born parents in Edinburgh, also considered low house prices in the Borders in making his decision to relocate. He stated: 'your disposable income is much greater than if you were, say, in London. Money that you would spend on that sort of quality of house here would be put towards a better quality of life.'

The reasons behind Catherine Parr and her husband's decision to migrate, however, were more complex, involving a fusion of factors including lifestyle choice, lifecycle stage, employment and circumstantial opportunity. She recalled:

> Well, life in London was lived at a very fast pace . . . I always had a yearning for
> a more quiet calm life without so much pressure on to do so many things and
> that's what we found here on Mull, although having said that we're more busy
> socially now than we've ever been in our lives. There's a much much better social
> structure and social atmosphere and getting together sort of thing here than there
> ever was. I mean we didn't really know our next-door neighbours in Northwood,
> we did, we knew them but we never socialised with them. We socialise all the
> time on Mull, not just with other English people, a lot of the people that we
> socialise with are Scots, not necessarily Mulleachs but some of them are, but a
> lot of them are Scots. So while we don't have pressures on us imposed by business
> in London we have pressures imposed on us by ourselves because of the way that
> we regard our business, it's a reflection of our, ourselves if you like and so if you
> don't do something well, for example if there's a mistake in [the newspaper they
> publish] Henry (pseud.) is mortified. I get very upset, I don't like to think that
> we've made a mistake through carelessness, so we put our own pressures on us
> but at the same time I can sit at my desk and I can look down Loch na Keal and
> I can see Inch Kenneth and I can see Iona and to me that's as much as I need
> from life. Ian Sainsbury (pseud.), who runs [an eco-tourist company] once said
> to me, we were going through a bit of a stressful time at this particular time, Ian
> came down one day, I think we were doing a wee job for him for the business, and
> he said to me 'you're going through all this and you only came here for a quiet
> life didn't you' and all I could say to him was 'yes'. So we felt very pressured in
> living in London for all sorts of reasons, going in to London in the morning on
> the train was quite safe, everybody was freshly showered and coffeed and quite
> sleepy and calm and doing their crosswords but coming home in the evenings was

a different matter altogether. They might have had an argument with the boss or the air conditioning in the office might have broken down and you never quite knew what was going to happen on the Underground. I mean we've seen some and experienced some pretty horrific things and we got the car scratched when it was parked outside the house and we lived in the Green Belt and we just didn't you know, expect that and I think as time went on we got more fearful of London life so coming to live on Mull, and it wasn't, we might just as easily have gone to live in south Cornwall, quite as easily. I mean we were torn because we had the first week of our honeymoon here and the second in Cornwall almost as far as you can go. It was only the circumstances, Ella (pseud.) [a friend who had lent them her holiday home for a few years] ringing and saying 'there's a business for sale that I think you should come and look at' that we came to Mull.

As in the case of Tom Bond (above), this quote reveals a complex amalgam of factors in deciding to move to Scotland. Having reached middle age the Parrs wanted to take control of their lives, and, rather than being employees, to run their own business. So they bought a printing company on Mull. They were not happy with their quality of life in London, where she was a commissioning art editor and he a university lecturer. Both commuted to their work and found this unacceptable, and they were also apprehensive of urban crime.

The Parrs knew Mull beforehand. They had been given two weeks in a holiday cottage over a three-year period as payment in kind for some editorial work Catherine had done. At that time she did not even know where Mull was. In some respects this was a modern form of social networks and chain migration at work.

So she [the publisher, Ella (pseud.)] said, 'Well I can pay you in kind'. I said, 'Oh yes what kind?'. She says, 'I've got a house on the Isle of Mull' and I said, 'Mull, where's Mull?' She said, 'It's the innermost island of the Inner Hebrides'...I said 'done'. So a little bit later that year, I think this took place in June or July, in the September Henry and I drove up to Mull from Chertsey where we were living and by the time we got to this little isthmus across the island at Gruline we were in love with the island already, we'd only been on it thirty minutes and we were already knocked out by the island and by the time we got to Tostarie which is where Ella's house is, we were just absolutely smitten...I think four days into this fortnight's holiday we were already talking about buying a place here for our own holidays perhaps to retire to one day and that was the way things were.

The Parrs conformed to the urban refugee construct, and sought escape and an enhanced lifestyle in a remote rural area. This was their prime motivation, as well as gaining control of their own lives by running their own business, rather than working for an employer. As her testimony indicated, this did not have to be in Scotland. It could have been in Cornwall, or elsewhere. Circumstances and the sale of the printing business brought them to Scotland.

Separately, analysis of the testimonies also revealed that post-rationalisation about quality of life contributed to people wanting to remain in Scotland. This was evident in the testimonies cited above but it was also an important factor for some 20 per cent of the sample who raised the subject of quality of life and who originally came to Scotland for different reasons. For example, Nick Johnston, who was the first MSP to resign from the Scottish Parliament, came to Scotland for three weeks in 1968 to help his employer, Gillette, launch a new stainless steel razor blade. He found he liked the lifestyle in Edinburgh, and when Gillette refused to transfer him to Edinburgh he resigned, and got a job selling advertising for *The Scotsman*.

> I decided my life was probably better in Scotland than it was in England . . . I found Edinburgh a terribly congenial place . . . [for a] 19-year-old to live . . . I really didn't know Scotland at all. I'd never been up on holiday. I had never really thought about it. And when they said to me 'you are going to Edinburgh' I had to look at a map to see where Edinburgh was. My first memory was that I picked up a hitchhiker somewhere north of Newcastle. I remember coming up the A1 and he was a student in Edinburgh. And I thought that would be quite useful to help me find my way, but in fact he was worse than I was. And we ended up driving into Arthur's Seat, Holyrood Park as I now know it was. And I saw this huge mountain I said 'we must be miles away', but he said 'no, no this is in the centre of Edinburgh'. And I think, I felt then, that this was a place I could do business with, because any, any city with such grandeur, natural grandeur as an integral part of it, I think, was eh was dear to my heart.

Here quality of life was defined in social and environmental terms. This exemplifies how different people employed the term. Another variation came in testimony from Peter Goodfellow who defined quality of life in terms of the spirituality he found in Scotland.

— LOOKING IN UNPROMISING PLACES —

Foucault encouraged historians to look in 'unpromising places'. Goodfellow's testimony highlighted the magnetism that the Findhorn New Age community had played in attracting him to Scotland. This prompted investigation into the role that spirituality might have played in attracting English-born migrants. First, an examination of what brought Goodfellow to Scotland. He had a successful career and was the managing director of a car dealership in Abergavenny, with 'a big detached house, a brand new car, expense account, and all the things that people aspire to'. And yet he admitted to feeling 'depressed and very lonely', so he went on a journey of self-discovery taking him to America, Australia and Europe before ending up at Findhorn. He explained that there was 'an aura' about Findhorn and Scotland that was 'very much more passionate and exposed to nature's forces, in a way for instance where it wouldn't be in London or even in the Home Counties.' He described this as a 'deep innate spirituality' that was 'quite wonderful' to live amongst.

These revelations raised the possibility that other English-born migrants might have been attracted in search of Scottish spirituality. The Findhorn Community was established by English-born Eileen and Peter Caddy in 1962.[17] The centre expanded into a world-famous New Age centre, attracting visitors from all over the globe. Goodfellow's testimony also confirmed that Findhorn attracted other English visitors to Experience Weeks and other events, with a small proportion returning as permanent migrants. Unfortunately the Findhorn Foundation has no records about place of birth of either residential visitors or permanent settlers. In her history of Findhorn, Carol Riddell confirmed that there was a significant English presence, but failed to give any quantitative data. In correspondence she could not be more precise, but did admit that 'the largest group of visitors to the Foundation was from England' and that 'some people from England have settled in the local area'.[18]

Were there other religious or New Age centres in Scotland that attracted English migrants? The answer proved to be yes. But, like Findhorn, the communities involved could not provide records showing country of birth of their resident visitors or permanent settlers. Nonetheless, three communities provided evidence, albeit not statistical evidence, of attracting English migrants. The first was the Beshara School, which was founded in 1973 in the ancestral seat of Clan Chisholme, near Hawick. It was founded by a Turk, Bulent Rauf, who was called by God 'to come to England [sic] to promote the knowledge in this world of the unity of Existence'.[19] Conversations with one of Beshara's three English-born directors revealed that Beshara was essentially an English community, and that out of around 10,000 English students some two-dozen had returned to live close to the school.[20] One of these, Sarah Thomas, confirmed in oral testimony that she had come to Scotland for spiritual reasons.

Some twenty miles from Beshara is Kagyu Samye Ling, the largest Buddhist monastery following the Kagyu tradition outwith Tibet. It was founded in 1967 in one of the Buccleuch Estate's shooting lodges in

Eskdalemuir. It expanded in the following decades, and the presence of a Tibetan Temple and Buddhist prayer flags fluttering from council house washing lines creates a strange prospect in the rugged hills of Dumfriesshire, as well as providing evidence of in-migration. Where did these migrants come from? The answer was that Samye Ling was essentially an English community. Ani Lhamo, the senior western nun, estimated that the scale of English participation amongst monks and resident laity had consistently been between 60 and 70 per cent. In addition, the monastery attracted some 1,500 English-born visitors a year to attend residential courses and long-term retreats. She also provided evidence of former English-born residents moving to live locally, and further afield in Glasgow and Edinburgh.[21]

Another religious community with links with English migration was on Iona. The Iona Community was founded in 1943 by George MacLeod, as a training centre for Church of Scotland ministers. According to Macleod's biographer, its role changed and 'Iona became a Christian education academy for ministers and lay people from different parts of the world'.[22] Many of the people, who were attracted to training, retreats and work on Iona, as well as those who became members of the internationally dispersed Iona Community, were English-born. Again, there was no firm statistical evidence. In oral testimony English-born Iona warden, The Revd Brian Woodcock, said that there were very few English-born people in the early days but that from the 1960s there were a disproportionate number of English people coming to be together 'to build a community on Iona'. By the end of the twentieth century, he claimed, 'the Iona community is only half Scottish and a lot of people from England'. Like Goodfellow, Woodcock also observed that Scotland had a distinctly classless and appealing spirituality.

These testimonies clearly illustrate that systems of belief and aspects of Scottish spirituality were factors in stimulating English migration to Scotland, albeit on a small scale. A reasonable conclusion might be to suggest that this form of migration was a subset of counterurbanisation migration, as many adherents of New Age beliefs formed 'a general consciousness movement, transcending the oppressiveness of culture.'[23]

— THE INFLUENCE OF RETIREMENT AND SEMI-RETIREMENT —

A common stereotypical image was of English people moving to Scotland in retirement. This was not reflected in the censuses, nor in the life histories. Analysis of the testimonies did reveal the influence of retirement and semi-retirement as a motivational factor, but only 6.9 per cent moved on retirement, and 5.17 per cent for semi-retirement. Of both these groups, 85.71 per cent retired to rural areas, mainly the Highlands. The average age of the retired group on moving was fifty-five, and fifty-four for the semi-retired. In terms of the statutory retirement age this was young, and perhaps this explained why three quarters of those who came for retirement took up some form of paid employment. In all cases Scotland was a deliberate retirement destination, but there were also other influences. In one case it was a wife accompanying her Scottish husband to his Scottish roots.[24] Another wanted to run a bed and breakfast business in a much-loved former holiday location to supplement pension income.[25] Another, on retiring from the RAF, found a local job that employed his specialist skills.[26] Another wanted to be within commuting distance of his younger wife's new job in Edinburgh.[27] And another had fallen in love with a Scottish widow on a business trip.[28] There were also instances of the impact of personal crises.

— THE INFLUENCE OF REDUNDANCY AND PERSONAL CRISES —

A small proportion of the sample, 6.9 per cent, indicated that some form of personal crisis created conditions for a lifestyle change, and that this stimulated migration. Personal crisis took the form of redundancy, job loss and marriage breakdown. In each case other factors contributed to making Scotland the destination of choice. For example, Mike Waters was made redundant by a multinational food company in London. He and his wife recalled how after receiving 'the brown envelope':

MW – Simon, who was our number two son, said: 'Well you are silly why don't you move to Scotland? You are always going up there. Why not go there?' So we then had another holiday. Touring didn't we? To see whether we could find anywhere suitable.

PW – We took *The Scotsman* paper and we also funnily enough *Exchange and Mart* we have now and again. So we wrote down a number of properties which looked . . . at the time we thought we would buy a little business you know, perhaps a little grocer's shop or something like that might fit the bill.

The Waters had taken holidays in Scotland for the previous ten years and were very fond of the Highlands where Mike practised his hobby of wildlife recording. The redundancy, Waters was sixty-two at the time, created the opportunity for them to realise their dreams, and they were encouraged to do this by their son. Family also played a further interest, as their daughter was a student at St Andrews University.

In the case of Pauline McLaren, her second husband lost his job in Cardiff in 1956 as the result of drunkenness. Her reason for migrating to Scotland was out of necessity. It just happened to be where her sacked husband found a job.

He [her husband] ended up losing his job because he would sort of have drinking bouts once or twice a month that were just absolutely tremendous and car accidents and all sorts of things you see. He really was getting intolerable. So anyway I was stuck down in Wales at this time and the children were going to school, this was . . . just outside Cardiff and he lost his job with ABC (pseud.) and after applying for lots and lots of jobs he eventually found one in Scotland through *The Times* or whoever, had interviews up in Scotland. And he came up to Aberdeen and of course he would charm anybody and get any job and knew lots of things about most things, one of those sort of men and he landed up here and of course he sent for us later.

Pauline McLaren subsequently divorced and, largely as a result of the drunkenness and money problems, faced difficulties in her early years in Aberdeen.[29] She remained in Scotland nonetheless, initially as a single parent and subsequently as a grandmother.

Marriage breakdown and related financial problems created the crisis or 'trigger' that brought June Williams to Scotland:

I knew I had to escape . . . Em, things went very badly wrong with my life in various ways . . . I was running away and I am not ashamed to admit it. There were some things I wanted to put, not only time but miles behind me and the em another strand that was arising out of that was an economic strand and the final thing was that I met somebody. I met somebody who had, he was English as well, he was from Surrey. He had already made the escape once and he'd lived along the east coast [of Scotland] em, but he'd gone back for family reasons and by the time we met he was on his own and he wanted to come back and so everything just came together and we came.

There was another factor involved here – a love of Scotland. Earlier in the testimony Williams explained how she felt after taking the first of sixteen annual holidays in Scotland: 'I have never forgotten the excitement of getting onto the M1, and there was this sign saying 'The North', and that's where I was going'. This feeling of attachment to Scotland was so strong that, even after the break-up of the relationship with the gentleman from Surrey, she decided to stay.

– A NEW FORM OF CHAIN MIGRATION –

A widely recognised cause of migration is the effect of family and social networks, often referred to as chain migration, where migrants stimulate further migration through communication with friends and family back home, and vice versa. This did not apply to late-twentieth-century English migration to Scotland. The evidence from the testimonies indicated that migration tended to be by individuals and nuclear families, and that there were hardly any pre-existing family or social connections. There were a few exceptions, such as the 5.17 per cent who came to live with Scottish spouses or partners, or the 3.45 per cent who accompanied returning Scots migrants. In one case, the Waters, their daughter was at a Scottish university, but this was a comparatively minor consideration.

Two enabling factors are important in chain migration: communication and the bonds inherent in family and social networks. These were relatively insignificant in the case of English migration to Scotland. There was, however, one significant factor, which arguably acted as a form of surrogate chain migration. Analysis of the testimonies showed that 36.21 per cent of the migrants had taken regular holidays in Scotland and that this factor was an important influence in the choice of migration destination. This was apparent in the testimonies of Parr, Waters, Goodfellow and Williams, mentioned earlier. Other testimonies also emphasised the role of holidays, respectively those of Paul Armstrong and Margaret Cox. Armstrong recalled:

> My parents used to come up here on holiday and bring me up ... generally [to] the Borders although they, we, used to go to Edinburgh, not really across to Glasgow. But we also had some friends up in Perth and then right up north in Thurso, so we would go up there as well, so quite a lot of exposure as a child. [This contributor migrated to the Central Belt and then moved to the Borders.]

And for Cox:

> The start of my arrival into the Borders was in about 1982 when I came and joined my parents on a holiday here, near where they had rented a cottage. My Dad's a fisherman and we had a holiday. We joined them for four or five days. That introduced me to the Borders which I'd never ever known anything about before and in about 1986 I bought a farm cottage that was, that needed some work doing to it and while I was still living in, actually living in Cambridgeshire then, I bought the cottage and had a good job and was able to pay for it as a second home and would drive up once a month ... and after about two or three years of this, I really realised that this is where I wanted to live and so in 1986 was when I moved here, lock, stock and barrel.

Holidays were a source of information, and, unlike communication through traditional chain migration, provided some experience of living in a new country. Important though this was, there were nevertheless people like Nick Johnston and Catherine Parr (above) who knew nothing about Scotland before their first journey north.

— STUDENT MIGRATION —

After two years tele-working from her renovated cottage in the Borders, Margaret Cox introduced a further change into her lifestyle. She became a mature student at Edinburgh University. Table 5.1 shows that another significant category was that of people migrating as students. Nearly one in ten of the sample, including Tim David, Paul Armstrong, Neil Bayfield, Elizabeth Bunting and Mike Wade, came from England to Scotland for their higher education. All of them chose to live and work in Scotland. Some got jobs immediately and others returned to Scotland later in life. Following Foucault's exhortation to explore connections and recurrences, how does this relate to the accusation, referred to by some observers as the 'Englishing' of Scottish universities,[30] and/or did English participation in Scottish universities stimulate net migration gain?

— CONCLUSION —

Much of the foregoing analysis has, of necessity, concentrated on single-issue migratory decision-making factors. Sometimes interrelated factors have been considered, but on the whole the full extent of the complex nature of the decision-making process, as it appears in testimony after testimony, has not been reflected. This would have involved producing a repetitive and dull explanatory narrative. Detailed examination of the testimonies, however, reveals that decisions to migrate to Scotland were generally multi-faceted and complex in nature.[31] This suggests how inappropriate simplistic theoretical models like push-pull can be.

General social theories may offer better explanations. In their study on the social history of migration, Pooley and Whyte postulated that structuration theory, as advanced by Giddens,[32] provided a useful framework. They argued:

> Migration itself is one of a set of social practices, which can be adopted when structural constraints place pressure on an individual or family: the migrant moves to a new location to modify particular structural constraints. In moving, however, a whole new set of constraints and problems will be encountered and the act of migration itself requires individual reactions to assimilate new circumstances.[33]

At first sight it would appear that this general theory accommodates the complexity identified in the testimonies. Its weakness, however, is the emphasis on structural factors, where migrants move when opportunities and constraints emerge as the result of the interaction between structures in society. Dickson, too, sought to explain migration between England and

Scotland in structural terms, citing the diffuse nature of economic interests in the United Kingdom. Leaving aside difficulties in defining what structural factors are, structural explanations ignore *mentalité*. In simple terms this can be defined as what people are thinking, why people are thinking what they are thinking, and how this influences behaviour. Also, in the context of this study, why do they think they want to migrate – and why to Scotland? Testimony after testimony revealed the importance of *mentalité* as a constraining, or enabling, influence affecting migration choice. Contributors provided insight into their innermost thoughts, revealing fears, aspirations, the impact of relationships, and that most-difficult-to-define concept, emotionally positive feeling towards Scotland.

One of the problems of theorising is that it often leads to semantic debate about the theoretical constructs themselves and so diverts attention from the people who themselves made history. What can be said with certainty is that the motivation behind English migration to Scotland, in the second half of the twentieth century, was extremely complex. It was possible, however, to identify some general trends and these were summarised in table 5.1. Going behind these data it was also possible to identify differences between English migrants and other migrant groups who came to Scotland. One of these was that the English came individually or in families. There were no pre-existing family or social networks to hinder early assimilation into local Scottish society. English migrants did not congregate together in national communities, unlike concentrations of the Irish in Glasgow's South-side or Dundee's Lochee, the Lithuanians in Lanarkshire, the Jews in the Glasgow Gorbals, or the first Asians in the Dundas and Roslin Street area of Glasgow. Compared with other migrant communities the English were, in this sense, invisible – a theme that will be returned to in later chapters.

– NOTES –

1. Ollila (ed.), (1999), *Historical Perspectives on Memory*, pp. 8–9.
2. Schacter (ed.), (1997), *Memory Distortion: How Minds, Brains, and Societies Reconstruct the Past*, p. 1.
3. Foucault, (1972), *The Archaeology of Knowledge and the Discourse on Language*.
4. Ibid., p. 76.
5. Ollila, (1999), *Historical Perspectives on Memory*, p. 9.
6. Ibid., p. 9.
7. Devine, (1999), *The Scottish Nation*, pp. 486–500.
8. Ibid., p. 488.
9. Maan, (1992), *The New Scots: The Story of Asians in Scotland*, Introduction.
10. Colpi, *Italian Migration to Scotland*, (conference, 'Race Curriculum and Employment', Glasgow, 8/3/86).
11. 28.13 per cent of the sample which mentioned employment fell into this 'improvement' category.

12. This is the first use of a 'thick' quote. A policy of open punctuation was used in transcription to ensure accurate representation of the spoken testimony. As people do not speak in the same way as written text some of the quotes may appear difficult to read. Some minor grammatical alterations have been incorporated to enhance readability without compromising the integrity of the original spoken word.
13. This conclusion is based on assessment of recorded and unrecorded conversations.
14. In this case her father was the decision-maker.
15. See, amongst others, Boyle et al., (1989), *Scotland's Economy, Claiming the Future*.
16. Elizabeth Bunting (pseud.), Tape MW0041, 28/8/01.
17. The Findhorn Foundation, *Who Are We?*, web site accessed 11/1/01.
18. C. Riddell, email to author, 20/1/01.
19. P. Young, *United by Oneness: Global Considerations for the Present*, (a talk delivered in Melbourne and Sydney, June 2000).
20. Conversation with S. Kenner at Chisholme House, 15/1/01.
21. Data about the Kagyu Samye Ling community was gathered from an interview with Ani Lhamo on 17/1/02, and the community's web site (accessed 1/2/01).
22. Ferguson, (1990), *George Macleod: Founder of the Iona Community*, p. 179.
23. Stone, (1976), 'The Human Potential Movement', in Glock and Bellah (eds), *The New Religious Consciousness*, p. 93.
24. Isobel Murray (pseud.), Tape MW0001, 1/11/99.
25. Pheona Sinclair (pseud.), Tape MW0054, 31/10/01.
26. James Dowling (pseud.), Tape MW0030, 21/6/01.
27. Tim David (pseud.), Tape MW0011, 30/3/00.
28. Source withheld for reasons of confidentiality.
29. Issues of assimilation will be covered in the next chapter.
30. See Chapter 2.
31. See unpublished thesis: Watson, (2003), *The Invisible Diaspora*, pp. 178–9.
32. Giddens, (1981), *A Contemporary Critique of Historical Materialism*.
33. Pooley and Whyte (eds), (1991), *Migrants, Emigrants and Immigrants: A Social History of Migration*, p. 13.

CHAPTER 6

Structural 'invisibility'

A common characteristic of most groups of migrants is their visibility in their new host country. They tend to stand out from the crowd. This was certainly the case in Scotland for the Irish, the Jews, Lithuanians, Poles, Italians and Asians. The English, by comparison, were less visible. This chapter will address the issue of structural 'invisibility'[1] or, in other words, the ways in which social practices and the structures of society relate to the relative visibility of migrants. It will attempt to explain why English migration has been ignored in the historiography. More importantly, by interpreting evidence from the oral testimonies gathered for this study, this and the next chapter will assess how degrees of visibility influenced assimilation and acculturation, and how this may have had a bearing on the impact English migrants had upon Scottish society.

So-called 'invisible migrants' have recently attracted the attention of migration scholars. Three main types of invisible migrants have emerged. Firstly, the work of Bean, Corona, Tuirán and others highlighted 'illegal border crossers' leaving Mexico for the United States of America. They classified those unauthorised Mexicans as 'invisible and ambiguous migrants'.[2] Helene Lackenbauer of the Swedish Red Cross also identified 'so-called illegal migrants' as a problem in Western Europe. She said, 'because of their illegal status, certain migrants are invisible before the law and are often denied even their most basic rights.'[3] Secondly, in 1992, Manolo Abella of the International Labor Organization estimated that in an increasingly interdependent global economy some twenty million skilled workers were employed in countries other than their own. He referred to these as 'highly invisible' migrants. Alan Findlay described this category of migrant as 'skilled transients' or 'the invisible phenomenon'.[4] The third category of invisible migrants is strictly European. The Institute of French Studies in New York has been studying repatriating or returning European colonists, referring to them as 'Europe's "invisible" migrants'.[5]

The first category of illegal immigrants clearly does not conform with the pattern of English migration to Scotland. The second, however, would appear to have some relevance. In Chapter 2, for example, there was evidence from the work of Firn, Scott, Hughes and others (and this was corroborated in the oral testimonies) that the transfer of capital and technology brought English migrants to Scotland. Whether this explains invisibility is less certain. A more rigorous analytical framework (see below) would be required to answer this supposition. Looking at the third category, the idea of the English migrating as returning colonists is rich in irony given the postulations of groups such as Siol nan Gaidheal and Scottish Watch that English migrants were active colonisers themselves. Recent interest in returning Dutch colonists,[6] however, may connect with one possible explanation why English migrants have been invisible to Scottish historians. The hypothesis here is that for the Dutch the history of colonial Indonesia is a taboo subject. This is where historical taboos are rooted in current and future interests, and where they are linked to the cultural politics of *forgetting* (author's emphasis).[7] Is there a similar taboo surrounding English migration to Scotland? Scottish historiography is dominated by Scotland's subservient role to England. Is there a case for a potential argument that this 'position of inferiorism' led to historians choosing to ignore the impact of English migration? Furthermore, the teleological nature of the historiography, related to the slow but steady growth of Scottish Nationalism (a journey to independence?) throughout the twentieth century, may have fed a possible reluctance to admit, or to recognise, the potential negative effects of English migration. It would, however, be difficult to prove or disprove such a hypothesis empirically. And, in spite of the temptation to follow Foucault's advice to continue looking in 'unpromising places', an understanding of English migration, and its relative visibility, will benefit only from the adoption of a more practical framework.

– Determining visibility –

There are a number of structural characteristics that differentiate newly arrived migrants from the host community. These include ethnicity, religion, family and social networks, migration patterns, places of origin and destination, language, social class, occupation, and cultural approaches to assimilation. Related to these are the issues of homogeneity and heterogeneity, and thus where homogeneity is greater the more likely it is that any differences will be apparent and visible. Conversely, the more heterogeneous the migrant group, the greater is its diversity and propensity to be absorbed by, and hidden amongst, the host community. The determinants of visibility that will be used in this analysis are set out in figure 6.1.

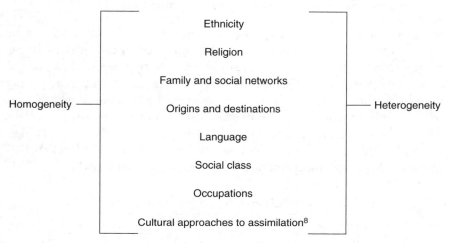

Homogeneity — Ethnicity / Religion / Family and social networks / Origins and destinations / Language / Social class / Occupations / Cultural approaches to assimilation[8] — Heterogeneity

Figure 6.1 Determinants of visibility

This framework facilitates comparative analysis with both the host community and other migrant groups, so providing the basis from which to clarify the question of 'invisibility'. A further and important justification for this approach is that it is informed by the weight given by oral testimony contributors to their early reactions to and experiences of living in Scotland.

– ETHNICITY –

In the 1991 census, the first census to ask about ethnic origins, the population was divided into eleven ethnic groups. But definitions of ethnicity are fraught with difficulty and are frequently confused with race and skin colour. Some academics even deny the concept of race, but in pragmatic terms the concept is generally known and understood.[9] The Race Relations Act (1976) made it illegal to discriminate on grounds of race, colour, nationality and ethnic origin. These terms inevitably required clarification and in 1983 the House of Lords was called upon for interpretation. The Lords defined an ethnic group as having some of the following characteristics:

- A long shared history
- A cultural tradition of its own
- A common geographical origin
- Common descent from a small number of common ancestors
- A common language

- A common literature
- A common religion
- Being either a minority or a majority within a larger community[10]

Such potential for confusion posed a number of difficulties for census administrators regarding reliability in the collection of census data. It was relatively straightforward for people to answer questions about their address or age compared with their ethnic origin. There was a risk that people would tick the wrong box. The example given by Ratcliffe is whether an Indo-Caribbean would tick the Black-Caribbean or Black-other box.[11] In spite of these difficulties Ratcliffe concluded that census data were of high quality.[12] The only likely problem was under-enumeration.[13] Table 6.1 illustrates the numbers and proportions of ethnic groups in Scotland in 1991.

Table 6.1 Ethnic groups in Scotland in 1991

Ethnic groups	Numbers	% of population
White	4,935,933	98.75
Black Caribbean	934	0.02
Black African	2,773	0.06
Black other	2,646	0.05
Indian	10,050	0.20
Pakistani	21,192	0.42
Bangladeshi	1,134	0.02
Chinese	10,476	0.21
Other groups – Asian	4,604	0.09
Other groups – Other	8,825	0.18
Persons born in Ireland	49,184	0.98

Source: The General Register Office for Scotland. The Census of Scotland 1991.

In terms of assessing the visibility of migrant groups, race or skin colour was an important factor. In *About Racism in Scotland*, the authors chose two phenotypic terms 'black' and 'white', where ' "black" is used to refer to people of African, Chinese, Indian, Pakistani origin, etc. who are perceived as *visibly different* [my emphasis]'.[14] In those terms less than 1 per cent of Scotland's population was 'black' in 1991. This increased to 2 per cent of the population in 2001.[15] The population was predominantly 'white', forming the 'visibly similar' majority. This would have included the majority of English-born migrants, along with the Irish, Lithuanians, Italians and Poles. In terms of colour, the English were essentially invisible. It should be remembered, however, that, in 1991, 1.77 per cent of English-born migrants were in ethnic groups other than white.[16] All the contributors providing oral testimonies for this study were white, although there was an unrecorded telephone conversation with a Bradford-born female, living in Edinburgh, whose parents were Punjabi immigrants.

– RELIGION –

The second half of the twentieth century witnessed the increasing secularisation of society and a significant decline in church membership. Callum Brown's running dataset of church communicants, members, adherents or claimed population shows a sharp decline in the Protestant churches after 1950, a decline in Roman Catholic numbers after 1975, and an overall increase in others, notably Islam, the Church of Latter-Day Saints and Jehovah's Witnesses.[17]

Table 6.2 Church adherence in Scotland 1950–94

	Church of Scotland	Free Churches	Other Protestant	RC Church	Others	% of population
1950	1,271,247	24,556	193,795	745,125	26,613	38.6
1975	1,041,772	14,198	146,851	813,000	44,568	33.3
1994	715,571	7,218	123,407	742,750	55,400	25.9

Source: Callum Brown's running dataset.

There is no reliable data showing the country of birth of these church members. The church traditionally associated with the English was the Scottish Episcopal Church, which, according to Brown, 'grew closer in doctrine and temper to the "high Church wing" of the Church of England'.[18] There was evidence in the *Third Statistical Account of Scotland*[19] that the Episcopal Church attracted English migrants, and in oral testimony English-born Mike Russell MSP, a one-time Episcopalian priest, commented that people coming from England automatically joined the Episcopal Church. Russell went on to point out that 'the Episcopal Church in Scotland is a very small church'. In 1950 there were 56,382 communicants[20] and by 1994 this had fallen to 20,350 adult and child attendees.[21] In view of these figures, compared with the volume of English migration, English participation in the Episcopal Church was likely to have been small. Brown characterised the Scottish Episcopal Church as 'the landed classes at prayer.'[22] He went on to suggest, though without providing evidence, that 'in the twentieth century large numbers of English Episcopalian immigrants find even the Presbyterian Church of Scotland more to their taste.'[23] There was evidence to support this conclusion from the oral testimonies gathered for this study.

Overall, 25 per cent of the oral history contributors raised the subject of religion – this figure is coincidentally similar to the proportion of church members in Brown's dataset. Of those who chose to raise the topic of religion, 18.18 per cent went to the Episcopal Church, 27.27 per cent joined the Church of Scotland, 36.36 per cent were associated with other Protestant churches, while the remainder were practising New-Agers. The oral testimony suggests a pattern of behaviour and church attendance similar to that described by Brown. Indeed, it seems to confirm his assertion that certain 'types', defined by their individual 'tastes' in worship, found themselves attracted to different churches, for a variety of reasons. Neil Bayfield, for example, said of the Episcopal Church:

> We go to the Episcopalian Church, another aspect of being English in Scotland. The Episcopal Church is known as the English Church. I don't know quite why it is known as the English Church but it does tend to have a majority of [sigh] quite a lot of English people go there, but also a lot of Scots who are Conservatives and landowners and all the nobs go there.

June Williams, for whom a combination of personal crisis and a strong desire to live in Scotland were the motivation for migration, received considerable support from the Church of Scotland, which, amongst other things, found her a caravan as a temporary home. She recalled:

> As far as the Church was concerned I've had an involvement there, I mean I was brought up Church of England. I was baptised into the [Church of England], I was christened into the Church of England but I was never confirmed... But em by the time I came up here things had changed and I was actually em confirmed, they didn't call it confirmation, but into the Church of Scotland. I had my classes when I was over at Gollanfield I was accepted into the Church of Scotland at Cawdor Church and so that I always say that now I'm a naturalised Scot because I was, I was received into the Church of Scotland.

In this case the church played an important role in assimilation, and it is significant to note June Williams' belief that she became a 'naturalised' Scot when she was 'received into the Church of Scotland'.

The Church of Scotland also attracted new members as in the case of Agnes Swift and Eileen MacDonald. Both women married Scots, and found that the Church introduced them to a network of new friends. Both were active in the Church for the whole of their lives, with involvement in the Sunday schools and the Mothers' Union. Mrs MacDonald was a cockney wartime bride, who had a very difficult first two years in Scotland at the end of the Second World War, not least with the deeply embedded tradition of Scottish sectarianism. She recalled:

I did find the Scots very very narrow. That was the set-off with Gran [mother-in-law]. Em you got the Papes which I had never heard this word a Pape...I had been brought up in the middle of London as you can understand and I didn't even know where Scotland was to be honest like everybody else until I came to it. Em my father was a strict disciplinarian but we never would we never discussed religion and you know Catholics and Protestants that was new to me. And that came up very much up here. Gran was terrible with that and I found that very disturbing 'cos it was all new to me. I mean you must remember...We didn't get on for that reason I suppose and many reasons I couldn't see eye to eye with her on anything, just anything, which was very difficult and I mean I was just twenty-one. You're young and you can't see it...We did have a bad start.

Religious bigotry continued to feature in Mrs MacDonald's life in Prestwick. Later in her testimony she continued:

People judge people and they shouldn't. I don't think they should anyway. But I have, I have, my brother-in-law, but I shouldn't speak ill of the dead, he's gone, em he and I used to cross swords because I wouldn't have this business about Papes and, we were going to Ireland for the first time about seven years ago and he says: 'What are you going over there for? What are you going over there for with those Papes?' And that I object to...and I used to say: 'You're supposed to be educated Billy (pseud.). You don't talk like that'. And we've got a very very dear friend that comes and I tell you something he wouldn't employ anybody that was a Catholic. He's retired now but he had a very responsible job and this, I mean, I just don't understand this. Why? It's very bad here. Why do they have this terrible prejudice about Catholics and I can't understand it. I've got a neighbour next door but one and she's a lovely girl and two children and they're growing up now, they've been here twenty year and I went to the Catholic Church when the wee girl had her communion and, they were wonderful people. I was made most welcome. And you know what someone said to me? 'You know why you were made welcome. Because they wanted you in there too...'. I said: 'Just don't be silly, don't be silly'. I said: 'I've been a Church of Scotland member all my life, well since I've been up here, I said: No no no.'

The issue of bigotry, which arose largely as a result of earlier migrations from Ireland (Catholics and Protestants), Lithuania (Catholics) and Italy (Catholics) was also raised in other testimonies. Christine Kirkton, who came to Scotland as a nine-year-old, started her career as a policewoman in Lanarkshire. She recalled being surprised at the enmity between Catholics and Protestants when she was ordered to police an Orange march in Motherwell in the 1960s.

That, that was probably the first time that, that I became aware of people being stigmatised, especially if they were perhaps Catholics...I was completely unaware that there was such a divide between the two and I was, I was really quite shocked and I, I had to talk it through with my colleagues and say, you know, 'But why! Why are they going on like that?' And, but nobody could explain it to me, but there was just this enormous divide between the two and it, it was the most amazing experience for me because I had never known that in my life.

There are, of course, numerous theories explaining the enmity between Catholics and Protestants in Scotland. It is generally accepted that one of the prime causes was the impact of Catholic and Protestant Irish migration into Scotland. Of relevance to this discourse was the visibility of these migrants, and the role that their religion played in making them more visible. Other migrant groups were also predominantly Catholic – the Italians and the Lithuanians. Religion was a factor in their visibility too, in a predominantly Presbyterian country. According to John Millar, the Catholicism of the Lithuanians contributed to 'bigotry, prejudice, intolerance, discrimination, fear, hostility, verbal abuse and even hatred'.[24]

In terms of religion, in this study's oral history sample, English migrants were more heterogeneous and therefore less visible.[25] In addition to the Episcopalians and those converted to the Church of Scotland there were those of other Protestant beliefs. The majority of the sample chose not to raise the subject of religion, and it would be reasonable to conclude that they, in the main, formed part of the secular majority, further mirroring the structure of twentieth-century Scotland as well as merging into Scottish society. Non-Christian religions contributed to the visibility of migrant groups, with Islamic mosques and Hindu temples further differentiating Asian communities. The Jews too were highly visible. In oral testimony recorded by broadcaster Billy Kay, a Mrs Aitkin described the Jewish community around the Oxford Street and South Portland Street Synagogues in the Gorbals district of Glasgow in the early years of the twentieth century: 'It was nearly all Jewish shops and Jewish firms in the Gorbals. There was the Fogels, the corner of Hospital Street and Cleland Street, there was the Jewish bakery at the corner of Dunmore Street. Gleiken, the gown people were there and the Ashers as well. The Gerbers, the Wolfsons...'[26] English migrants by comparison did not belong to homogeneous religious communities and as a consequence were less visible. The only exception were the relatively small numbers of New Age practitioners referred to in Chapter 5.

– PATTERNS OF MIGRATION –

Using evidence from the oral history sample, one of the distinct characteristics of English migration was its exclusivity. Migrants came as individuals

(25.00 per cent), or as couples (16.07 per cent), or as part of a nuclear family (58.93 per cent). There was no evidence of group migration or, with a few exceptions, of migrants moving to join family groups or pre-existing social networks. Only 8.93 per cent of the sample cited migrating to be close to family members and only 3.57 per cent were followed by close family. Unlike many other migrant groups there were no formal structures to stimulate or facilitate migration, as was the case with the role of the *padrone* in Italian migration,[27] the assisted emigration packages to the Dominions in the mid-twentieth century,[28] or the emigration societies supporting migration from the Highlands in the nineteenth century.[29] English migration to Scotland was an essentially personal affair with inevitable consequences for assimilation and visibility.

Another feature that differentiated the English from other migrant groups was that theirs was a land-based migration – the exceptions being onward ferry journeys to the Islands. The majority of the migrants in the oral history sample came by car with the remainder coming by rail. Indeed, a number of the contributors highlighted their journey north of the Border; for example, Nick Johnston, who picked up a hitchhiker to navigate him to Edinburgh, and Amanda Green who combined her migration with a vintage car rally *en route* to Lewis. Another was Sarah Brown, who recalled:

> We had got two cars when we moved up and because we couldn't drive the two cars up we had actually put my Mini in the removals van, it wasn't a problem, we put the furniture in, then we drove my Mini in with the house plants in and then the rest of the furniture went in and so of course when what people saw was the furniture coming out and then this bright orange Mini being driven out.

English migrants did not arrive as part of a group or a surrogate group, formed on board a ship or aircraft. Nor did they settle amongst their kith and kin. They arrived on their own and were obliged to integrate with their host communities, be they neighbours, work colleagues or other groups. The English, by comparison with the Irish, Italians, Asians and Lithuanians, were not part of a homogeneous group, and, as shown in Chapter 3, their heterogeneity was emphasised by the fact that they came from a diversity of locations as well as settling all over Scotland. This contributed to their structural 'invisibility'.

– LANGUAGE –

One discernable difference between migrants and their host community was language, particularly the choice of language used by migrants to communicate amongst themselves and their ability (or lack of it) to communicate in English within the host community. Examples of this would be found amongst first generation migrants from Italy, Eastern Europe and Asia. This is very much so where audibility increases visibility. English and Irish migrants shared the same language with the Scots but with significant differences in accent and dialect. More than three fifths of the oral testimony contributors commented that they were very conscious of accent and/or dialect at two levels. The first was the issue of comprehending the local accent or dialect when they first arrived; the second concerned what Mugglestone refers to as 'phonetic propriety'[30] – this concerns the way in which the listener perceives the class and status of the speaker.

Comprehension of Scottish accents and dialects was a common problem for newly arrived English migrants, although this tended to be short-lived. English migrants soon overcame initial difficulties and many adopted Scottish terminology, as can be seen in a number of the extracts quoted throughout this book. Examples include the use of words such as 'wee' and 'outwith'. Reading these extracts, however, will not reveal how some English accents contained tinges of Scots and how two of the English-born contributors had acquired distinct Scottish accents.[31] Typical examples of the early experience can be seen in the following three transcript extracts.

> Sarah Andrews – I couldn't understand a word they were saying to start with, being broad Buchan but that didn't seem to [matter], I mean people were very kind and slowed down and took care not to speak so that you couldn't understand what was going on when they realised that as soon as you opened your mouth you were English. (Date of arrival 1976 in Peterhead.)

> Elizabeth Bunting – I had a dreadful [West Riding] accent and nobody would ever understand me. My first teaching-practice [in Edinburgh] the kids that I had said: 'You're foreign aren't you?' And I said: 'Yes' . . . they said to me: 'Where are you from?' And I said: 'Well where do you think I am from?' 'Well you're not from round here.' And this went on . . . at great length. 'It must be from a very very long way away 'cos you are definitely foreign. You talk funny'. So they decided I was from Glasgow because that was the furthest place they could think of that was far away you know. So I just said: 'Yeah'. I thought I am not going to get into this 'I'm English bit' because you were never quite sure how people would react. I thought that was quite funny. It was one in the eye for the nasty tutor who said I would never make a teacher because the kids wouldn't understand me. The kids understood me well enough. (Date of arrival 1968 in Edinburgh.)

> Jack Brown – As soon as I came into contact with anyone here [Hawick] it was quite a foreign language. I just did not know what they were saying. And of course, they didn't know what I was saying because I was speaking with a fairly broad Yorkshire accent. (Date of arrival 1937 in Hawick.)

What these extracts illustrate is an underlying consciousness of being different because they were English. Isobel Murray observed, on arriving in the Borders:

> I felt odd simply because I felt English. I just felt that my voice was embarrassingly English and to have to speak up and ask for something in a shop, felt quite awkward. I felt I was wanting to actually say to people, 'Look, I live here. I'm not a tourist'.

Sarah Brown reinforced this reaction, providing clear evidence of being invisible but audible, when she commented:

> I think one of the difficulties is that you are immediately marked out as being different the minute you open your mouth. I can be in the car in Shetland. I can be sitting in a concert. I can be doing anything and nobody would know I was English but the minute I open my mouth I am English.

Finally, mention should be made of contributors' references to Gaelic where 14 per cent of the sample referred to encountering Gaelic when they first arrived. Indeed, of that number two fifths went on to learn the language with varying degrees of fluency.

— ACCENT AND THE NOTION OF ARROGANCE, OR SUPERIORITY —

In her study *'Talking Proper': The Rise of Accent as a Social Symbol*, Lynda Mugglestone argued that:

> Accent was itself to be regarded as a marker of social acceptability, facilitating or impeding social advance; it alone could secure deference or disrespect, acting as an image of 'worth' in a culture increasingly attuned to the significance of phonetic propriety.[32]

Here she was referring to social class but, as the testimony from this study demonstrates, accent also acted as a marker of nationality with consequent influences on the behaviour of the individual concerned, as well as the behaviour of others towards that individual. One of the most striking effects of an English accent was the perception by many Scots that this ascribed middle-class status to, or upon, the speaker. This was routinely commented on in testimony after testimony, regardless of the regional or phonetic origins of the speaker. A cockney or North Country accent was as likely to be perceived as middle class as someone using 'Standard English'[33] and/or 'Received Pronunciation'.[34] For example, Catherine Parr said: 'People in

Scotland probably still think of me as middle class and I don't subscribe to [that], I don't like that idea because I don't see myself as middle class.' This positioning of the English as middle class conforms to McCrone's assertion that 'the narrative of class in Scotland is one in which issues of national identity play across class'. He argued that Scotland's relationship with England had taken on 'class' connotations, and that this was related to the role of Anglicised lairds.[35] This was a point brought up in the testimony of T. C. Smout. After retiring as a history professor at St Andrews University in 1990, English-born Smout was appointed to a number of quangos (quasi-autonomous non-governmental organisations). He observed that in his work on various committees the predominant accent was English but that this did not necessarily mean that all the participants, whom Smout referred to as the 'great and the good', were English. Reflecting on the nationality of trustees, committee and board members, Smout observed: 'It is very difficult to tell, unless you have the birth certificates in front of you, who is Scottish and who is English'.

This blurring of Englishness and middle-class status created difficulties for some English-born migrants. In cases where accent acted as a marker of social acceptability, 'securing deference or disrespect',[36] it could position English migrants as fitting the stereotype of being arrogant and superior. Dot Jessiman explained:

> I work with quite a few Scots who said to me . . . I can get away with things because I walk into somewhere with an English [accent] and Scots will stand, stand back. There's an acceptance, almost it's [a] dreadful thing to say but amongst a lot of Scots the mere fact that you've got an English middle-class accent gives you [a] sort of a one up and I think it has to do with this whole feeling of having inferiority pushed upon them. Do you know what I mean? that in some way your ways are inferior to those of England.

Dot Jessiman was a cockney by birth. She proudly recalled her East End working class roots of 'Vote Labour, never cross a picket line, never shop your neighbours to the police sort of thing'. She came to Scotland in 1975 with her Scots-born husband who got a job as a radio engineer. She bought and ran a croft before becoming an SNP activist. She was elected onto the National Council, stood as an unsuccessful list candidate, and became convenor of 'New Scots for Independence'. Her comments about accent reflect Beveridge and Turnbull's theories about inferiorisation,[37] a theme that will be explored in greater depth in Chapter 10. Of interest here is the corollary that the common perception was that ownership of an English accent conferred a position of superiority. This, according to Jessiman, exacerbated the stereotype of arrogance and superiority. She provided examples of people with 'cut glass' accents with whom she had appeared on television programmes.[38] She argued that this created difficulties for English migrants:

> I remember sitting in one of the Land Commission hearings in Inverness with a dreadful little man and sitting there and I felt very uncomfortable because he was English and he was saying: [uses upper-class Home Counties accent] 'Of course I've bought this croft' he said. 'Since I've had it the whole thing has been improved. The person who had it before really couldn't do anything. I've bought this and I've done that and I've made these improvements.' . . . And you could see every Scot in the room, including the journalist, you could see the hair on the back of their necks standing up. He was a dreadful little man . . . when you've got people like that you will have trouble.

Accent created difficulties in other ways. Trevor Steven, the Rangers and England footballer, suggested that he experienced discrimination as the result of his English accent. He recalled that in the early to mid-1990s:

> I was a regular on TV here because I was part of the Rangers' Scottish scene, football scene and I was injured a lot and the TV companies were using me on a regular basis once a week if not twice a week and I was happy to do that. However, when I stopped being a Rangers player I became an Englishman abroad as far as TV was concerned and I think what you do find if you look at television you find that Scots voices are welcome and promoted and encouraged on English television or in English-produced programmes whereas in Scotland there's far more em Scottish voices for Scottish subjects, no matter what your speciality is or where you have been in your experience I tend to think that there's more, it's difficult for an English voice to be heard on Scottish sports programmes.

Another English broadcaster shared Steven's experience. In May 1997 Mark Souster,[39] who had presented BBC Scotland's *Rugby Special* for three seasons, brought a legal action for race discrimination against BBC Scotland. When his contract ran out the BBC changed the format of the programme and brought in a Scottish presenter, Jill Douglas, from Hawick. Souster claimed he had been the target of anti-English jibes, and complained, 'he had been ousted by anti-English bosses wanting a Scottish voice for their rugby coverage'. He said at the time: 'Anti-English feeling is woven into the fabric of BBC Scotland. There's always been a traditional hostility but with devolution there's a feeling that only Scottish voices can now be heard.'[40] After protracted legal proceedings the case ended with Souster receiving an out-of-court settlement reported to be 'substantially less than five figures'.[41]

— ACCENT AND VICTIMISATION —

The principal area where an English accent caused problems was with bullying of children in schools. This was referred to in a third of the testimonies where accent was discussed. Jim Grant said his son, who had a strong Liverpudlian accent, needed 'guts' when he went to school in Prestonpans in 1982. Sarah Thomas said her daughter developed a 'protective coat' by adopting a local accent for use at school and with her peers. This appeared to be a common survival strategy, with a number of contributors observing that some, or all, of their children were 'bilingual'. Stuart Brook referred to his English-born sons' schooling:

> They spoke with a Lancashire [accent]...they sort of spoke with a north of England accent at home. If you brought them into school by the time they had got to the hospital [opposite the school] they were talking in a broad Hawick accent and I don't think that they, they got into trouble because they were English.

English-born Kenneth Silver, who was rector of Jedburgh Grammar School between 1971 and 1984, provided written testimony for this study:

> Reaction to English-born people was very varied. Among the native pupils, many of whom spoke a slovenly form of English with broad vowels, there was a quite obvious reaction on occasions to those English-born immigrants who joined them. Those with strong local regional accents (e.g. cockney, West Midlands) were allegedly not able to be understood; and they were often poorly mimicked and/or ridiculed.[42]

Judging from the testimonies, bullying tended to take the form of verbal abuse and no examples of violent behaviour were cited.[43] Bullying children with different accents, however, was not restricted to Scottish schoolchildren. Mike Wade came to Scotland as a seven-year-old, went to school in Kirkcaldy, acquired a Scottish accent, and returned with his parents to England. In Kirkcaldy he was 'picked on' for his English accent, and six years later in Lancashire he was 'picked on' for his Fife accent. Further evidence of children's responses to different accents came in Peter Goodfellow's testimony. He went to school in Wales and was bullied because he was English. He recalled: 'I clung to my Englishness and refused to develop a strong Welsh accent and defended England against all comers'. It is outwith the scope of this study to explore the psychology of bullying; interest here is in examining the role accents played in contributing to the visibility of English migrants in Scotland. One of the English-born MSP oral history contributors, Mike Russell, made interesting observations in which he dismissed the idea that bullying was a serious problem.

> At school I got teased and bullied sometimes. Why? Not because I was English, but because of my accent, it sounded English to people I was at school with in Troon, but kids get teased and bullied at all times for lots of different reasons, because they're fat or because they wear the wrong trainers or something. To act against that you need to act against the problem of bullying not the symptoms but the cause.

Here Russell admitted there was a problem, one that he had personal experience of, but argued that it had nothing to do with his country of birth. Instead, he emphasised the issue of differences. Arguably, his hypothesis that being English is like wearing a different pair of trainers is politically disingenuous. Russell had frequently been deployed by SNP leader Alex Salmond to rebut accusations that the SNP was anti-English.[44] Another contributor, Mary Mulligan (Labour), a Liverpudlian-born MSP, also denied that bullying of English children was a serious problem.

Nevertheless, judging from the testimonies, bullying of English children was a problem throughout the period under review. Furthermore, this arose from the children's visibility, or should that be audibility? In addition, this did cause difficulties for the children concerned as one of the three school-age contributors in this study confirmed. In an interview in her school, Hannah Green said:

> I found that I've become quieter since I came up here. Believe it or not, I'm starting to come out of it now but, yeah, I became quite withdrawn. I didn't like to say anything out loud. You know, kept my voice down in case my accent. It just wasn't worth it. It wasn't worth, it wasn't worth you know, sort of, 'Oh, she's so posh! She's from down south and luvvy, daahling' kind of thing, which we don't do anyway but they sort of make it out as though we do. I think also there's an element of, if you work hard as well. If you're from England, you've got a posh accent and you work hard, it's not a good combination really.

Coincidentally, the ascription of middle-class status contributed to Hannah's difficulties. She went to a school in a predominantly working-class community. Kenneth Silver also raised the issue of class confusion in his written testimony. He commented that, 'those [English schoolchildren] whose spoken English was more refined and totally comprehensible were widely regarded as "posh" or "snobs"'.[45]

Lynda Mugglestone argued that through the nineteenth and twentieth centuries there had been a supplanting of the heterogeneity of regional accents and that there had been an influencing trend towards the homogenisation of the 'correct way' to speak, in terms of 'educated accents, talking proper and BBC English'.[46] Listening to the tapes of the English-born contributors there is a diversity of regional and class accents. Paradoxically, Scots listeners frequently perceive this heterogeneity as homogeneous and middle class. Thus accent is rendered a complex topic, one subject to extensive study by phoneticists and others. What clearly emerges from the testimonies in this study is that it is an important factor in defining the origins of English migrants in Scotland, both for the migrants themselves and for other members of the community. This audibility is clearly a form of visibility. The role of accent is perhaps best summed up in Patricia Yeaman's testimony in an answer to a question about how often she was conscious of being English:

PY – That's a really good question. I'd say daily and I have been heard to say that my one great regret is speaking with an English accent, I think Scots speech particularly in this area of Scotland is just beautiful and I hear my own harsh tones and vowel sounds against this backdrop of the vernacular in Dundee and then kind of work with spoken Scots, I hear it all the time and I'm very very aware of being English. But that's also political 'cos I'm aware of Scots feelings about England and Englishness to which I'm sympathetic to.

MW – Is it only when you open your mouth or are there other occasions?

PY – It's mostly when I open my mouth or, there've been a lot more English voices come to Dundee recently, you hear English spoken in the street quite a lot and I'm alert to it all the time but then on the other hand I'm very language oriented, I'm a listener to language and speech and have been professionally conscious of speech patterns. Yes. Awareness all the time.

– OCCUPATION –

The penultimate determinant of visibility (see figure 6.1) was that of occupation. A common feature of a number of Scotland's migrant communities was the homogeneous nature of their employment patterns. Early Indian settlers tended to be itinerant pedlars, and in the late twentieth century this developed into the familiar pattern of the Asian-owned 'open-all-hours' corner shop.[47] The first wave of Italian migrants came from Lucca and Frosinone, selling figurines and statuettes made at home. In the early part of the twentieth century the Italians ventured into catering, specialising in ice-cream and fish and chips. According to Colpi, business grew, based on family networks, up until the Second World War, after which there was increasing occupational heterogeneity.[48] The Chinese too specialised in the catering trade and were especially visible from the late 1950s through to the arrival of Chinese restaurants in towns and cities throughout Scotland.[49] The early Lithuanians were also occupationally homogeneous, the majority ending up in the Lanarkshire coalfields.[50] The largest group, before the English, were the Irish. Their employment patterns were more varied than those groups mentioned immediately above, but they still tended to homogeneity, largely working as unskilled and semi-skilled labourers.[51] According to Tom Devine the visibility of the Irish in Scottish society was significantly increased by: 'their tendency to concentrate in particular areas . . . Above all else, it was the jobs generated by industrialization that drew them and ensured that substantial communities of Irish descent grew up.'[52]

The English by comparison were quite different. The census analysis in Chapter 3 clearly demonstrated the heterogeneity of English migrants, both in terms of industrial classification and occupational category, and this applied throughout the second half of the twentieth century. Looking at industrial classification, although there was a marginal bias towards the public services, the English were also working in professional and scientific services, chemicals and allied industries, miscellaneous services, other manufacturing industries, insurance, banking and finance, and gas, electricity and water. Equally there was a diverse spread of occupational categories from unskilled to semi-skilled, skilled, technical, professional and managerial.

This heterogeneity was corroborated in the analysis of the oral history sample. Further corroboration was evident from the testimonies cited earlier in Chapter 5. These included people coming to Scotland as: a police constable, a personnel executive, a footballer, the head of the Scottish Gas Consumers' Council, a sales representative, an insurance manager, a trade union official, an oil company project engineer, a university lecturer, an army private, a farmer, a dentist, a writer, a teacher, a sales assistant, an holistic healer, a clergyman, a bed and breakfast proprietrix, a flight simulator trainer, a voluntary worker, a manufacturing manager, and a printer. This heterogeneity contributed to 'invisibility' through its diverse spread of industry and occupational types.

Furthermore, subsequent occupational and geographic mobility within Scotland also contributed to 'invisibility'. This mobility was not evident from census data, but analysis of the sample questionnaires and testimonies provides widespread evidence of both types of mobility. Of the two thirds of the sample who undertook paid employment, the number of jobs ranged from one per person to five (producing an average of 1.97 jobs per person). And these data underestimate the true rate. In the questionnaire a number of the contributors only put one description, such as journalist or academic, against the question for previous occupations in Scotland. Detailed examination of the testimonies reveals that this concealed a number of jobs held for the same and different employers. The average length of residence for this cohort, not including time spent in retirement, was twenty-four-and-a-half years, meaning that, on average, people changed their jobs every twelve-and-a-half years. This calculation ignores the contributors' previous and subsequent employment outwith Scotland.

In terms of geographic mobility, nearly half the sample lived in more than one place in Scotland. The number of moves ranged from two to eight, evenly split between local and inter-regional moves, with an average of 2.84 moves per person. The average length of residence for this cohort, including retirement, was twenty-five years exactly, meaning that, on average, people moved every 8.8 years. This calculation, however, excludes the initial move from England. In work carried out in 1971, P. H. Rees found that in the United Kingdom each individual was likely to make between seven and eleven migrations (moving place of permanent residence) during a lifetime, with five to ten being within regions and only one to two between regions.[53] Evidence from the oral history sample shows a greater propensity amongst English migrants to Scotland to migrate inter-regionally, but they settle to a similar pattern in terms of lifetime migration. The latter may have been slightly higher but no data was collected about prior moves outwith Scotland.

– CONCLUSION –

The final determinant of 'invisibility' (see figure 6.1) was cultural approaches to assimilation. As this is a major theme this will be fully explored in the next chapter. Reviewing the other determinants, clearly the concept of 'invisibility', when applied to migrants is, in a physical sense, absurd. Yet the term is being used increasingly by scholars to describe different categories of migrants who remain somewhat concealed from society at large, as well as from the scholars themselves. Some groups of migrants, regardless of their numbers, are more visible than others, and structural factors play an important role in this process. These include ethnicity, religion, language, patterns of migration, social class, and occupation. The English are different in many respects from other migrant communities in Scotland. And it is these differences that have tended to conceal their presence. For most of the twentieth century the English have outnumbered all other migrant communities and, even when compared with the numbers of Irish in the nineteenth century, formed the most significant migrant group in modern Scottish history. The main difference was the heterogeneous nature of the English compared with the homogeneity of the others. In twentieth-century Scottish society the homogeneity of migrant groups, other than the English, served to emphasise their structural differences, and so make them more visible. Mike Russell MSP illustrated the tendency of some migrant communities to keep to themselves when he said:

I mean there is a Lithuanian Club in Edinburgh and a Latvian Club; I don't think there is an English Club as far as I know. The New Club might regard itself as such but there is no such thing. . . . [And referring to the English] Maybe they blend very well with the surroundings.

This blending into the surroundings was, in part, a function of English heterogeneity. They tended not to live, work and pray together. Their diversity and pervasive spread throughout Scotland meant that they did not live and work within more traditional migrant communities or 'ghettoes'. And, because they were similar in many respects to the Scots, they merged into society and were, relatively speaking, 'invisible'. The only significant area where the English stood out was through their speech. Accent was the main area where they appeared visible, both within society at large and within themselves.

— NOTES —

1. Recent studies have introduced the concept of 'invisible migrants'. This, of course, is an inaccurate descriptor. Invisibility is an absolute condition and in the sense of H. G. Wells' *Invisible Man* it cannot apply to migrants, other than in fiction. More precise language should refer to relative visibility. The term 'invisible migrants', however, has slipped into general usage, and will be applied here in spite of its obvious limitations.
2. Bean et al., *Circular, Invisible and Ambiguous Migrants, Components of Differences in Estimates of Unauthorized Mexican Migrants in the United States*, web site accessed 29/7/02.
3. Lackenbauer, *VIth European Conference of the International Federation of Red Cross and Red Crescent Societies*, (Berlin, 19/4/02).
4. Findlay, 'Skilled Transients: the Invisible Phenomenon?' in Cohen (ed.), (1995), *The Cambridge Survey of World Migration*.
5. Smith, *Europe's 'Invisible' Migrants*, (conference, 'Europe's "Invisible" Migrants: Consequences of the Colonists' "Return"', New York, 9/4/99).
6. Williams, *No Homecoming: The Repatriation of the Dutch from the Indies* and *The Invisible Dutch: A Reconstruction of Academic Involvement*, (conference, 'Europe's "Invisible" Migrants: Consequences of the Colonists' "Return"', New York, 9/4/99).
7. Trouillot, (1995), *Silencing the Past: Power and the Production of History*.
8. This topic will be covered in the next chapter.
9. Ratcliffe, (1996), *Ethnicity in the 1991 Census*, p. 2.
10. Cant and Kelly, (1995), 'Why Is There a Need for Racial Equality Activity in Scotland?', p. 25.

11. Ratcliffe, *Ethnicity*, p. 6.
12. Ibid., p. 12.
13. Cant and Kelly, *Racial Equality Activity in Scotland*, p. 10.
14. The Community Work Training Company, *About Racism in Scotland: A Case Study*, web site accessed 23/2/01.
15. The Census of Scotland, 2001.
16. See Chapter 3.
17. Brown, 'Religion', in Cooke et al. (eds), (1998), *Modern Scottish History 1707 to the Present*, pp. 145–7.
18. Brown, (1987), *A Social History of Religion in Scotland since 1730*, p. 2.
19. See Chapter 4.
20. Currie et al., (1977), *Churches and Churchgoers: Patterns of Church Growth in the British Isles Since 1700*, p. 129.
21. Brierley and MacDonald, (1995), *Prospects for Scotland 2000*, p. 82.
22. Brown, (1987), *Social History of Religion*, p. 2.
23. Ibid., p. 48.
24. Millar, (1998), *The Lithuanians in Scotland*, p. 4.
25. No one in the sample mentioned they were a Roman Catholic, although there were two 'high church' Anglicans/Episcopalians who left their church when a woman was appointed minister.
26. Kay (ed.), (1980), *The Complete Odyssey: Voices from Scotland's Recent Past*, p. 228.
27. Colpi, (1986), *Italian Migration to Scotland: Settlement, Employment and the Key Role of the Padrone*.
28. See, amongst others, Hutching, (1999), *Long Journey for Sevenpence*.
29. See, amongst others, Smout, (1997), *A Century of the Scottish People, 1830–1950*, pp. 62–9.
30. Mugglestone, (1995), *'Talking Proper': The Rise of Accent as a Social Symbol*, p. 1.
31. Christine Kirkton (pseud.) and Mike Russell are clear examples of this. Others, like Trevor Steven, are thought, by some, to have a mild Scottish accent, especially when they are in England.
32. Mugglestone, (1995), *'Talking Proper'*, p. 1.
33. Sweet, (1908), *The Sounds of English*, p. 7. Standard English is defined as pronunciation and language least betraying the locality of the speaker.
34. See Bauer, (1985), 'Tracing Phonetic Change in the Received Pronunciation of British English', pp. 61–81.
35. Cited in Devine and Finlay, (1996), *Scotland in the Twentieth Century*, pp. 115–16.
36. Mugglestone, (1995), *'Talking Proper'*, p. 1.
37. Beveridge and Turnbull, (1989), *The Eclipse of Scottish Culture: Inferiorism and the Intellectuals*.
38. Amongst other programmes Dot Jessiman claimed appearances on BBC's *Now You're Talking* and Grampian's *You the Jury*. This author watched a recording of the latter and can confirm Dot Jessiman's testimony.
39. Souster would not accept an invitation to be interviewed for this study.
40. G. Chamberlain, 'BBC Scotland Settles "English" Race Case', *Scotsman*, (28/5/02).
41. Ibid. The Souster case had one particularly interesting outcome. In Souster v. BBC it was found that, although there was only one British nationality, Scots, English, Welsh and Irish people did have distinct 'national origins', and that the Race Relations Act 1976 could therefore apply if a person suffered discrimination on the grounds of such origins. Source: *Scots Law News*, web site accessed 14/8/02.
42. Correspondence with the author 21/1/01.
43. The media did provide evidence of violence, though not always accurately. See Chapter 9.
44. See amongst others, E. Quigley, 'Gibson Unaware of Star Role in SNP Drive', *Scotsman*, (1/9/95). M. Russell, 'Braveheart Points Up Positive Nature of Independence', *Scotsman*, (20/9/95).

45. Correspondence with the author 21/1/01.
46. Mugglestone, (1995), *'Talking Proper'*, p. 5.
47. See Maan, (1992), *The New Scots*.
48. Colpi, (1986), *Italian Migration to Scotland*, pp. 1–25.
49. Murray and Stockdale, (1990), *The Miles Tae Dundee: Stories of a City and Its People*, p. 63.
50. Millar, (1998), *The Lithuanians in Scotland*, pp. 25–66.
51. Devine, (1999), *The Scottish Nation*, p. 488.
52. Ibid., p. 487. See also Kenefick, (2000), *Rebellious and Contrary: The Glasgow Dockers 1853 to 1932*. The Glasgow Dockers were largely Irish-born, at least up until 1914. This is a good case study of the formation of an Irish occupational community. Ironically, the leader of the Dockers' Union, the Scottish Union of Dock Labourers, was an Englishman, Joseph Houghton.
53. Rees, (1979), *Migration and Settlement*, cited by Coleman and Salt, (1992), *British Population: Patterns, Trends and Processes*, p. 395.

CHAPTER 7

Fitting in – the process of integration

Coming to Scotland affected different people in different ways. Migrants adopted a range of strategies in order to integrate into their new way of life, as the following three testimonies demonstrate:

Stuart Brook – There were four of us joined Pringle [a knitwear company] at that time [1968]...I didn't get very much flak from the people in Hawick because I was English and they were Scots. Um, one thing, which I did realise, was that Hawick is a very clannish town and I was, I could see that I was, looked on as being a Dawson man,[1] obviously intruding into what had been a nice cosy little relationship with all Hawick people and so I deliberately set out to become a Pringle man. And everything that I did was associated with Pringle as opposed to being Dawson. I mean, Dawsons appointed me and I said very quickly well forget about that I'm employed by Pringle, Pringle pay my salary not Dawsons even though they are part of the Dawson group and um I'm living here, my children are going to school here, and I'm working here, so therefore I'm identifying myself with Hawick as much as I can. I didn't try and play a part in the Common Riding to do this and try and become a Scot because that wouldn't wash and it's not my character anyway but I did insist that my car had a Roxburghshire registration and not a Kinross registration.

Roger Smith – There are a lot of cultural differences of course, which you gradually get used to over the years. I mean our first Hogmanay up here [1975] was a bit of shock. It was not something we were used to at all. We got into it and it was great. And we you know – could have done with a bit of education about things like that...We were up and down all these houses in the street and it actually happened in Peebles that all the houses were open and you just went along and people came into your house and we just went along, and it just seemed to go on and on and on [laughs], which was nice. I mean we were used to it but it was tremendous but again it made, we met more people. And having a baby as well that might have helped, a sort of bringing together...And my wife, my first wife that is, was always very interested in everything to do with Scotland. She found out that there was an evening class in Peebles in elementary Gaelic and she went to that. [After a few years the Smiths moved to Oban.] . . . I remember that the Gaelic teacher that we had in Oban, she was a bit taken aback when I joined the choir but she realised that, of course I was prepared to work very hard, and though I am not fluent in Gaelic you know that also I can sing in tune, which was quite useful, I think I won her over in the end. She was a very strict taskmaster, which you had to be because you know the choir had a long proud history. My main concern was just not to let them down. And I know that within myself that I didn't. And we were on television. It [the Mod] was in Govan that year . . . We were on television and of course I had to wear a kilt, which again, I thought I looked quite good in a kilt. I've got no right to wear one as such but certainly I didn't feel out of place and I have worn a kilt since to weddings and things like that. So people said as an Englishman you shouldn't wear a kilt. And I told them why not? I don't stop Scots wearing trousers.

Sarah Thomas – I don't actually feel the Border personally I don't feel, I never have done and I know this is an anathema for some but I don't feel Scotland is a separate country I never have done. When I lived in Wales I didn't feel Wales was a separate country. To me you can look at it on the map it's one island there's no reason to have any break in it, I never have understood it. So I don't share some of the local what shall we call it, strength of feeling about such matters and quite possibly this creates a distance between me and them because I have never really made much of an attempt to cross it.

The testimonies of Stuart Brook and Roger Smith both display an awareness of the process of integration, and this led to the adoption of behavioural strategies to help them 'fit in'. Indeed, in the case of Dr Brook he was attuned to the subtleties of unique local nuances. Less typical was the response of Sarah Thomas. She rejected the idea that there was a need to integrate, on the basis that England and Scotland were part of the same country, although she did recognise that there was 'distance between me and them'. Who the 'them' are is not clear. Closer inspection of her testimony revealed the distinction could have been based on nationality, class, religion,[2] or a combination of all three. In any event, she chose not to integrate with the new communities into which she migrated. In terms of this study's oral history sample her behaviour was exceptional.

The previous chapter concentrated on structural differentiators such as ethnicity, class, religion, networks, geographical dispersal and language. Here the emphasis will be on the influence of cultural change at a personal/family level and how this may have had a bearing on the impact English migrants had upon Scottish society.

— Some thoughts on acculturation and assimilation —

The act of migration is complex, and one where, initially at least, the migrant is an outsider in the host community. At first, the migrant is separate from the host culture; this is usually followed by a blurring of cultural lines. Many societies formalise the integration of migrants. That is, and has been, the case in the USA, where Americanisation policies are 'institutionalised in both government and civic society.' This led to naturalisation through the 'Oath of Renunciation and Allegiance'.[3] Similar practices were employed elsewhere. For example, the New Zealand government employed information officers on board immigrant ships to lecture and advise travelling migrants.[4] The Czech government introduced a re-education and assimilation programme for the Roma (referred to by some as Gypsies) in 1952, but had to abandon it in 1968 when this form of social engineering failed to produce the desired outcome.[5] Institutionalised integration, however, did not apply within the United Kingdom, although Home Secretary David Blunkett proposed the introduction of an oath of allegiance for immigrants in 2002.[6]

What these governments were trying to achieve was the acculturation and assimilation of migrants from different cultural, ethnic, religious and social backgrounds. Acculturation is the adaptation to, and adoption of, a new culture.[7] It describes a process of cultural change in which the migrant acquires and learns the ways, behaviour, habits, values and attitudes of the receiving society.[8] Assimilation, and, in the context of this chapter, behavioural assimilation, involves a process whereby migrants become, or are, 'integrated into a common cultural life with other groups as a result of sharing the experience and history and acquiring the memories, sentiments and attitudes of those other groups'.[9] What was the process of acculturation for English-born migrants to Scotland, and how did they assimilate into Scottish society?

These are not easy questions to answer. To what extent did the English-born migrants retain their former way of life, and to what extent did they adopt and adapt to Scottish cultural habits? By clinging on to Englishness they would stand out and be more visible. Conversely, by becoming Scottish they would be less visible. Migration specialist Maurizio Catani argued that 'one of the most striking and recurrent factors one comes across is the immigrants' maintenance of their former systems of ideas, representations and values'.[10] He went on to suggest that this occurs in spite of numerous material changes that are created by the act of migration itself. Significantly for this study, when there are definitional problems relating to whether migration from England to Scotland was inter-regional or between nations, he concluded that this arose for both international and internal migrations. His findings were corroborated by Edwin Muir, in his *Scottish Journey*, when he found 'Maidenhead all around me in Dunkeld, Brixton in Ullapool and Tunbridge Wells in Scourie'.[11] He argued that some of the English had a 'strange and exasperating habit of filling it [Scotland] with the local atmosphere of some provincial or suburban district of their own land'.[12] What is not clear from Muir's journey is whether he was referring to English tourists, residents, or both. This distinction is important. Sixty-four years later, in 1998, Mike Russell wrote a book based on Muir's original journey.[13] In oral testimony Russell observed that tourists carried their English culture around with them, and complained when they got the *Scottish Daily Mirror* rather than the *Daily Mirror*, and the *Scottish Daily Mail* rather than the *Daily Mail*. When it came to English-born residents, however, Russell cited the example of the English-born head teacher of Tighnabruaich School who became so involved in the local community that she had not, in Muir's sense, 'turned Tighnabruaich into Surbiton'.[14]

Detailed analysis of the oral testimonies demonstrates that 93.1 per cent of the English-born migrants consciously adopted personal assimilation strategies, although these varied in intensity and effectiveness, therefore confounding both Catani's and Muir's hypotheses. They experienced, in the words of Malcolm Dickson, 'some form of "Scottishing" effect',[15] unlike the Irish, who, according to Tom Devine, were 'strangers in a strange land'.[16]

Migrants thought about the interrelated processes of acculturation and assimilation in different ways. Emma Wood referred to becoming 'part of life up here', as a form of 'engagement'. Amanda Green talked about gaining community acceptance. One of the ways she achieved this was through communal peat-cutting on Lewis, an activity that she would not have experienced in her former Leicestershire home. James and Lucy Dowling referred to 'acceptance', pointing out that this was a two-way process. Other descriptions included 'fitting the bill',[17] 'being prepared to muck in',[18] 'mixing in',[19] and 'to socialise'.[20] What this showed was a consciousness about the need to assimilate, as amply demonstrated by the first two extracts at the beginning of this chapter.

The processes of acculturation and assimilation are inherently complex and vary from individual to individual. Furthermore, analysis becomes more problematic at an individual level, given that there are behavioural variations depending on time and place. Assimilation is essentially about immersion into the receiving society, in particular absorbing its culture and history in terms of habits, roles, attitudes, sentiments, values and knowledge.[21] A problem is that these are all imprecise terms, with an added difficulty being that, in the host society, they change over time and are reflected in different ways in different segments of that society. To overcome these difficulties the following discourse will be informed by the testimonies of the migrants themselves. The result will fall short of a structured analysis, but it does reflect the untidy realities faced by English-born migrants settling into a new cultural environment.

— THE UNTIDY REALITIES OF ASSIMILATION —

An effective way to measure assimilation is through some form of participant observation, but this is not usually an option for historians. Fortunately, however, there is a scattering of participant observation studies available for historical analysis. In their study of 'locals' and 'incomers' in North-West Ross, MacLeod and Payne observed that 'the archetypal ideas of "community" and "neighbourliness" inform and pattern everyday practices that stress solidarity'.[22] Their study found that some incomers actually preferred to remain outsiders, but most tried hard to be accepted by locals, and, in this group, some were while others were not. This was also reflected in the oral history sample, with nineteen out of twenty trying hard to gain acceptance. The majority of these claimed success with few observations about failure. Because human nature is reluctant to admit failure some caution should be applied here, and, as Macleod and Payne found, 'some [incomers] found the negotiation of social boundaries easier than others'.[23] This was also apparent from the oral testimonies. Stuart Brook, whose sophisticated assimilation strategies were quoted above, modestly recognised: 'So I think really we've not gone out of our way to become assimilated and to become Hawick folk, um, yeah it's just the way we are, people take us as they find us and we do the same with them.' Paul and, particularly, Amanda Adams found it more difficult to negotiate the social boundaries:

> AA – I found it [Scotland] slightly different. I felt it was a different country. The money was different and also the language, the accent was different. I just felt I was in a different country for a little while, not for long though. [Laughter].

> PA – I think it was more difficult for Amanda because obviously I was out at [work] and really

> AA – Until I joined, '97, went back into Guiding, and helped with the Brownies. I did find the Guiders, a little bit of sort of towards the Scots, they didn't really want to know [how Guides were run in England]...I went to Scottish camp last year, a big Scottish camp; I pushed myself forward to help...I was working with our County Commissioner and Assistant County Commissioner and I got to know her really very well and you got to know other Guiders from other parts of the County.

This extract paints only part of the picture. For the Adams the process of assimilation was multifaceted, like it was for most of those trying hard to 'fit in'. Amanda Adams joined the Scottish Women's Rural Institute (SWRI), the Trefoil Guild, the North Berwick Swimming Club, and attended weekly keep-fit classes. Paul Adams met people through playing golf. He joined the North Berwick Horticultural Society and was elected its president; he chaired the residents' committee, and joined Probus when he retired. Of those who chose to remain on the outside, like Sarah Thomas (see above), there were sometimes factors involved that were not directly connected with a change to Scottish culture. Take the case of teenager Jennifer Roberton: her parents bought a farm in the Borders and she was sent to the local High School, which had a largely working-class intake. She was unhappy there, and transferred to an Edinburgh boarding school. She recalled:

JR – I definitely prefer it because people from all round the world and they've got different, although they're different they've got like the same experiences as me. And they're not all Scottish. They're, quite a lot of them are English and I've made a lot of close friends there. I'm definitely glad that I went and I don't regret leaving for school there.

Mum – Say what you said to me yesterday about why you didn't feel that there was any Scottish/English.

JR – Because people all have English accents, nobody has a Scottish accent at my school because they're all . . . sort of middle-upper class, Scottish people . . . Well, yeah, I mean, I am not the sort of person to just change myself to fit in really. I don't think I'll ever do that. [I'm] very stubborn.

While there was a Scottish/English dimension here – Jennifer retained her English accent while her sister did not – her motives were clearly class driven. She was happy to assimilate into the Scottish upper-middle class, but not to cross class boundaries.

Some two thirds of the contributors raised the subject of community and community spirit. This was frequently done in a comparative way where Scotland was cited as having closer communities than England. It was also evident that the Scottish sense of community facilitated assimilation. James and Lucy Dowling moved to Blairgowrie when James got a new job near Perth. They were both struck by the friendliness and community compared with the south west of England:

JD – We have often said that the last house we were at before we moved to Scotland, a little village at Etchilhampton just outside of Devizes, and we lived there for seventeen years and even when we left we were still known as the people that live in the new house and really we were not considered locals . . . But as soon as we came up here the folk were so friendly. In fact when we came to look at the plot of ground we were made to feel at home and the farmer from whom we purchased the plot took us round to meet some of the neighbours around and we felt as though we had known them for years.

This recognition of community was commented on time and again. Sarah Brown in Shetland noted that 'it worked out really well because we are accepted in the community'; Sarah Andrews in Inverness remarked, 'I got very involved in local community stuff and all the school stuff, the mother and toddler stuff, the school board; you name it I seemed to be on it'; Chris Smout found the people of Anstruther 'regard outsiders with a kind of wry amusement and affection, very often'. He explained that this combined 'a very subtle and interesting sense of identity' with a 'sense of welcome'. Tim David, who bought a house near Eyemouth, observed:

> We have taken part in as much as we can of the activities of the local community and we like to consider ourselves as incoming natives. So we're against the idea of being called English or anything else. We are, we have set ourselves here and we want to be as good members of the local community as we possibly can.

This sense of community and its role in assimilation varied and was largely dependent on location. Migrants who lived in both urban and rural locations commented on differences. Paul Armstrong compared Coldstream with the Central Belt.

> [I live] just north of Coldstream so I'm right on the border. I think if you move into any community no matter, the fact that I was English moving into a community made no difference. You know, when you move from one area to another you're a stranger aren't you and er, I said I've had absolutely no problems the community . . . The small village I live in, they couldn't have been more welcoming. [In] the Central Belt I found the people a lot more harsh . . . Um the people in the housing estate where I lived, again I didn't have any problems with. There were a number of English families on the estate although we certainly didn't, we certainly didn't keep together if you will, the majority of my friends were Scottish but, so from that point of view, the sense of community was mixed. You know there was English and Scottish all mixing in. There isn't the sense of community where I was there that there is in the Borders but that's probably because it is a lot smaller.

Roger Smith also recognised the feeling of community in the small town of Peebles: 'There was a feeling of a community, a definite community there, which we hadn't had, certainly hadn't had, living where we did in the Midlands [of England].' Smith lived in eight different locations in Scotland and commented on the relative lack of community in urban environments, as well as indicating differences between coastal and inland locations. Armstrong stressed that he was not a member of an exclusive English social network, and that he had Scottish friends. This sentiment was repeated time and again throughout the testimonies. The English visibly assimilated into predominantly Scottish social networks. This contributed to their relative invisibility.

— GENDER AND THE ROLE OF FAMILY —

There were significant gendered differences in assimilation and this could be broken down into four categories. First, there were the males and females in work where the workplace provided opportunities for assimilation. This was evident in a number of the testimonies including those of Jimmy Smith, Jack Brown, Chris Smout, Mary Mulligan, Ron Curran, Neil Bayfield, Patricia Yeaman, and others. The second category was wives and partners, either with no children or older children. Paul Adams recalled, 'I think it was more difficult for Amanda because obviously I was out at work all the time and Amanda was at home so harder for her to become integrated'. The absence of young children played a role in making assimilation more difficult for non-working wives and partners. Janice Grant highlighted this:

> I was absolutely devastated [when her husband was transferred to Edinburgh] and it did take a couple of years to settle down, basically I think because the children didn't need me to take them anywhere so consequently, I think you get to know more people when you do take them around and you do take them to places whereas they didn't need me to take them.

This leads conversely to the third category, women with younger children. Sarah Andrews (above) demonstrated how children facilitated assimilation. This experience was reflected elsewhere and is probably a general migratory experience and not just for moves between England and Scotland. But children did not always produce an easier route for assimilation. Patricia Yeaman recalled, 'the first thing that ever happened was that I pushed this baby out in a pram and little Dundee wifies in bonnets would lean over the pram and talk to the baby: "Are ye gettin a hurl then?"' In spite of this she was 'so, so lonely'. The fourth category was single females, divorcees and single parents; all of the latter, in this sample, were female. This group faced the greatest difficulties with assimilation. June Williams 'escaped to Scotland' after marital breakdown.

> Moving up here, I have said this many times, moving up here was the most sensible thing I did on a personal level but it was career suicide. And em what with the relationship break-up and you know losing everything financially I found myself in the situation of having to claim benefits and I didn't know what they were.

Arguably Williams' problems were unrelated to the act of migration and were the consequences of her marriage break up and would have occurred wherever she had 'escaped to'. Her love of Scotland, however, had a therapeutic effect and amongst other behavioural strategies she used her new membership of the Church of Scotland as one of her routes to assimilation.[24] Shortly after arriving in Aberdeen, Pauline McLaren divorced her alcoholic husband and became a single parent with four children. In addition to financial problems, McLaren talked about the difficulties she faced in making friends with other families in 1960s' Aberdeen without a husband. Similarly, one single female contributor explained that her partner-less status created difficulties:

> I actually went into the flat next door to Alice (pseud.). Apart from her I wouldn't say I have made any good friends in Dundee. It's an odd place to sort of make friends. And again I think it's because I am a foreigner. I am very aware of being a foreigner. The other thing about Dundee is people stay in Dundee. They are born here they live here they stay here. There is an awful lot of people who have never really been anywhere else. So you're an oddity if you have moved around and that you've been places. And again I am single and [unclear] per cent of women my age are married so I am a real peculiar bird . . . I go out on my own which is also extremely peculiar [laughter]. So I am definitely not your average normal female in Dundee terms. Em, but in spite of all that I still like living up here.

Elizabeth Bunting also observed that Dundee family networks were closed, and this hindered assimilation. This was also the experience of Dundee-based Patricia Yeaman: 'Your Dundee friends are very busy with their [extended] families as well, they don't have so much time, they've got other demands on their time.' Here the Dundee University babysitting circle, made up largely of incomers, formed a valuable surrogate family role: 'we were like each others' uncles, cousins, brothers, sisters because we missed our families, they were so far away and we did a lot of childcare swapping.'

At the beginning of this chapter Stuart Brook commented about the clannish nature of a small Borders town; this was also commented on by Peter Crown:

> They do all know each other. It has its disadvantages as well. Sometimes it's a terrible thing. Everybody knows everybody else, including their past . . . It's mind-boggling how you actually keep track of all these people and know who they

all are . . . You obviously struggle when there are not a lot of school friends and acquaintances.

MacLeod and Payne referred to this type of social boundary as a 'concept of difference' of 'being rooted in the place; the identity of belonging; bounded social horizons; and a sense of antiquity and continuity over time'.[25] Their study was corroborated by anthropologist Jonathan Hearn who also recognised the density and interconnectedness of Scottish social networks that often shared the same mutual history.[26] In spite of these barriers, which evidently hindered assimilation, none of the contributors who raised the issue gave up and returned to England. Indeed only two people mentioned homesickness, and in both cases this was short-lived.

– BELIEFS, VALUES AND *MENTALITÉ* –

One of the benefits of life history testimonies is the insight they provide into *mentalité*, or what people are thinking and why people are thinking what they are thinking. This is especially revealing because an important part of the process of assimilation is the acquisition of values, attitudes and sentiments of the host society. Each life history unravelled layers of experiences that the contributor felt important in connection with migrating to, and living in, Scotland. Each life history experience was extracted from a mass of complexity and reconstructed in the form of oral testimony. Sometimes the narrative was presented in an apparently logical framework, but more often than not it was not. Trains of thought were interrupted (or contradicted) when a contributor remembered a link or connection that influenced his or her recall of the 'event' being described. This should not be a surprise; after all it is the way the human mind works, thinks and remembers. The output, for historical analysis, is a richness and diversity that inevitably impedes reasonable levels of coherent categorisation. Analysis becomes more problematic because of the imprecision of the concepts of 'values', 'attitudes' and 'sentiment', and the fact that their overlapping nature does not remain constant, changing, as it does, over situational time. Foucault's genealogical approach provides a means to disentangle these interrelated complexities. His starting point to supplying a foundation of intelligible elucidation was to go back to the 'origins', in this case the testimonies themselves. Here, a number of themes emerged within the processes of acculturation and assimilation. These included: reactions to Thatcherism and adoption of Scottish political perspectives, feelings of national identity, involvement in Scottish culture and community activities, the adoption of Scottish iconography, and interest in Scottish history.

One of the topics that was raised by one in four of the contributors was the role played by Margaret Thatcher in Scottish politics in the 1980s and early 1990s. This was revealing in three respects. First, most of the contributors raised this spontaneously, without prompting. Second, Mrs Thatcher resigned as prime minister up to ten years before the interviews took place. And third, only three other prime ministers, Churchill, Heath and Blair, were mentioned, and they were mentioned only once by two different contributors. Why then did Mrs Thatcher feature so strongly in the consciousness of this representative quota sample, and was this a common reaction? The answer to the latter was yes. In most cases Mrs Thatcher was criticised as not understanding Scotland, and, by implication, represented the 'worst' of England. The following four extracts are typical:

> Yeah don't let's forget Margaret Thatcher because one of the reasons for getting away from England at that time was 'that woman' and what she was doing and people were lapping it up and, in England, whereas of course here things were very different.

This was the recollection of Emma Wood who was politically active, and her political leanings were clearly influential in her moving north. Margaret Cox, who was not active politically, came to live in the Borders in 1986. She observed:

> I think Margaret Thatcher for a while was on lots of people's tongues to the point of derision . . . I, oh, well her attitude and not necessarily her policies. I think, I think because of her attitude. Yeah. A railroading, steamrolling, you know, who are those people, who are the people out of, you know, beyond Westminster.

Referring to Thatcher as a 'nanny figure' who bossed Scotland around, Elizabeth Bunting said:

> The poll tax was one of their worst mistakes I think. I think the fact that they imposed it on Scotland first, and not just the poll tax I mean every every sort of grotty policy they wanted to implement was tried on Scotland first. There really was a feeling that they didn't give a shit about Scotland at all.

Bunting was an active trade unionist and naturally anti-Thatcher. The same could not be said about June Williams, a self-confessed Tory from Sussex:

> I can remember going to the, this was back in the early days, going to Eden Court [Theatre in Inverness] and seeing the Corries and I can remember one song that

they did and the lyrics went: 'The English didn't give a toss when the poll tax came up here but now they've got the same as us they're crying in their beer' [Laughs]. So you know it's em. I voted SNP when I came up here . . . As an aside to that I can never vote Conservative again.

Only two out of the four MSPs interviewed mentioned Mrs Thatcher. Mary Mulligan, Labour, was understandably critical. The Conservative, Nick Johnston, was surprisingly blunt, but also critical:

There were some policies, which the Tories carried out in their 18 years in power, which frankly didn't help the cause terribly much up here. I think any party, which decides to use a part of the United Kingdom as a test bed for policies, which may or not work, is asking for trouble.

Johnston went on to criticise the superior colonial attitude of English MPs, commenting that this lack of understanding of Scotland contributed to the Conservatives' decline:

And just last week [mid-November, 2000] we had a bunch of seven of them [English-based MPs] up from Westminster, none of whose names are known beyond the boundaries of their constituencies I would venture to suggest, with the exception maybe of Dominic Grieve . . . And their attitude to me, I mean as an Englishman, who has lived here for a number of years, was frankly patronising. Um . . . almost colonial. Um . . . the, the, you know. We are still an outpost of the Empire, that needs to be controlled, and we get far too much money. And you know, I have said to them, and I have said it fairly forcibly, and I have fallen out out with people in the party because of it, unless we can find some way of muzzling the more rabid dogs of our party in Westminster then we haven't a hope in hell of making ourselves electable to the people of Scotland again.

Significantly, what comes through in these extracts is an appreciation of Scotland's feeling of being the junior partner in the United Kingdom. Johnston, as an Englishman living in Scotland, railed against the patronising attitude of his English party colleagues. And Williams, a former Conservative voter, evidently approved of an anti-Thatcher folk song. Arguably this demonstrates an appreciation of Scottish political feeling and is an example of migrants adopting one of the host country's values.

Margaret Thatcher was very unpopular in Scotland, and this was reflected in election results.[27] Angus Calder argued that Thatcher's unpopularity was 'fuelled by an especially Scottish "civic" consensus . . . and a more generous attitude to the wider world.'[28] Tom Nairn concurred when he wrote, in 1988, that the 'Thatcherite formula . . . is meeting [in Scotland] the unforeseen obstacle of a civil society structurally hostile to many of its implications'.[29] Another explanation of Thatcher's unpopularity was her strident nature and the Englishness of her manner. This was certainly the view of Ludovic Kennedy,[30] but this opinion, even after challenge, was not shared by any of the sample's contributors with the exception of Bernard Crick. He said, 'yes I think the stereotypical English-lady accent does rather grate on Scottish ears but then so did Ted Heath's.' Crick was more inclined to the view that Thatcher's policies were out of step in Scotland, and that she did not help herself by referring to 'Scotland' as 'England'.

Thatcher certainly generated hostility in Scotland, and this was mirrored by a quarter of the English-born migrants, some of whom would have been amongst her supporters in England. As such this can be partly explained by the adoption of Scottish political perspectives and values, especially the appreciation of the notions of Scottish civic society and community. Political commentators, political scientists and historians[31] are generally agreed that the Thatcher years, and the so-called 'democratic deficit' after the general election of 1992, provided a stimulus for Nationalism and the 'home rule' movement. Furthermore, throughout the nineties the press and broadcast media upped the tempo in terms of its coverage in this area, including widespread reporting about the growth of anti-English feeling and protest. These issues are all closely inter-connected and affected English migrants living in Scotland during these years. How they responded, and what effects this had on assimilation and acculturation, merits detailed examination, and will be covered, in depth, throughout the next three chapters.

Evidence from the *Third Statistical Account of Scotland* (see Chapter 4) showed how English-born migrants involved themselves in community and voluntary activities. This was also reflected in the oral testimonies. Altogether the contributors claimed membership of 134 voluntary and non-governmental organisations. There was a wide range of activities covered, from membership of sports clubs to participation in the Campaign for Nuclear Disarmament (CND), a women's singing group, village hall committees, community councils, trade unions, and parent-teacher associations. Twelve per cent of the sample did not mention any membership but this did not mean they were not members of any organisations, given the free-format nature of the interview. For the same reason, it is likely that there is an underestimate of participation from those people who talked about voluntary activities. Not accounting for underestimation, each migrant, in this cohort, participated in an average number of 2.62 voluntary organisations. This ranged from one to eight. Another feature was the proportion of office bearers. Nearly one in four were committee members or officials, such as secretaries or chairmen.[32] Membership of voluntary organisations provided a means to meet people, integrate and understand differences in Scottish society and culture. But involvement with voluntary groups continued long after the initial assimilation phase. The fact that many of these groups were concerned with specifically local and Scottish issues implies an immersion in Scottish values, political and cultural *mores*. At a local level, this ranged from the Galashiels Rotary Club to the Lewis Keep NATO Out group, the Prestwick Scout troop, the Royal Northern University Club and the Hawick Pleasant Sunday Afternoon choir. At a national level, involvement at office-bearer level included the Scottish Wild Land Group, the National Trust for Scotland, New Scots for Independence, the National Museum of Scotland, Scottish Natural Heritage, the Guide Association, the [S]WRI,[33] and Citizens' Advice Bureau. The SWRI was the most popular organisation and given it is open only to women it assumes added significance. Indeed, all the SWRI members in the sample related how important this organisation was in getting to know people and as a means for continued socialisation. Only one of the contributors had been a member of the [English] Women's Institute. All expressed opinions that the SWRI was a more inclusive less 'Jam and Jerusalem' type of organisation. This acceptance of the Scottish model, and rejection of one of the most recognisable English icons, provided further evidence of a shift from English to Scottish values.[34]

Table 7.1 Participation rates of Scots and English migrants in local organisations and activities

	Long-term residents	English [migrants]	Scots [migrants]
Cultural group			
Active participation	18 (10%)	12 (12%)	43 (12%)
Hold office	1 (0.6%)	9 (9%)	15 (4%)
Community activity			
Active participation	24 (14%)	18 (18%)	59 (17%)
Hold office	17 (10%)	9 (9%)	18 (5%)
Community council			
Active participation	5 (3%)	1 (1%)	8 (2%)
Hold office	2 (1%)	2 (2%)	2 (1%)
School board			
Active participation	10 (6%)	9 (9%)	17 (5%)
Hold office	2 (1%)	3 (3%)	10 (3%)

Source: D. Short and A. Stockdale, 'English Migrants in the Scottish Countryside: Opportunities for Rural Scotland?', *Scottish Geographical Journal*, vol. 115, no. 3, 1999, p. 190.

In the Roxburghshire volume of the *Third Statistical Account of Scotland*, the editor, Kenneth Silver, observed that the English had a 'quite disproportional representation on local committees, voluntary and charitable organisations'.[35] This conclusion was partially corroborated by Short and Stockdale's study of six rural districts in 1997.[36] Table 7.1 shows the levels of participation of English and internal Scots migrants to be similar, and in all cases exceeding those of longer-term residents.

Short and Stockdale concluded that from their participation rates 'it seems that they [the English] wish to involve themselves in the life of both a community and environment which they value highly'.[37] This demonstrates that reasonable levels of precision can be applied when measuring acculturation and assimilation in terms of participation in voluntary activities.

Precision is more problematic when it comes to assessing the adoption of other cultural values. But what is culture? Jonathan Hearn argued that the concept of 'culture' is poorly understood, ill defined and embraces a 'loosely cohering set of assumptions and beliefs.'[38] Christopher Harvie attempted definition from two perspectives:

> The first is historical, an extension of the history of ideas, paying special regard to the social conditions in which a society either accepted or rejected an ideology . . . The second approach, recently more salient, concentrates on the text and mode of discourse, language symbolism, relationship to audience, and so on.[39]

Beyond academic debate, 'culture' would normally be associated with the arts and even here there would be disagreement about whether classical music or popular music represented 'culture'. With the exception of the testimonies of T. C. Smout and Bernard Crick, there was little evidence of consciousness of 'culture' as represented in the definition presented by Christopher Harvie. There were, however, many references to what might loosely be referred to as 'tartanry'. Scottish iconography was seen as distinctive. But this needs to be put into perspective. Awareness of cultural differences was raised at other levels, particularly related to community and national identity.[40] Recognition and adoption of Scottish customs and traditions were manifested throughout the testimonies in a variety of different ways. A number of these have already been mentioned, including kilt-wearing, learning Gaelic, appreciating performances by the 7:84 Theatre Company and participation in hogmanay festivities. Jack Brown arrived in Scotland on the 15 December 1937 and was about to experience a 'culture shock':

> . . . and what horrified me was that they [the Scots] worked on Christmas day and I thought, 'What a bunch of pagans' . . . I got on quite well with the folks

eventually. Once they'd begun to understand me and I understood them and actually, we got settled down into the place. Had church connections and that was useful. I joined the Scouts as a Scouter. I got a kilt. Did the whole thing in style . . . Oh at Christmas, Christmas time of course or New Years time of course they had the celebrations and connected with the churches, it was the Old Year's Night Soirée at the Home Mission, which is now defunct.

Coincidentally, this interview took place on the sixty-second anniversary of Brown's arrival in Scotland – surely confirming, in this case, successful integration. Eileen MacDonald, another long-stay migrant (fifty-five years) enthused about what she perceived to be a Scottish institution: 'I quite like, I like a Burns Supper. I do like Burns Supper. We used to go to some lovely ones with the local Philharmonic in Ayr'.

Other Scottish icons were adopted by English-born migrants in their pursuit of Scottishness. One middle-aged lady wore a transfer-type tattoo of the saltire on her face to support Scotland at Murrayfield, and Trevor Steven, the Rangers and England soccer player, admitted to singing the *Flower of Scotland* anthem. However, because he had represented England at international level, he cautioned: 'But if it was England/Scotland I wouldn't sing along to it.' Christine Kirkton, whose son played representative rugby for Scotland, said she would support Scotland in a Calcutta Cup match because 'my blood has totally turned to supporting Scotland. I believe that Scotland is really my home.'

One of the more unusual examples of iconographic transfer involved Scotland's only morris-dancing team and their alter ego, an English-born Scottish ceilidh band. Neil Bayfield and half a dozen Englishmen, living in the Banchory area, set up the morris-dancing team in 1974. Morris dancing, according to Jeremy Paxman, was evocative of the English idyll,[41] but Bayfield did not wholly agree:

Curiously it [morris dancing] used to be very much a Scottish thing as well as English. It was actually suppressed by John Knox and other Scots, Church of Scotland early Church of Scotland people. It was too much like good fun I think. In fact there are records of people being prosecuted for morris dancing in Elgin, in Aberdeen, and indeed in Edinburgh somebody was nearly hanged for it.

A sense of history and tradition were important to Bayfield: 'The music and the dance are a perfect match and they are very old, some of them go back to the thirteenth century and they just so beautifully fit together and some of the tunes are so I don't know it just gets in your veins.' This interest in tradition was not limited to morris dancing:

I also play in a ceilidh band . . . *We* are a Scottish ceilidh band . . . We are called the Flying Piemen and we are a six-piece band . . . We are all English. But I mean musically musically we play essentially Scottish ceilidh music. Because ceilidh bands in Scotland are different to in England. *They* play off a different repertoire . . . There are some things in common but the Scottish ceilidh is fairly distinct and *we* are a traditional Scottish ceilidh band.

One of the most significant parts of this extract is Bayfield's use of the first person, when referring to Scotland, and the use of the third person when referring to England. His use of '*we*' and '*they*' indicates a personal alignment with Scotland. A number of other contributors also used the first and third person in this way.[42] Perhaps this could be used as a marker of assimilation?

— The past remaining as part of the present —

Understanding and sharing the sense of history of the host community is an important measure in the process of acculturation. According to MacLeod and Payne, 'events of the past are used to re-state cultural values and norms of behaviour' and this frequently creates a conceptual barrier for assimilation.[43] Clearly in the case of Neil Bayfield, and through his hobbies, he acquired a deep knowledge and understanding of a specific area of Scottish history. This sense of history pervaded the testimonies. At the beginning of this chapter Stuart Brook referred to the Hawick Common Riding. Another Borders resident, Peter Crown, commented on the relationship the locals had with their history, and how it acted as a barrier to the incomer:

A bizarre, a bizarre event [The Common Riding] that you know, as an outsider, seeing a melting pot of historical things that also are definitely twentieth century that most of the people in the town use the event as just, just for a jolly good time. The historical things, maybe sometimes, just matter to some of the people . . . It's an amazing event. I have always felt that it was an event for local people and that, as an English person, you went along and was made welcome but em you never feel part and parcel of the whole event . . . And at the end of the day it is celebrating Hawick youth routing part of an English army [in 1514] so I have always kept a healthy distance from it. Just out of respect.

The previous two testimonies demonstrate a relatively sophisticated understanding of aspects of Scottish history and the role of the past in the twentieth and twenty-first centuries. Other contributors too showed an appreciation of subtle differences between Scottish, English and British history, as well as a desire to learn about the Scottish past. Overall, the subject of history was raised in 43 per cent of the testimonies. Three of the contributors went as far as joining local history societies, and Catherine Parr, who was secretary of the Mull Historical Society, said that they had Scots and Mulleach members but that 'the majority were English'. The importance of history in Scottish culture was something that was recognised by all of the contributors who raised the topic of history. And, in many of their contributions, 'history' was interwoven into the fabric of their testimonies, being raised in different contexts, and often making connections to contemporary events. For example, Tim Underwood made references to history throughout his testimony. Shortly after he arrived in Scotland, the Stone of Destiny was stolen from Westminster Abbey in 1950. Underwood could not understand what all the fuss was about. Three years later at the coronation he showed he appreciated why some Scots were against the Queen being crowned Elizabeth II and not Elizabeth I of Scotland. And later on in the testimony, he began to use historical analysis to explain contemporary events, in this case sectarianism:

> There are people I know who feel very strongly about it [religious bigotry] still and I think the Scots generally do think more about their history than the English do. I mean quite honestly it's not a subject that's I've ever really been, modern history yes but something that happened three or four hundred years ago is to my mind. I am afraid I am very short-tempered say when it comes to things religion in Scotland. Before I came up here I had never come across any bigotry . . . I'd never come across it and this was one thing that surprised me when I came to Scotland, this strong feeling in the west of Scotland that is very real.

There are a number of other examples in this vein. Other contributors, some from a self-confessed position of historical ignorance, came to view Scotland as having been hard done to by England, and here, in Foucault's terms, there are symmetries, proximities and connections with issues surrounding national identity (and these will be considered further in Chapter 10). Emma Wood, who wrote *Notes from the North*,[44] subtitled *Incorporating a Brief History of the Scots and English*, believed she had a mission to help English migrants understand Scottish history – from 'the decidedly unsubtle Edward I' to 'Butcher Cumberland's genocidal campaign of revenge' and 'the historical guilt of the clearances'.[45] Targeting her book at English migrants she felt there was a need to improve historical understanding. Consciously and unconsciously she was recognising the role played by sharing historical memory with the host society.

— CHILDREN AND ASSIMILATION —

According to teenager Neil Andrews the unfortunate thing about his mother is that she 'speaks with an English accent'.[46] Neil and his sister were both born in Raigmore Hospital, Inverness, to English-born parents. Sarah, his mother, confirmed that both her children considered themselves Scots in 'contrast to other friends that I have who have children who . . . see themselves as English because they've got English parents'. Sarah went on to explain that through her children identifying with Scotland both she and her husband began to consider Scotland, rather than Portsmouth, their home. Here the role of family, and especially children, was a key component in completing the acculturation cycle. The Andrews children also played a part in facilitating assimilation for Sarah, as she met a lot of people through mother and toddler groups and school activities (see above). This raises questions about the impact children had in the assimilation process, as well as considering the implications of assimilation for children.

Looking at the contributors as a whole, 18.18 per cent did not have children and of the remainder 13.33 per cent had children who had left school at the time of migration. The average number of children was 2.4 per family unit; 48.51 per cent were born in Scotland, 43.56 per cent were born in England, with the balance being born elsewhere. While there were no routine questions about the perceived national identity of the children, close analysis of the testimonies revealed, regardless of place of birth, that there were four distinct categories, as seen in table 7.2. These were: family units where all the children saw themselves as Scots; family units where all the children saw themselves as English; family units where there was contested nationality, that is where some siblings saw themselves as Scots and the others English;[47] and finally, family units where the data were unclear or inconclusive.

Table 7.2 Estimated perception of perceived national identity of migrants' children

Family unit type	Approximate percentage
All children perceived themselves as Scots	54
All children perceived themselves as English	8
Contested nationality	16[a]
Insufficient data	22

Source: Data gathered from this study's oral testimonies.
a. 57% of this group perceived themselves as Scots, 43% as English.

Interpreting this data requires caution. There were no specific questions about this in the interview, and there are inevitable risks in extracting the data. This was minimised to a degree by rejecting around one in five of the testimonies, but this in itself is problematic because it represents a large proportion of the available information. Nonetheless, some interesting hypotheses can be advanced, a matter that will be returned to shortly. But first we need to examine the category of contested nationality. The testimony of Chris Smout, who had a Scandinavian wife, was fairly typical. He had two children. They went to the same schools in Edinburgh, and to the same university in England. They both married and returned to live and work in Scotland. Speaking about his daughter, Smout said, 'nobody ever considers her anything other than Scottish. And indeed I think that Penny has two languages. One to use with us here and one with everybody else.' Referring to his son: 'I think he thinks of himself as English . . . it is remarkable to me how one child unhesitatingly thinks herself Scottish and the other one English'. No explanation for this different behaviour was offered,[48] and neither was it in all the other testimonies where there was evidence of contested nationality.

Returning to the aforementioned hypotheses, there is evidence in the testimonies to suggest a correlation between ease of assimilation by the parents and the desire of the majority of their children to want to be seen as Scottish and not English. Equally, the behaviour and attitudes of the children could have had a bearing on their parents' approach to life in Scotland. To prove or disprove these ideas would require, at least, investigating the attitudes of children of returned migrants to see whether this had a bearing on their parents' choice of home. Unfortunately this was outwith the scope of this study. What also emerged from the parents' testimonies was that, by attending Scottish schools and mixing with a predominantly Scottish peer group, their children were exposed to different aspects of Scottish culture and society, often in a more raw form. This was brought into the home, providing an additional source of information and experience which added to the process of assimilation.

– CONCLUSION –

Analysis of the testimonies paints a picture of successful integration, but this could also present a false impression, given the self-selecting nature of the sample where only 4 per cent of the contributors had returned to England. The 1981 census data showed a return migration rate of 31.55 per cent.[49] There can be little doubt that failure to assimilate would have been one of a number of factors behind this return movement, as demonstrated in some anecdotal testimony. Referring to a colleague who came to work with him in Edinburgh, Jim Grant said: 'He unfortunately didn't settle, he didn't get on with the people at head office or rather some of them tended to have a go at him because he had a southern accent.' There was a range of factors influencing return migration including job transfer, the weather, midges,[50] and returning to be nearer family. Distance from family was mentioned by a number of contributors, and clearly was a dilemma for migrants who had successfully integrated into Scottish society. For example, Sarah Brown, after saying her husband wanted his ashes scattered in Scotland, failed to answer her own rhetorical question, 'well what are we going to do?' when their eighteen-year-old son heads south for employment.

Given the rigour of the sampling and oral history methodology it is reasonable to make generalisations about the group as a whole, and therefore English migrants as a whole. Overall, the evidence points to successful integration and that this was an evolving process. Combined with widespread geographical dispersal, and socio-economic diversity of English migrants, the nature of their assimilation and acculturation added to their 'invisibility'. What the foregoing analysis proves is that assimilation and acculturation are profoundly interconnected with issues of structuralism, attitudes of various host communities, fears, aspirations, a personal sense of identity, and place in society. This is part of a lifelong process of negotiating identity, difference, flourishing and failing in a new context – in this case Scotland and all its societal sub-groups. Like personal motivations behind the reasons to migrate, assimilation and acculturation were complex and multifaceted.

– Notes –

1. The Dawson Group, a textile conglomerate and holding company based in Kinross, owned Pringle of Scotland, a knitwear company, when they employed Brook in 1968.
2. Sarah Smith was a member of a New Age community, the Beshara School. (See Chapter 5.)
3. Fonte, Hudson Institute, web site accessed 28/8/02.
4. Hutching, (1999), *Long Journey for Sevenpence*, p. 114.
5. Holomek, *Roma in the Former Czechoslovakia*, web site accessed 28/8/02.
6. S. Israel, 'David Blunkett', *Channel 4 News*, 7/2/02.
7. Mayhew, (1997), *A Dictionary of Geography*.
8. Johnston, *Dictionary of Human Geography*, (Oxford, 2000).
9. Ibid.
10. Catani, 'Social-Life History as Ritualized Oral Exchange', in Bertaux (ed.), (1981), *Biography and Society*, p. 211.
11. Muir, (1935), *Scottish Journey*, p. 72.
12. Ibid., p. 72.
13. Russell, (1998), *In Waiting: Travels in the Shadow of Edwin Muir*.
14. Mike Russell, Tape MW0025, 13/6/01.

15. Dickson, (1994), 'Should Auld Acquaintance Be Forgot?', p. 131.
16. Devine, *Strangers in a Strange Land? Two Centuries of the Irish in Scotland*, (Royal Society of Edinburgh Regional Lecture, University of Dundee, 21/11/01).
17. Tim Underwood (pseud.), Tape MW0034, 28/6/01.
18. Isobel Murray (pseud.), Tape MW0001, 1/11/99.
19. Rob Nicholson, Tape MW0018, 10/5/01.
20. Charlotte Howe (pseud.), Tape MW0052, 29/10/01.
21. See Mayhew, (1997), A *Dictionary of Geography, Dictionary of Human Geography*.
22. MacLeod and Payne, ' "Locals" and "Incomers" ', in Baldwin (ed.), (1994), *Peoples and Settlement in North-West Ross*, p. 394. (43 per cent of the study's incomers were English-born.)
23. Ibid., p. 397.
24. See Chapter 6.
25. MacLeod and Payne, (1994), ' "Locals" and "Incomers" ', pp. 409–12.
26. Hearn, (2000), *Claiming Scotland*, p. 84.
27. In the 1987 General Election the number of Scottish-based Conservative MPs was reduced to nine out of a possible seventy-two, the lowest number since 1910. In 1992, after John Major took over party leadership, the number increased to eleven. In 1997 there was only one Conservative MP representing a Scottish constituency, and the Shadow Secretary of State for Scotland represented an English constituency.
28. Calder, (2002), *Scotlands of the Mind*, p. 164.
29. Nairn, (1998),'Tartan and Blue', *Marxism Today*, p. 33.
30. Kennedy, (1995), *In Bed with an Elephant: A Journey Through Scotland's Past and Present*, p. 300.
31. See, amongst others, Marr, (2000), *The Day That Britain Died*; Crick, 'For my Fellow English', in Campaign for a Scottish Assembly, (1989), *Claim of Right for Scotland*, pp. 150–5; Harvie, (1994), *Scotland and Nationalism: Scottish Society and Politics 1707–1994*.
32. All the contributors used this descriptor. Even the women who were 'chairmen' used this term.
33. More commonly referred to as the WRI or 'the Rural', this is one of the few organisations that does not require the prefix Scottish.
34. See, amongst others, Isobel Murray (pseud.), Tape MW0001, 1/11/99.
35. See Chapter 4.
36. Short and Stockdale, 'English Migrants in the Scottish Countryside: Opportunities for Rural Scotland?', *Scottish Geographical Journal*, pp. 172–92.
37. Ibid., p. 191.
38. Hearn, (2000), *Claiming Scotland*, p. 10.
39. Harvie, 'Culture and Identity', in Cooke et al., (1998), *Modern Scottish History*, p. 277.
40. See Chapter 10.
41. Paxman, (1999), *The English*, pp. 166–8.
42. See, for instance, testimony from Nick Johnston above.
43. MacLeod and Payne, (1994), ' "Locals" and "Incomers" ', p. 409.
44. Wood, (1998), *Notes from the North*.
45. These three 'quotes' come from Wood, 'Bad Vibes Up North', *Guardian Unlimited, Special Reports*, 31/8/99, web site accessed 15/09/00.
46. Sarah Andrews (pseud.), Tape MW0047, 30/9/01.
47. Only three of the children were interviewed. Deciding how to categorise the perceived national identity of the others was determined from the contributor-parents' observations.
48. Smout later wrote that his was 'a comfortably muddled family'. See Devine and Logue (eds), (2002), *Being Scottish: Personal Reflections on Scottish Identity Today*, p. 245.
49. See Chapter 3.
50. The weather and midges were cited by Donald MacKenzie, of the Lochalsh and Skye Housing Association, *Scotland on Sunday*, 29/9/02, p. 12.

CHAPTER 8

Anglophobia

In the weeks preceding the 1997 devolution referendum, editorial writers on *The Herald* turned their attention to the growth of 'disgraceful attacks on English residents in Scotland'. According to them there was 'some anti-English feeling in Scotland because there is a tradition of such behaviour.'[1] A few months later a message was posted on the St Andrews University Bulletin Board from someone called Ken, from the south west of England, saying that he was thinking of relocating his family to St Andrews. He wanted to know: 'Is there any anti-English feeling?' A reply, from Pete, read: 'Not that I've noticed. I came here [from Somerset] as a student in '73 and never had any hint of difficulty . . . I can't say I've noticed any anti-English feeling in Scotland generally'.[2]

So which is the correct analysis? Pete went on to say that he had noticed 'anti-*England* [my emphasis] feeling', especially around the time of rugby and soccer matches between England and Scotland. Perhaps *The Herald* was confusing anti-Englishness, that is, feelings and behaviour at a personal level, with anti-England where feelings and behaviour are directed at a state. Tom Nairn subscribed to the latter view, arguing, 'there is of course antagonism towards "England" among Scots (though far less towards English individuals).'[3] He argued, as did Rab Houston,[4] that this form of Anglophobia had been there since long before the Union, 'after which it settled down into a steady . . . grumbling and narkiness, a "chip on the shoulder." '[5] He suggested that this was due to the structural inequalities of the Union.

One of the problems with Nairn's prognosis is that it was not based on empirical research, and unfortunately this is a scarce commodity. In their work on racism in Scotland, Robert Miles and Anne Dunlop identified, amongst other things, discrimination and harassment affecting Asian and Irish migrants, but made no references to the English. They argued that in the post-1945 period the 'national question' in which *England* was 'a political and ideological signification' was a dominant theme in the political agenda, and that this was sustained by a long-term decline of the Scottish economy overlaid by the historical experience of loss of nationhood.[6] In their words, Scotland and the Scots were 'the object of a different form of "colonial" domination by England'.[7] Whether this was the 'dominant theme' of the post-1945 period is open to doubt, but what is evident is that the relationship the Scots had with *England*, the state, was significant.

More recent empirical research, however, did identify the existence of anti-Englishness. A team of researchers from the Centre for Education for Racial Equality in Scotland (CERES) conducted an audit of studies on racial equality in 2000. CERES identified experiences of anti-English racism, but commented, without quantification, that some English people interviewed saw these issues as different from racism. Frustratingly their paper did not say why, although they did comment about the 'marginalisation of Scotland and Scottish issues within the UK'.[8]

This chapter will address the issue of anti-Englishness using the oral tes-timonies gathered for this study as the empirical basis for analysis. This is potentially problematic, however, because 94 per cent of the sample indi-cated that anti-Englishness was not a serious problem.[9] This directly contra-dicts *The Herald*'s editorial writers whose arguments about the tradition of anti-Englishness were corroborated by their large archive of articles, letters and features about anti-Englishness.[10]

– SOME THOUGHTS ON ANTI-ENGLISHNESS –

Issues surrounding racism are complex and, in the case of the English in Scotland, complexity is compounded by the confusion between England the state, and English, the people. Furthermore, analysis becomes additionally problematic because perceptions and definitions of racism changed during the period under review. Indeed, it was very difficult to find documentary references to racism before the 1960s, when the issue of Commonwealth immigrants entered the political lexicon, and even then this was very much confined to race relations in England. Between 1962 and 1988 there were ten Acts of Parliament concerned with immigration and race relations, the most important being the 1976 Race Relations Act.[11] This legislation was primarily directed at Commonwealth immigrants, but, as was seen in the Souster case, it came to be employed in anti-English cases in Scotland.[12]

But what is racism? According to Solomos: 'Racism is broadly defined in the sense it is used to cover those ideologies which discriminate against others on the basis of their putatively different racial membership.'[13] Peter Jackson, who argued that racism 'involves the attempt by a dominant group to exclude a subordinate group from the material and symbolic reward of status and power', offered a Weberian definition.[14] But how was racism manifested and experienced, and to what degree did this affect English migrants in Scotland? The first of these questions is much easier to answer than the second. In terms of legislation, racism was defined as discrimination (such as unequal employment opportunities) and harassment (for example, through violence or verbal abuse). The legislation, however, was concerned only with *acts* of discrimination and harassment. Sociologists like Michael Banton[15] stressed the significance of the *processes* of discrimination. According to Jackson:

> Processes are established, routine and *subtle* [my emphasis]; only occasionally will an individual act of racial discrimination become visible within these processes, and only intermittently can one individual actor be identified as responsible for the exclusion of another from rightful opportunities.[16]

To establish the extent of anti-English racism, the testimonies were analysed, looking first at acts of racism in terms of verbal abuse, violence and discrimination, and second at the more subtle processes of discrimination or social exclusion. Before considering this, we need to attempt to resolve the complication raised by John Solomos, when he observed that racism was not a static phenomenon. 'In societies such as Britain', he argued, 'racism is produced and reproduced through political discourse, the media, the educational system and other institutions.'[17] In the 1940s and 1950s racism was not recognised in the way that it was later. Even after the 1976 Race Relations Act, and the advent of political correctness from the late 1980s, much of what became understood as racism was hitherto acceptable social behaviour for many sections of society. Inspector Rob Nicholson provided examples of this social and political change. Nicholson, from Leicestershire, joined the Berwick, Roxburgh and Selkirk Constabulary in 1972. He was surprised at the attitude of his colleagues, and to find that he was an 'Englishman abroad'.

> Not long into my new job, and all the rest of it, and I was being called things like an English bastard and nobody had ever used a phrase like that to me in my life . . . I did grow a thick skin very quickly and anecdotally one of my colleagues, an experienced officer, who took me under his wing and we had an awful lot of fun on usually on a Friday or a Saturday night, because early on we would stand in a particular spot and as the trouble makers, whatever you might call them, were coming along he would prime me to speak at a certain time and whenever I did speak I would get the reaction 'an English bastard' and we would lock them up. [Laughter] So it worked extremely well. Provocation or whatever, it certainly worked.

On what basis these people were locked up was not clear, but some twenty-five years later, Nicholson, now an Inspector in the Lothian and Borders Force, became community liaison officer responsible, amongst other things, for race relations. He explained how social and political change affected his job:

> I also have evidence of people using . . . the race card, for example, [in] neighbour disputes that have gone on for years and years suddenly are now being reported to me as racial incidents because over the fence one has called the other an English bastard. They've maybe said it time and again over the years but now it's reported as a racial incident because people think if they hang that race label on it something else will happen; it has more gravity because it's now got this race label . . . The law has changed slightly. I think it's more an attitude of the people who wish to report it has changed . . .
>
> MW – *Now I'm not making any value judgements here but you imply that this is verbal abuse, I mean is there any violence?*
>
> RN – Not, in the cases that I've got, they're all verbal, the cases I have are all verbal. The cases I've had reported to me are all verbal . . .
>
> MW – *In your opinion or maybe you have got some form of facts, and if you go back to 1973 when you first came here, would you say that the situation was the same, better or worse?*
>
> RN – Well as far as reported incidents are concerned there is no comparison because we didn't have race relations legislation then, so [no] reported incidents. I know that if somebody came in to a police station in 1973 and reported that they had been abused because of their Englishness they would have been chased, quite honestly, but by the same token in 1973 the possibility is if a black man or an Asian man or a woman had come in and reported the same thing they too would have been chased in 1973. So that legislative difference, it's also a social difference I think.

What these last two testimony extracts demonstrate is the influence of legislative and social change over a very short time span. When Nicholson came to Scotland he suffered what would later be recognised as racial verbal abuse. Uncomfortable as it made him feel, this was acceptable in legal and social terms. Overall, the implications from this analysis are that this makes it difficult to make historical comparisons.

Even when statistical evidence is available it is far from reliable. From 1988 the Scottish Police were required to report annual statistics on racial incidents of a criminal nature, excluding employment discrimination and certain types of harassment. According to Elinor Kelly, police officers played down the 'racial' element in incidents and their resistance to recording them underestimated the levels of occurrence.[18] A further issue, which suggests an under-reporting of racial incidents, was identified in a Scottish Executive study. This found that in many small communities and towns there was a real fear that going to the police with complaints could attract reprisals from the perpetrators of harassment.[19] In terms of reported cases, the Commission for Racial Equality (CRE), set up under the 1976 Race Relations Act, maintained that around 5 per cent of their case load in Scotland concerned complaints about anti-Englishness.[20] While these figures cover discrimination and aspects of harassment they ignore the subtler processes of discrimination. One significant element of the CRE data is the relatively small number of reported cases involving people of English nationality. Given that English-born migrants outnumbered all other migrant groups by nearly two to one, the incidence of anti-English problems was relatively small, further corroborating the findings in the oral testimonies.

– VERBAL ABUSE –

Turning now to the oral testimonies, the most common type of anti-Englishness came in a verbal form. This was variously reported as banter, teasing, joking, or occasionally abuse. In many cases it was difficult to assess whether it was abuse or inoffensive conversation. For example, one day Isobel Murray was sitting on a bench in Tayport, admiring the view, when a man, walking his dog, stopped for a chat and during conversation said 'you're English'. Isobel commented that this was just conversational, but she observed that some other English migrants might have offered a more sinister interpretation. This was certainly the case when Amanda Adams admitted feeling uncomfortable when a guest at a coffee morning said 'oh you're English'. This may have been a form of verbal rejection, but hardly amounted to the type of racist name-calling, common in Scotland, like 'Paki or wog'.[21] And, as Isobel Murray observed, there would have been no thought of racism if the comment had been 'you're an American?' The testimonies did throw up examples of potentially racist comments, and indeed most people referred to comments about their English origins, either first hand or anecdotally. On the whole this was not seen as a problem, and its occurrence was rare, or it was not considered important in the grand scale of things. Liz Potts could only recall one instance in forty years and Tim David denied any experience of anti-Englishness at all. Indeed, it was noteworthy that, in many cases, anti-Englishness was only discussed after questioning. Pauline McLaren mentioned, spontaneously, that she had been on the end of 'snide remarks' from her work colleagues in Aberdeen, but that did not put her off liking Scotland where she has lived for forty-five years. Sarah

Brown's comments were typical. 'I think on the whole we have been accepted wherever we are, wherever we've been [in Shetland]. You get the odd comment but not to any great extent'.

Another theme of anti-English comments was their use in teasing, joking and banter. Sarah Andrews explained:

> I've never really actually had it [anti-Englishness] thrown in my face in anything other than a sort of joking way which is not the same thing. I've never had anybody; I've never had any fear that somebody's going to come and you know do anything horrible just because I'm English. Wherever I've been living I feel quite secure. [This was an important observation because Sarah was attacked shortly after her arrival in Scotland. Later in her testimony she mentioned this attack had nothing to do with her being English.]

Surely significant here is her feeling of security, hardly the sign of a racist environment. Good-humoured comments occurred with work colleagues, and in relationships with close Scottish friends. Paul Armstrong referred to shop-floor banter, and Peter Goodfellow recounted:

> I have never had any prejudice because I'm English and what is interesting is that I've got some friends who are very Scottish, real Scots Nationals and when they've had a few drinks their old hatred comes out and what has always fascinated me is that in the safety of our friendship we are able to really explore that old dynamic of the Scots feeling[s] about the English.

Unpleasant remarks about being English tended to surface where the perpetrator was unknown to the contributor. Mike Wade told of an incident in Edinburgh:

> I can tell you, a guy came up to me at a cash machine late at night and said 'have you got any money?' And I said 'actually I haven't, that's why I'm at a cash machine and I'm not giving you a fiver'. And he said, he was really pissed, and he said 'you're English aren't you?' I said 'I am' and he said 'you fucking English bastard, you fucking English bastard up here, what are you doing up here?' And I said 'I'm shagging your women and I'm taking your jobs' and he just kind of like kind of disappeared. [Laughter.]

Paul Armstrong experienced a similar incident:

> I was up in a pub just to the west of Edinburgh and someone took exception to my accent . . . We had been for a meal and we went in, we went to, a group of us from work, we went into this pub and I went to the bar to order a drink and the guy standing next to me, he obviously heard my accent, turned to me and asked

me if I was effing English. I told him yeah I was AND? And he just sort of grunted at me, turned back to his pint and carried on. So, not very welcoming. [Laughs.]

A common feature of the last three extracts was alcohol. This, according to Charlotte Howe, 'loosened tongues', and she and her husband did not patronise their local pub in Mull to avoid anti-English comments. What was also common in the previous extracts was the behaviour of the English-born contributors in dealing with the situations, and this is a subject that will be returned to below.

Overall, however, verbal comments and abuse were not perceived to be a problem, although that is not to say abuse did not exist. More serious, perhaps, was the potentially racist environment they could create. In his influential study *The Nature of Prejudice* Gordon Allport argued that:

> Racist name-calling, verbal rejection, even when it occurs in an environment where banter is common, creates a fertile environment for other forms of racism. Racist name-calling is usually associated with avoidance – distaste not just for particular individuals but for their ethnic group, whether neighbours, clients, customers, colleagues or even strangers.[22]

Another form of verbal abuse was graffiti. Anti-English graffiti routinely appeared all over Scotland, and was especially visible when the Watch groups were active in the early to mid-nineties. Only four of the contributors mentioned seeing graffiti, of the 'English Go Home' type, as far afield as Glasgow, Edinburgh and Broxburn. Three of them dismissed this as inconsequential, but the fourth, Mike Russell, mentioned how he had taken legal action, when he was chief executive of the SNP, to bankrupt one of the perpetrators, Scottish Watch. Russell's initial interdict was to prevent distribution of leaflets, some of which were particularly virulent. According to Jonathan Hearn, 'the second incarnation of Siol nan Gaidheal (1988) expressed extreme antagonism towards the English (sic)'. One of their posters showed a person wearing military gear, a balaclava and a rifle, with the well-known slogan from the Declaration of Arbroath in 1320 'So long as 100 of us remain alive we will never submit to English rule'.[23] Most of this graffiti was directed against England, the state (as above), rather than English people, although this was not always the case. The Scottish Separatist Group (SSG), one of the perpetrators of graffiti, has as one of its objectives:

> Among our immediate demands [the SSG in partnership with the Russian Maoist Party] is halting English immigration into Scotland, a process that is artificially changing the ethnic balance in Scotland and turning the Scots into a national minority in their own country.[24]

Examination of all the testimonies indicated that the activities of these groups, in spite of the media publicity some of them received, failed to impact upon or touch the lives of the contributors to any extent.

— VIOLENCE AND HARASSMENT —

The testimony from Inspector Nicholson indicated he had no experience, in the Borders, of reports of violence associated with anti-Englishness. Similarly, no other contributor mentioned violence. That is not to say that English-born residents did not suffer violence as a result of their origins. The media would have us believe that this was not uncommon, but, as shall be seen in the next chapter, their reporting was more than occasionally inaccurate or misleading.

The closest any of the contributors came to violence would probably be better described as aggravated harassment. One incident involved Charlotte Howe, a guesthouse owner on Mull, and her family. They lived on a hilly spot and to move their caravan to a new location secured permission from their neighbour to hoist it over a boundary wall. Her husband, father and friend were hard at work:

At this point in time they heard a screech of tyres and wondered what the devil was going on and the local farmer who lives just down the glen from us came screaming up saying 'what' I won't use all the expletives, but basically 'what did they think they were doing?' And Harry explained to him he was just popping the caravan over the wall to use it as a garage store. Now at the time, okay fair enough Harry had actually removed well you can't really call it removed, trampled down a bit harder a wire fence, it wasn't a barbed wire fence just a wire fence, to lift the caravan over our boundary wall. The fence was actually on the floor it wasn't doing anything but anyway the farmer concerned basically started and we honestly thought he was going to have a heart attack. He was hanging on to the side of his Land Rover, he was actually beetroot in the face, Harry thought he was going to have a heart attack and he was basically saying 'English public school [sic][25] b b b coming on to the island and running your b b b little businesses thinking you can do everything here'. It was almost laughable because he was shouting so hard that one of the local garage owners across the glen could hear him and this was like a mile and a half away but I mean it was almost laughable because what he was actually saying was, he must have been watching for days because he knew what was going on. He must have been waiting for them to go up the drive to take that caravan over the wall because there was no way he would know, he just happened to know when it was going to go over the wall so he could come and have a go. Anyway my father as I say was here and Harry actually said to the farmer concerned to calm down otherwise he was going to have a heart attack. But it was actually getting rather nasty and my father said you know if you've got anything else to say could you say it to the police. He did actually call the police who were quite willing to come out but by this time things had cooled down. My father also reported him to the Race Relations Board who were very interested because this isn't the first time it had happened but again it didn't actually come to fruition but they said if they had any more trouble at all they would be more than willing to come out and sort it out because it was, it was under their jurisdiction. So all in all it leaves a nasty taste you know.

Compared with race incidents affecting other migrant groups in Scotland this was comparatively mild, and on the contributor's admission a little comic. It did not create an ongoing climate of fear or uncertainty for the Howes – indeed they 'love living on Mull'. Mrs Howe's reaction to the farmer, who also ran a bed and breakfast business, was that he was a hypocrite for taking English tourists' money. Intriguingly, she used her own form of racial stereotype to discredit him: 'he's not a Mulleach, he's just from Scotland but that's the sort of attitude you come across'.

Another incident proved more upsetting for Elizabeth Bunting, and did affect her long-term attitude to living in Scotland. Although she remained in Scotland long after the incident she provided a number of examples where she modified her behaviour to minimise the risk of something similar happening again.

EB – Those who typically attack are usually drunk but I have been attacked [verbally] on a couple of occasions for being English and being in Scotland and taking a job away from a Scot . . . The worst occasion was when I bought my house in Auchtermuchty and I think it was probably the previous owner who would phone up and scream abuse at me down the phone for being an English cow and a bitch, he was very drunk and I listened to him for a few minutes and told him exactly what I thought of him and put the phone down. But you know that was again it was couched in terms that you were a female and so a lot of filth about being a female and then stuff about me being English as well, how much he hated the English di da di da di da.

MW – What prompted this do you think?

EB – Probably because I didn't give him the price that he wanted for his house because it was a bargain and he needed to sell.

The perpetrator here, whether he was motivated by the low house price or not, was fuelled by alcohol. He sought to be abusive on the grounds of gender and nationality. Indeed, close analysis of the testimony indicates that the issue of Bunting being a female ('a lot of filth about me being a female and then stuff about me being English') indicated that the perpetrator might have resented losing money to a female rather than to an English person. The question of racism intersecting with issues of gender, class and religion is interesting, and will be discussed more fully below.

Evidence of anti-English violence was hard to find, but that does not mean it did not exist. In a twenty-five year period from the late 1960s to the early 1990s there were outbreaks of violence and bombings, described in Chapter 2. The important point to note is that these were primarily directed against England, the state, and not English people living in Scotland. Compared with other migrant groups in Scotland the English were exposed to significantly less violence and harassment. In the case of the Irish there is a large body of evidence. Taking one example, during the interwar years there was an upsurge in Protestant (anti-Irish/Catholic) extremism. In 1923 the Church of Scotland endorsed a report entitled *The Menace of the Irish Race to our Scottish Nationality* and this ultimately contributed to a climate in which priests and Roman Catholic shop assistants were assaulted and threatened in the streets of Edinburgh.[26] Another example involved Asian migrants. In 1986, the Scottish Ethnic Minorities Research Unit found that in Glasgow 49 per cent of Pakistanis and 55 per cent of Indians had experienced damage to their property; and that 18 per cent of Pakistanis and 22 per cent of Indians had experienced physical attack.[27] The English never suffered to this degree.

— DISCRIMINATION —

The final indicator of racism employed in this analysis is discrimination. This is another area where evidence is hard to find, especially the subtler, less visible forms of discrimination. One of the most obvious forms of discrimination is when people are excluded from employment opportunities on the grounds of their national or ethnic origins. This is not a problem normally associated with the English in Scotland. On the contrary, Alistair Moffat and George Rosie, in their 1986 film *The Englishing of Scotland*, argued that you had to be English to get the top jobs, and that it was the Scots who were being discriminated against.[28] The testimonies do, however, throw up examples of discrimination. The first involved Amanda Green on Lewis. She claimed that she did not get a teaching post because she was English. She had to wait two and a half years for her English-teaching qualifications to be recognised and then had to work without pay for nearly three months, before waiting ten years to be offered a permanent part-time contract. Amanda eventually applied for a new modern languages job. She got on to the shortlist with a Lewis-born teacher, who incidentally had been trained by Amanda. The local was offered the job. Amanda recalled:

When it came to the job interviews apparently we both did extremely well but they decided to give her the job rather than myself which I think shocked a lot of people who felt that this wasn't really fair in the view of my record for the community that perhaps I should have been given the job. But she did have parents from the island although she had been living away and had moved back so she did have island connections, which I didn't have.

It is impossible to conclude from the testimony whether there was any discrimination here and whether the education authority had failed to comply with the Race Relations Act. What is evident is that during her years on Lewis, Amanda's Englishness held back her teaching career. The second case of discrimination also involved an education authority. Neil Bayfield recalled how his wife, the deputy head of a large primary school, applied for the headship of a smaller, rural primary school. She didn't get the job, although she felt she had the best qualifications for it. She was told afterwards: 'We thought you were too English for it, you know we felt we needed a local person.' This testimony provides a clear example of discrimination, and illegal discrimination at that, but it needs to be pointed out that this is anecdotal, uncorroborated evidence. According to her husband Mrs Bayfield's disappointment was short-lived, and she even agreed with the decision:

> I think they were probably right and my wife thinks they were probably right as well. We can understand why they chose a local person because it is a very rural community, very Scottish and my wife has got a very English accent, a very Essex accent. And they felt you know she was just too, she was just too English really.

The final example of discrimination, and this time more subtle, came from Ian McGeechan, one of Scotland's outstanding rugby players. McGeechan was born in Leeds of a Scottish father and English mother. He was educated in Leeds, taught in Leeds and played rugby for Headingley RFC in Leeds. He was offered, and turned down, a trial for England, preferring to aim for a Scottish cap. McGeechan had an affinity with Scotland as a result of his father's patriotism and his closeness to his extended family in Scotland. In the late 1960s the route into the national team was through trials matches, and it took McGeechan four years of appearing in Scottish trials before gaining selection. While there was particularly strong competition for McGeechan's position, he observed: 'I think undoubtedly you had to be, you had to be seen to be a better player than a home-based Scot.'

These were the only examples of discrimination cited. Generally the English had few problems in securing positions of power in employment, trade unions, the arts, politics, voluntary organisations and so on. Compared with other migrant groups this type of discrimination was not a serious problem for the English-born.

— WHERE PREJUDICES INTERSECT —

The testimony from Elizabeth Bunting clearly showed that the drunken man from Auchtermuchty displayed prejudice against her gender and nationality. Prejudice was often confused on the grounds of ethnic origin, gender, class or religion. As Peter Jackson argued, 'racism frequently parallels or intersects with other axes of discrimination'.[29] This was evident from the testimonies, and is an added difficulty in trying to assess the role played by anti-Englishness. Take the case of Patricia Yeaman. She recalled an incident at the start of a new teaching job in 1978:

> My second day there I wore trousers and he [the head teacher] sent his deputy to tell me that he didn't like trousers and women were to wear skirts. And I challenged him and won the challenge and he was dressed down. Then he took me into his room with his deputy and read me out some order which was his way of putting me down even though I'd won the right to wear trousers. Can you imagine? And he told me 'when I started my job at Harris Academy [in Dundee] in 1950 the very first day I wore a kilt and I was summoned before the Rector and told that men wore suits and sent [me] home and I knew from that day onward that the proper dress for men, gentlemen, was lounge suits and the proper dress for women was costumes. You are here to mother the children and mothers wear skirts' was what he said, but of course I told him I was a mother and I wore trousers and I was here to educate the children. But anyway the kilt reference was really meaningful as well, and I think that [this] was a classic example of how he saw English accent, middle class, bossy, patronising English and 'I'll get one over on her' and he spent the whole time we were together in that school trying to find ways of putting me down. [Laughs.]

Patricia described herself as a 'convinced feminist', and she carried on wearing trousers. She was also proudly working class, with a Yorkshire accent, and resented being perceived as middle class. What the source of this head teacher's prejudice was is not clear. There was evidently a gender bias. The role of women was to mother children and 'mothers wore skirts'. Her Englishness was also a factor and elsewhere in the testimony Patricia said, 'the fact that I was English compounded his hatred I think.' The issue of class, as a basis for the head teacher's prejudice, is unlikely in this case, as he saw Patricia as middle class. David McCrone, a sociologist, explained Jackson's conceptualisation about the intersection of different axes of discrimination in slightly different terms. He argued that ' "English" is undoubtedly a shorthand for some complex and contradictory terms'.[30] He suggested that this shorthand 'obfuscated' between different identities. The testimonies of Patricia Yeaman and Elizabeth Bunting provide classic examples of more than one form of intolerance, and, while gender was evidently an issue, their Englishness was abused, and was perceived by both to be a significant factor in the incidents described. Mary Mulligan MSP provided an interesting example of gender discrimination. She recounted how her Englishness was not a problem during her selection as a Labour candidate for the Scottish Parliament. A bigger problem was that she was a woman.

Other forms of discrimination, which frequently intersect with racism, include social class and religion. The discourse on accent and social class in Chapter 6 provided evidence where working-class English migrants were perceived as being middle class. While this was not a conventional form of negative prejudice it nevertheless made some working-class English migrants feel uncomfortable. In terms of religion, Jewish and Asian migrants to Scotland were frequently abused and discriminated against on the basis of their faiths, as well as, or instead of, their ethnic origins. The same can be said about the Catholic Irish. Indeed, the subject of bigotry and sectarianism was raised by a number of the contributors. In the context of this discussion on anti-Englishness, what is significant is that the contributors were all surprised by the level of hate sectarianism generated[31] and that, compared with the level of anti-Englishness, this represented a much more serious social problem.

Two other forms of contradictory prejudice emerged from the testimonies. The first came from the Rangers footballer Trevor Steven. After the Heysel disaster, in 1985, the Rangers manager Graeme Souness brought a number of English players to Ibrox. One of these was the black English international Mark Walters. According to Steven, the white English players, after a settling-down period, were accepted and welcomed by the Rangers supporters. Life was more difficult for Walters.

> I think Mark Walters got a little bit for being a coloured man and I don't think there was a coloured player playing at Rangers before then and I'm not sure all the while back. But he was an easy target and people in Scotland were not used to seeing a coloured footballer . . . I think it was more colour than English because there [were] several other English there and we weren't getting the attention that Mark was getting.

The issue of colour prejudice being a more significant problem than anti-Englishness was also raised by a number of other contributors. Mike Wade, an anti-racist campaigner, criticised middle-class English people in Edinburgh for 'bleating about anti-Englishness'. Dot Jessiman witnessed racial violence, discrimination and harassment when she lived in Brent, Notting Hill and Brick Lane. Comparing Scotland with what she saw in these areas of racial tension, she said: 'I've never been made to feel that, [discriminated against] because I've always been accepted . . . I have never encountered anybody being nasty to me, because I am English and therefore that gives you confidence.'

The other aspect of discrimination that was identified was homophobia. During her testimony Patricia Yeaman revealed that, after her divorce, she fell in love with another woman. Amongst other things, this involved socialising with the gay community in Dundee. One of the early controversies of the new Scottish Parliament was the Clause 28 affair, concerning teaching about homosexuality. Opposition was mounted and financed by the millionaire bus-company owner Brian Souter.

> I mean he [Brian Souter] whipped up and encouraged homophobia to the surface of Scottish life I found horrifying and personally very frightening. I had never been afraid to walk the streets. I had had girlfriends that I would hold their hand. I have straight girlfriends whose hands I hold. I didn't see why I shouldn't hold my partner's hand but knowing that I was taking risks and to be frightened to walk home, to be frightened to walk out of known gay places at night . . . That was a terrifying time. It really was.

Compared with her earlier experience with the head teacher this contextualises experience of anti-English behaviour. Homophobia was a far worse experience, as was black racism and sectarianism. That is not to say that anti-Englishness was not an issue, but in comparative terms it was a less serious problem for English migrants than other forms of discrimination and harassment for other groups, and society at large.

'IT'S SORT OF COOL TO BE RATHER HORRIBLE TO THE ENGLISH'

This observation from Emma Wood somewhat contradicts the findings in this study, where 94 per cent of the contributors claimed that anti-Englishness was not a problem. Wood's own oral history research identified that English migrants, who lived mainly in the north-east Highlands, did experience anti-Englishness. Although there were methodological weaknesses in Wood's work (see Chapter 2), her conclusions need to be taken seriously, especially as respected sources like *The Herald* claimed that there was a tradition of anti-Englishness in Scotland. Indeed, some contributors to this study suggested that there was an undercurrent of anti-English feeling. Mike Hadrian said his first wife was always conscious of an 'anti-English feeling that was underneath all the time, most of the time'. Jim Grant found that: 'there was always this sort of edge that you know "you English were swine to us Scots"'. This comment was made when Grant was talking about a post-war England v. Scotland football match, and, in this respect, there were distinct resonances with Pete's St Andrews Bulletin Board comment. Tim Underwood also hinted at the background climate of anti-Englishness, but made an important behavioural observation when he said:

> I'm one of these people who don't go around looking for trouble. I have never have. I take people as I find them and all right I am a gregarious character I mix well and I think it, not to be accused of boasting, to say I have always been quite popular wherever I've gone with people. But if you want trouble you can find it. If you want to take offence.

Significantly, all of the last three contributors were amongst the 94 per cent who admitted not finding anti-Englishness a problem. Underwood was typical when he said, 'I had friends all over Scotland. I can't speak too highly. I have always been made welcome.'

In spite of this, there were clearly sections in the host community where English migrants were not welcome. Emma Wood explained this in terms of a continuum of behaviour and response to the English. At one end there would be extreme anti-Englishness and at the other an open welcome. This might be interpreted as in figure 8.1.

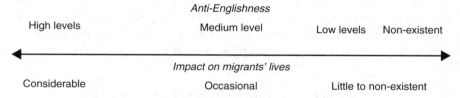

Figure 8.1 Anti-English Behavioural Continuum

'High levels' would encompass the activities of extremist groups such as the SSG, Settler Watch and Scottish Watch, as well as individuals like Adam Busby and a pub landlord in Annan. As has already been seen the extremist groups were small, their activities were short-lived, and they failed to have an impact on the lives of the contributors – many of whom were not even aware of their existence. Adam Busby, in terms of the jail sentences he received, was perhaps the most notorious of the 'tartan terrorists'. Referring to 'Flame'[32] and the Scottish National Liberation Army, Malcolm Dickson, who studied political violence in Scotland, said in oral testimony:

> The prime instigator was a man called Adam Busby who had got himself into bother in relation to activities of this nature in the early 1980s and had fled to Dublin in 1984 and had subsequently continued to be a thorn in the authorities' side right up to the present day. And Mr Busby is still at large in spite of having spent some time behind bars over the last five or six years for various activities, still pursuing his activities through his new front called the Scottish Separatist Group, and still dabbling in this type of kind of extremist activity. However, if you look at the kind of history of this the kind of peak of this type of violent kind of response, which was largely about a reaction to the British state *and not necessarily based on an anti-English feeling* [my emphasis] the peak was really in the 1970s and the early 1980s when a number of groups and quite a few organised individuals made an attempt to try and get up to the kind of level of violence we might have associated with Irish republicanism. They never really got there. It died away in the mid-1980s and has subsequently remained at the kind of activity [level] of one or two individuals who have continued to kind of perpetrate this type of activity, and I see no great evidence for any return to the kind of activity levels of the 1970s and early 1980s.

The case of the Annan landlord had a direct bearing on two English-born migrants, Frank and Sandra Walters, who alleged they were barred from the pub because they were English. Their case was taken up by the CRE and they were awarded £4,000, with £40,000 costs. They moved back to England, albeit to Longtown only a few miles from the border. After the case the Walters said, 'Scottish people are the best people in the world, we have lived here for a long time and they are wonderful. It's just a small few.'[33] This was not an isolated case, there were also incidents involving pub landlords in Inverness[34] and Errol, where an English customer responded to anti-English 'intimidation' by taking a sawn-off shotgun into the pub.[35] Perhaps the latter was evidence of anti-Scottishness?

But, as the Walters said, these types of incidents were only perpetrated by a 'small few', although their significance was exaggerated by media coverage. The most common pattern of behaviour experienced by English migrants, from the host community, appeared at the right hand end of the continuum. Using British Election Survey data, Malcolm Dickson pointed out that 'the actual number of people who think that there has been . . . fairly [high levels] or serious conflict between Scotland and England has actually doubled in the last twenty years'. He went on to point out that the annual surveys were attempting to find out what people thought, and that this was about perception, possibly quite different from reality. He explained:

> This is completely different from the actual measurable empirical evidence for anti-English behaviour activities, harassment, discrimination or anything like that. This is what people perceive to be the case, just in the same way you could ask people to say how frightened are you of crime, how frightened are you of being mugged? OK people might express a fear but it might not actually be reflective of the reality of crime statistics or whatever.

Behaviour and perception are near impossible to quantify, but are nevertheless important considerations in assessing the impact of anti-Englishness. The earlier testimonies of Mike Wade, referring to an incident outside a bank in Edinburgh, and Paul Armstrong, referring to an occurrence in a Central Belt pub, demonstrated how their behavioural reactions defused potentially unpleasant situations. Tim Underwood had a strategy of avoiding trouble, and Nick Johnston argued that there was a certain type of person who naturally found trouble.

> I often wonder whether people actually invite discrimination by their attitudes...I mixed with all sort of people. Funnily enough [in the 1970s] when I chummed up with someone, who was also English and even more English than I was. I mean he was very, almost English to the point of being camp and we used to go drinking in some terribly insalubrious places down in Leith. Whether they left us alone because they thought we were gay or not I don't know but even then we never had any sense of, of being [threatened]. Funnily enough, later in life, I met a chap who seemed to attract trouble like a dog attracts fleas. Um...he was a Scot, about the same age as me, and whenever he went out he seemed to get into some sort of fight or other. And I mean I have to say, you hear stories of people getting into fights in pubs, and I mean in my thirty-three years in Scotland I have never ever been involved in any trouble, whatsoever. It's not that I have avoided it. I haven't consciously avoided places where there may be trouble. I've been out in Edinburgh on Friday and Saturday nights, in a worse-for-wear state in my early years. But trouble never came to me.

Behaviour is difficult to assess and measure. Dot Jessiman made an interesting observation, explaining that, when English people were involved in incidents, there was a temptation to diagnose racism when it was often just a case of 'a nasty person being nasty', a view incidentally recognised by Emma Wood, who also said 'nasty people do nasty things'.

— CONCLUSION —

So what does this tell us about the role of anti-Englishness in the lives of English migrants in Scotland? The most significant finding of this research is that 94 per cent of the contributors felt that anti-Englishness was not a problem. This suggests that *The Herald*'s contention that there was a 'long tradition of anti-Englishness in Scotland' could be misleading, possibly another myth in Scottish history. The role of the media in generating and/or exaggerating anti-Englishness, often confused with 'anti-Englandness', was raised by a number of the contributors and this will be discussed in the next chapter.

It was clear, however, that anti-Englishness did exist, and that in spite of changing attitudes towards 'racism' the dynamic of the historical relationship between England and Scotland did impact on the lives of English migrants. It is also clear that there was a climate of anti-English feeling, but this tended to be in the background and very much to the right-hand end of the Anti-English Behavioural Continuum. If the host nation had been accused, under Scots law, of anti-English feelings, the likely verdict would be that of 'not proven', which a cynic might interpret as probably guilty, but there was insufficient evidence for a guilty verdict.

Compared with other migrant groups in Scotland, the English did not suffer from violence, widespread abuse, serious harassment or discrimination. For those other groups, survey after survey cited examples of racist behaviour. A black schoolgirl said, 'there wasn't a day that passed when I wasn't racially harassed . . . and I was showered in spit.'[36] A Mr Raman said that 'a large number of people treat us like . . . we are second-class citizens'.[37] There was no evidence to suggest that English migrants suffered in the same way. Raman's observation about being second-class citizens emphasises the point that racist behaviour turned on those who were perceived as inferior. The Community Work Training Company pointed out that it was not only 'black' people who suffered in this way. 'The Irish have also been treated as an inferior "race" by the Scots'.[38] But this was not a fate suffered by the English, who were generally perceived as superior. Does this imply an inverse form of racism when incidents of anti-Englishness occurred? It certainly confounds most theories of racism. A further theoretical complication emerged from the CERES survey, which found that anti-English experiences were often seen as different from racism in a Scottish context.[39] This undoubtedly arose from the confusion between anti-Englishness and anti-England, the state, what Peter Jackson referred to as the 'politicisation of Scottish identity'.[40]

– NOTES –

1. 'Racism in Scotland', *Electronic Herald*, web site accessed 22/2/01.
2. Re: Relocation (February 18 2000), web site accessed 22/2/01.
3. Nairn, (2000), *After Britain: New Labour and the Return of Scotland*, p. 213.
4. Houston, *The State of Scottish History*, lecture (Edinburgh International Book Festival, 17/8/02).
5. Nairn, *After Britain*, p. 213.
6. Miles and Dunlop, 'Racism in Britain: The Scottish Dimension', in Jackson (ed.), (1982), *Race and Racism: Essays in Social Geography*, pp. 132–4.
7. Ibid., p. 133.
8. SWSI Race Equality Audit, ceres@ed.ac.uk, (summer 2000), web site accessed 10/10/02.
9. This does mean, however, that 6 per cent of the sample admitted that, to some degree, it was a problem. A few did not raise the issue at all.
10. See *Glasgow Herald* Indices under English, Immigration, Population, Race and White Settler, (1964–2002). For example, in 1973 there were 20 related stories or readers' letters.
11. Solomos, (1993), *Race and Racism in Britain*, p. 81.
12. See Chapter 6.
13. Solomos, *Race and Racism in Britain*, p. 9.
14. Jackson (ed.), *Race and Racism*, p. 12.
15. Cited by Solomos, *Race and Racism in Britain*, pp. 79–80.
16. Jackson (ed.), *Race and Racism*, p. 12.
17. Solomos, *Race and Racism in Britain*, p. 9.
18. Kelly, (2000), 'Racism, Police and Courts in Scotland', pp. 141–59.
19. Scottish Executive, *Audit of Research on Minority Ethnic Issues in Scotland from a 'Race' Perspective*, chap. 9, p. 4, web site accessed 13/5/02.
20. This data was provided in a series of conversations the author had with the CRE in September and October 2002. In spite of requests for documentary evidence the CRE only provided copies of annual reports.
21. Armstrong (ed.), (1989), *A People Without Prejudice? The Experience of Racism in Scotland*, p. 10.
22. Cited by Kelly, 'Racism, Police and Courts in Scotland', pp. 142–3.
23. Poster description from Hearn, *Claiming Scotland*, p. 65.
24. Joint Declaration by the Russian Maoist Party and the Scottish Separatist Group, web site accessed 15/10/02.
25. Harry (pseud.), her husband, was a printer by trade and had not been to a public school, providing further evidence of class confusion.
26. Gallagher, (1985), 'Protestant Extremism in Urban Scotland 1930–1939: Its Growth and Contraction', pp. 143–67.
27. Kelly, 'Racism, Police and Courts in Scotland', p. 4.
28. Conversations and correspondence with A. Moffat and G. Rosie, spring 2002.
29. Jackson, *Race and Racism*, p. 13.
30. McCrone, 'Who Do We Think We Are?', p. 1.
31. See particularly: Christine Kirkton (pseud.), Tape MW0002, 12/11/99, and Eileen MacDonald (pseud.), Tape MW0050, 5/10/01.
32. Flame was a code name for a bombing campaign. It is often mistaken as an extremist group.
33. A. Denholm, 'Couple in Anti-English Case Settle Out of Court', *Scotland on Sunday*, 13 August 1999.
34. See Dot Jessiman, Tape MW0036, 9/7/01.
35. D. Maule and J. Rougvie, 'Anti-Englishness Feud Blamed for Errol Pub Gun Incident', *Scotsman*, 13/11/97.

36. The Community Work Training Company, *About Racism in Scotland: A Case Study*, p. 2, web site accessed 23/2/01.
37. Ibid., p. 4.
38. Ibid., p. 6.
39. SWSI Race Equality Audit, p. 6.
40. Jackson, *Race and Racism*, p. 134.

CHAPTER 9

Sport, politics and the influence of the media

According to Emma Wood, people were more conscious of the differences between England and Scotland at the time of elections and of football and rugby matches between the two countries. Indeed, 43 per cent of the contributors felt the same way, citing raised levels of anti-Englishness and increased awareness of issues of national identity surrounding sport and political events. Bernard Crick explained this in terms of the situational effects of the behaviour of the Scots and English. This chapter will investigate these situations, in particular the interconnectedness and influence that the contributors ascribed to sport, political events and reporting in the media.[1] Treated as genealogies, in Foucauldian terms, a complex set of parallels, symmetries and connections emerge. Let us look first at sport before moving on to the media and politics.

— 'NINETY-MINUTE PATRIOTS' —

After the 1992 General Election, Jim Sillars blamed the SNP's disappointing performance on the fact that 'Scotland has too many ninety-minute patriots whose nationalist outpourings are expressed only at major sporting events'.[2] What was being expressed here was recognition of the importance and 'obsession'[3] Scots placed on sporting events, especially football and rugby matches between England and Scotland. According to Grant Jarvie and Graham Walker, Sillars' comment was 'a classic expression of the view that sport has functioned as a substitute for political nationalism in modern Scotland.'[4] This was recognised by contributors to this study, including the historian T. C. Smout, who argued that sport 'helped to reinforce a locality and a national Scottish identity',[5] and the sociologist Neil Blain, who postulated that the political and economic relationship between England and Scotland was mediated through sporting occasions.[6]

Given this environment, it was not surprising that sport touched the lives of English-born migrants in Scotland. Jim Grant attended the first Scotland v. England football international at Hampden Park after the Second World War:

> We went up to Hampden Park on the train and we just bought tickets anywhere and we went in into the ground and everybody, I can vividly remember, everybody round about they were all wearing flat hats, all were Scots and they were shouting abuse at the English players and what not, and then I think England scored a goal and of course I was sort of leaping up and down shouting *Yeah* and this fellow sort of looked down and said 'are you supporting England?' and my friend's father said 'yes we've come up from Carlisle to watch the game'. 'Fair enough' . . .

The atmosphere at football grounds began to change in the 1960s, crowd segregation was introduced, and the annual fixture between the 'auld enemies' was scrapped in 1984[7] because of repeated crowd trouble. This fixture, and Calcutta Cup rugby matches,[8] continued to be the basis for national rivalry, both on and off the pitch, throughout the period under review. Martin Robson recalled 'banter' on the oil rigs where he worked in the 1970s. Paul Armstrong talked about 'shop-floor banter' in the 1990s in factories in Livingston and Jedburgh. The 'biggest surprise' for Paul Adams was the passionate way Scots felt about their sport and the 'desire to see the English . . . lose at all costs'. It was not only men who found this. Margaret Cox, in the Borders, observed that there were 'digs at the English' around Calcutta Cup matches, and Sarah Brown found that Shetlanders used sport as a distinction between locals, the Scots and English. On the field of play, rivalry was more intense. Trevor Steven, who played for Rangers and England, provided several examples, not least at international level:

> Friendships go by the wayside, completely in an England Scotland challenge, in a match between the two. I've seen some ferocious tackling going on and I remember Graeme Souness [Scotland] and Ray Wilkins [England] albeit they were never team mates apart from when they got to Rangers but in an England/Scotland game at Wembley when Graeme Souness was trying to knock Ray Wilkins' head off with his elbow there was absolutely fury, you know tension and aggression that's on the field between England and Scotland teams.

Tensions between the two countries even surfaced on Rangers' Ibrox training ground where there were a number of English-born players on the books:

> If you go to any football club you will get the locals against the rest in five-a-sides for instance in training, and we always used to have on a Friday morning England against Scotland games, which were competitive to say the least.

On the rugby pitch the atmosphere was the same, if not even more fero-cious. David Hilton,[9] who played prop for Scotland forty-one times, recalled playing in Calcutta Cup matches:

> I think supporters all over the world want to watch the Calcutta Cup because it is so *brutal* [my emphasis], you know, I think every player in the Scottish side that play against England will raise their game by at least 40 per cent, maybe 50 per cent and you know they play out of their skin and they try their best . . . You saw real battles between Carling and Hastings. They didn't like each other, one was English one was Scottish and it was the actual very, very good example of players in [the] Calcutta Cup, you know in the Calcutta Cup, you know they hated each other and these games were great to see. [Laughter.]

This was a view shared by Scottish international and coach Ian McGeechan, who observed that playing in Calcutta Cup matches was the nearest thing to going to war, fighting battles. Similar opinions were expressed elsewhere. Catherine Parr, from the isolation of Mull, said: 'I think that football and rugby and those contact sports are like legal battles, it's like legal war and if we can thrash them then we've won this battle'. And as if to emphasise this point, on the second weekend of the Iraq War in 2003, Jeff Connor wrote in *Scotland on Sunday*'s rugby pages that 'As every newspaperman will confirm, the first casualty of war is the traditional language of the sports pages'. He recommended avoiding terms like 'aerial bombs, prolonged blitzes, bullet-like headers and explosive efforts'.[10]

– THE BILL MCLAREN HYPOTHESIS –

Bill McLaren, who saw his first Calcutta Cup match in 1936, and commen-tated for the BBC between 1952 and 2002, advanced a similar hypothesis:

> Well there's no doubt that in most Scots' minds the desire to beat England is uppermost, there's no doubt that in the Five Nations and now the Six Nations championship I think that most of Scotland's rugby players would say that the team they would prefer to beat above all are England. And, I think that's quite understandable when you consider the history of English and Scots both in warfare and in other aspects of life . . . It's all about English aggression towards poor Scots, it's all about the history of being invaded and being the wee country against the big one and it's been handed down . . . I think there's a resentment there that is handed from one generation to another and I don't know that it'll ever change.

Here we return to the cultural legacy of history,[11] interwoven with perceptions of national identity. McGeechan, Parr and McLaren are not academics, but scholars, too, shared their opinions. Bert Moorhouse suggested that Scottish football supporters' biennial trips to Wembley were a modern recreation of historical invasions, and this was a metaphor that was employed by the media.[12] Blain et al. argued that sport, especially football and rugby, was a 'vitally important channel for collective resentment',[13] and 'fighting the "old enemy"'.[14] The latter, in some respects, reflected 'characteristics of tribalism'.[15]

According to Jarvie and Reid, sport reflected the images of nationhood, and provided an arena in which submerged nations, like Scotland, could assert themselves and play a role in international affairs.[16] They went on to argue: 'The quest for identity, nationhood or independence usually draws upon romanticism, mythology, invented tradition and cultural artefacts (e.g. flags, songs, and great sporting moments depicted in local heroes and heroines)'.[17] Jarvie and Reid were referring to expressions of nationalism and identity, both of which were commented on in the testimonies. Benedict Anderson stressed the important symbolic value of national anthems:

> No matter how banal the words and mediocre the tune, there is this singing, an experience of simultaneity. At precisely such moments, people wholly unknown to each other utter the same verses to the same melody. The image: unisonance . . . [provides] occasions for unisonality, for the echoed physical realization of the imagined community [the nation or national identity].[18]

By the 1970s the national anthem, God Save the Queen, was being booed by Scottish football supporters at Hampden Park and Wembley, and to the surprise of Alan Bairner the more conservative Scottish Rugby Union (SRU) adopted the Corries' song, Flower of Scotland, years before the Scottish Football Association (SFA).[19] We have already seen, in Chapter 7, how Trevor Steven enjoyed singing Flower of Scotland, except when watching Calcutta Cup matches. In his testimony, Ian McGeechan recalled how the SRU introduced the anthem because it was essentially anti-English. In his testimony, Bill McLaren commented how the English stand-off half Rob Andrew told him after the 1990 Calcutta Cup Grand Slam decider that the crowd's singing of Flower of Scotland was a vocal challenge far greater than he had experienced in the Welsh stadium, Cardiff Arms Park. The following year during the World Cup semi-final between Scotland and England The Guardian commented on the singing: 'the message of Murrayfield . . . seemed etched on the faces of the players as they sang Flower of Scotland. It boiled constantly around the arena . . . Murrayfield was a message of Scottish identity and nationhood.'[20] The famous 1990 game, won by Scotland 13–7, was only the third time in over a century that Scotland had won a Grand

Slam in the Five Nations Championship, and represents one of Scotland's most remembered 'great sporting moments'. This match featured large in Ian McGeechan's testimony and, intriguingly, McGeechan, then the coach, used a novel form of anti-Englishness to motivate the team – in this case, the Scottish team's dislike of the 'poll tax' and prime minister Margaret Thatcher. And, as will be seen below, McGeechan went out of his way to avoid public references to Bannockburn and other traditional historical romanticism.

What is evident here was the intersection of politics with sport as well as with issues of national identity. Just as in Chapter 8, where we saw how racial prejudice intersected with class, gender and religion, similar processes affected sport. Moorhouse, Jarvie and Blain emphasised the influence of gender, class, politics and sectarianism,[21] as did Bernard Crick in his testimony. These issues, however, tended to be submerged in the other testimonies. There were only two references to sectarianism in sport. Trevor Steven, referring to 'old firm games' between Protestant Rangers and Catholic Celtic, said, 'There's a hatred thing isn't there. There's a real enemy type of thing.' Elizabeth Bunting was also aware of the sectarian divide and its intersection with her Englishness:

> I was in Glasgow . . . with my French god-daughter and she wanted to go to an Irish pub and we went into this Irish pub and it was obviously a Celtic supporters' pub and they were all pretty drunk so I just gave her the money and said: 'You go to the bar'. And I just kept my mouth shut the whole evening. I have never been so uncomfortable in my entire life. [Laughter.] I really felt threatened.

On the whole, however, contributors' observations about sport dwelled on issues of national identity, anti-Englishness and Scottish passion for beating the English, or the desire to see England lose, regardless of their opponents. There was recognition that sport in Scotland, whether through nostalgia, mythology or invented traditions, contributed an important ingredient to the relationship that the host nation had with its English-born migrants. Whether this was sufficient to prove McLaren's hypothesis, on its own, is open to doubt. Proving the hypothesis of the 'Voice of Rugby'[22] needs more evidence. Will that be forthcoming from the following analysis of the media?

– THE MEDIA AND SPORT –

It was not only on the field of play, or in pubs, or the workplace where national sporting rivalries featured. One of the most significant arenas for this discourse was through the back pages of the press and the airwaves of radio and television. Reporting on sporting and political events was commented on, with some passion and at length, by a number of the contributors. For example, Emma Wood referred to 'the tabloid bastards'. Peter Crown suggested that anti-English attitudes were 'whipped up by the media' especially around sporting occasions. On his arrival in Scotland in the early 1980s Jim Grant recalled:

> When I first came up here I used to read the papers and steam used to come out of my ears by some of the comments about the English [football team]...I don't think the media help. I think they hype it up, maybe it sells papers, I suppose that's the only reason for doing it, isn't it? It's to sell papers but I do think they do tend to pump up the aggression beforehand, and also if Scotland win they pump up the jubilation. I do blame the press for an awful lot of the feeling that there is going about.

Jim Grant used to respond to his 'getting steamed up' by writing letters to the papers, the *Daily Express*, the *Daily Mail* and *The Scotsman*. After one letter to *The Scotsman* he received a bomb threat:

> I got a letter in the post saying, this fellow told me exactly what he thought you know that I was an Englishman of dubious parentage and this that and the other and that he was going to come and put a bomb through my letter box because he knew where I lived, which I found to be a little bit disturbing but then I realised that the man was just a nutter and didn't bother.[23]

Reporting in the media also affected the sportsmen involved. Trevor Steven, commenting on 'media hype', said:

> You get full attention of every newspaper, every radio station, every television channel, one focuses on this, builds it up, looks back in history at all the things that have gone [on before], the clashes, the this and that. You know England, Scotland beat England and it's you know Bannockburn and everything comes out from the history. It's never taken for what it is. It's a match. Let's take it from the whole context of what England and Scotland have been about over the centuries.

A similar scenario tended to accompany rugby matches. In 1990, Ian McGeechan deliberately restricted press access to the players before the game.

> The press do go over the top but it's the press more than anybody who get the nationalistic drum beating and they can have a massive influence and it's individuals again, it's individual press people who almost want to, you know, get

back to Bannockburn and get back to, they are drawing these comparisons and in 1990 we actually tried to defuse that by only allowing certain players to speak to the press, talking everything down, talking England up because we knew that all they wanted was a quote or something in which they could go totally over the top from a nationalistic point of view and a historical point of view because the majority of our papers I would say are very nationalistic in their approach to sport.

McGeechan's strategy was to minimise press comment about historical rivalry, to encourage articles about how well the English team had been playing, and so lull his opponents into a false sense of security. In terms of the match result his plan worked.

Assessing the influence and impact of the media is extremely complex, involving, as it does, a multifaceted mix of social, economic and political dynamics. According to the Governance of Scotland Forum, 'the media pursue, under political, economic and ideological constraints, a changing relationship to the national character they imagine their audience and market to possess'.[24] In the period under review, social and political change was far reaching. This, combined with changes in media ownership and editorial direction, as well as different positions taken up by the tabloids, broadsheets, radio and television, produced an ever-changing tableau of reporting. This was evident from examination of files of press cuttings and the work of Moorhouse,[25] Smith,[26] and Blain et al.[27] A significant finding from this study, however, was the extent to which media coverage of sporting and political events impacted upon the lives of English-born migrants resident in Scotland.

All of the testimonies mentioning media reporting of sport referred only to the last twenty years of the twentieth century. Could this have been a result of short memories? Or was there a scarcity of reporting about Scottish and English issues before 1980? Or did the tone of reporting change? Evidence from elsewhere in the testimonies indicated that there were clear and verifiable memories well before 1980, so short memories can be discounted. The most likely explanation was a change in tone of the reporting. Moorhouse cited, from the beginning of the twentieth century, numerous examples of how the press reported the good-humoured, if sometimes boisterous, nature of Scots fans' biennial trips to Wembley.[28] The tone of reporting began to change in the 1970s. For example, there were two quite different reports, both involving Scots fans running onto the Wembley pitch after Scottish victories. In 1967, a *Daily Express* reporter wrote: 'I could have stood and cheered as their [Scotland's] ecstatic fans kissed the Wembley turf which had borne their heroes, pocketed tufts of grass and danced massive reels.'[29] Ten years later, under the headline 'Tartan Rip-Off', the same paper reported:

The famous Wembley pitch had the look of an allotment yesterday as groundsman Don Gallacher surveyed his devastated domain. Back over the border had gone the Tartan hordes who got so drunk with victory that they dug up the pitch with daggers.[30]

The emergence of football hooliganism undoubtedly contributed to this change of tone, but another likely influence was the ongoing publicity surrounding the electoral success of the SNP in the 1970s, and the debate about Scotland's oil. Another study, by Maurice Smith, also argued that political change altered the nature of press comment. Whether it was reports of Mrs Thatcher saying, 'we English, who are a marvellous people, are really very generous to Scotland', or Chancellor Nigel Lawson suggesting the Scots were a 'nation of spongers', Smith argued that the Scottish media emphasised the negative aspects of the Englishness of the Thatcher governments.[31] Regardless of what caused this change of tone, it was certainly picked up by the English-born contributors to this study. The testimonies (cited above) had a common theme, that is, the way in which the legacy of history and use of military metaphors were employed to highlight the sporting differences between the English and Scots. Their observations were corroborated in a study about sport and national identity in the European media, in which the authors observed that military metaphors were frequently used by 'other nations' journalists to describe their teams' performances. But in Scotland it is at the core of the nation's perception of itself'.[32] Writing in 1994, they ascribed this to 'the impossible difficulties' which always face journalists to 'justify to the Scots [their readers] their own political inaction'.[33] *Scotland on Sunday* journalist Murdo MacLeod explained in oral testimony that the use of military metaphors went beyond journalistic clichés about Bannockburn and Culloden and had a commercial and political purpose. In this respect he agreed with contributor Jim Grant (above) who thought that anti-English 'media aggression' was employed to sell newspapers. Macleod described editorial policy on *Scotland on Sunday*:

It [stories about the English and Scotland] serves to be a so-called 'talker', in other words it's something that people will talk about, something that's going to get a reaction. It's something that's going to get letters, people see it as something which very obviously gets people going and makes, if you are trying to make the newspaper the centre of people's conversations in the way that you know the *Sun* has managed to do with punchy headlines and Page Three or whatever, that's the way you're going to do it.

In its sister paper *The Scotsman*, English-born journalist Mike Wade offered a similar explanation for running England/Scotland stories, confirming that

Scottish editors, sometimes English-born, were 'sensitised' to whether there was an 'English angle' on a story. He went on to corroborate Blain's findings (above) when he said, 'the media overplays the differences [between England and Scotland] I mean that would be my [opinion], there's far less separating people than many media stories would have you believe.'

Wade went on to argue that, because most Scottish newspapers were pro-Union, sport offered them a platform to wave the Scottish flag without compromising their political stance. Evidence to support this theory was forthcoming through the *Daily Record* on 11 September 1997. This was devolution referendum day, which co-incidentally was the 700th anniversary of Wallace's defeat of the English at Stirling Bridge. Jarvie and Reid cited how the paper exploited Scotland's other romanticised patriot, Robert the Bruce, who 'would have loved the Wembley weekend'. The report glorified previous Scottish sporting successes against the English. It referred to when the Freuchie cricket team from Fife 'thumped the English' in 1985,[34] and commenting on the 1990 Grand slam triumph, '1314? Scottish rugby buffs are more interested in 13–7 – the final score that historic day . . . in an action replay of Bannockburn Proud Edward's Army went into hasty retreat.'[35] This one story on its own would surely support McLaren's hypothesis, but add this to the wealth of evidence from other sources and the proposition that sport in a Scottish/English context is a surrogate form of war is a convincing one.

– ANTI-ENGLISHNESS AND THE MEDIA –

More often than not submerged in the testimonies, but sometime explicit, were comments about how the media stimulated anti-English feeling. One contributor, more than the others, provided in-depth testimony about the media. That was Dot Jessiman, the SNP convenor of New Scots for Independence. In her case, some care needs to be taken in interpretation because it was in the SNP's interests to minimise criticism they received for sending out coded anti-English signals. One incident bears close scrutiny. On 28 June 1998 the *Sunday Times* ran a front-page story, 'Anti-English feeling grows in Scotland',[36] followed up on the inside pages by a *Focus* feature, 'It's all over now – Anti-English feeling is clearly on the rise'.[37] Both articles were illustrated with pictures of 'Tartan Army' football supporters in 'see-you-Jimmy' hats. In her testimony Jessiman said:

> The *Sunday Times* did a most appalling . . . did a truly appalling poll from which they deduced all sorts of things about racism from a Scottish, from a poll about football [sic] . . . Alex [Salmond, the SNP leader] rang me up and said 'Do you know, can you have a look at this and see if you can do something. It's atrocious.'

The articles were based on a National Opinion Poll (NOP) survey, from which the *Sunday Times* concluded that 'after the historic vote for a separate parliament, Scottish antipathy towards the English is hardening',[38] and that 'anti-English sentiment is rising'.[39] To arrive at such conclusions the *Sunday Times* would have had to produce comparative findings over time. They did not do this. They quoted only six survey results. Two, concerning Scots' views on the monarchy and opinions on the likelihood of independence, had little relevance to anti-English feelings. The other four results hardly supported the newspaper's case. When asked 'do you think senior jobs in the public sector should be offered to Scots first?', three fifths of the respondents said no. When asked 'do you think anti-English sentiment is increasing among the Scottish?' only two fifths agreed. Again, only two fifths thought that Scottish relations with England would become worse under devolution – more than one third thought they would improve, with the remainder 'don't knows'. Finally, three fifths of the sample, with a tenth of 'don't knows', hoped that the England football team did well in the World Cup.

These findings hardly merit headline treatment that anti-English feeling was on the increase, especially as there was no time series data. Checking the articles for internal consistency there is further evidence that the headline treatment was misleading. The journalists cited, as supporting evidence, opinions from Timothy Clifford, the English-born director of the National Galleries of Scotland. His only comment was that he had noticed an increase in correspondence on the subject to newspaper editors, and that there were 'some very clumsy Englishmen who do offend the Scots'. Lord Archer, who was subsequently jailed for perjury, was quoted as saying that if the Scots gained independence they might turn round and say 'well the English aren't so bad'. Right wing Conservative MP, Teresa Gorman, commenting from her Essex constituency, said that the Scots were 'xenophobic about devolution'. The journalists also quoted people expressing opposing opinions. A schoolboy from Currie High School[40] said there was only 'friendly rivalry', and Professor David McCrone pointed out that the poll results could be viewed positively with 83 per cent of Scots saying they felt no personal dislike for the English. However one looks at it, from the evidence provided in the small print in these two articles, it is hard to justify the exaggerated headlines about the growth of anti-English feeling in Scotland. This was clearly a case of media exaggeration, a topic that will be returned to below.

Jessiman's immediate response was to write a short letter of complaint, marked <u>NOT FOR PUBLICATION</u>, to the editor of the *Sunday Times*, in London.[41] In the meantime the SNP issued a press release quoting Mike Russell.

As the English-born Chief Executive of the SNP, the detail of this poll confirms my own experience that – despite a sensational approach by some of the media – anti-Englishness is not a factor of any importance in Scottish politics... Only a minority of this poll think that relations with England will deteriorate post devolution, or that anti-Englishness is rising.[42]

On not receiving a reply from the *Sunday Times*,[43] Jessiman lodged a formal complaint with the Press Complaints Commission on 17 July 1998.[44] A month later the Commission found that there was no breach of the code and that it did not consider that the front-page article would mislead readers 'when read as a whole with the *Focus* piece'.[45] In this respect, the findings were correct. The small print, and the paragraphs embedded in the articles, certainly suggested that anti-Englishness was not as serious a problem as implied by the headline treatment. A case could be made out, however, that for those readers who only read the headlines, these were misleading or exaggerated propositions.

To use a journalistic cliché, it could be argued that this was a case of not letting the facts get in the way of a good story. When it came to other stories about anti-English racism there were further examples of the media either exaggerating the facts or presenting a misleading analysis. A significant example brings us back to Currie High School. In November 1997 a former pupil of the school, Mark Ayton, was beaten up and murdered in the nearby village of Balerno. Reporting the case in *The Scotsman*, Tanya Thompson wrote that detectives were following this up as a racially motivated killing, as Ayton was English-born.[46] By the time of the trial the media were reporting an anti-English murder. In May 1998, Katie Grant, writing in the London-based *Spectator*, under the headline 'A very Scottish death', claimed Ayton died for 'being thought English'.[47] Close inspection of Thompson's original story reveals there may have been other factors. A Balerno man was quoted as saying 'There have never been any problems of that kind here. I don't think there are that many English people in the village, but we all seem to get on fine'.[48] An unnamed youth from Currie was quoted saying, 'He [Ayton] used to go to Currie High School and was a big Rangers fan, which annoyed people round here. There were often fights about the football but I don't think he was killed because he was English.'[49] Perhaps a more likely scenario was testosterone-fuelled sectarianism. Further doubts about this being an anti-English racist killing come from the fact that one of the youths convicted of the murder was also English-born.[50] And, acknowledging media misrepresentation, the Currie Community Council minuted 'the council regretted very much the false picture painted of life in our community'.[51] This widespread media coverage, however, left an image of an anti-English racial murder. The case was even recalled as such, four years later, by one of the contributors.[52]

Mike Wade's earlier testimony indicated how editors were always looking for a confrontational English/Scottish angle. He also provided valuable insight into how these types of stories could spread. Journalists frequently rely on press cuttings as their sources; academically acceptable levels of verification are not applied. This was likely to have been the case with the *Spectator* and other articles. According to Tom Nairn this story conveniently supported *Spectator* editor Peregrine Worsthorne's pro-Union political stance.[53] Wade provided a perfect example of this journalistic practice. In 2002, on the day of the Calcutta Cup match, he wrote a story for *The Scotsman*, saying that Edinburgh's Lord Provost, Eric Milligan, had watched England's World Cup match against Argentina in 1998, with the Queen in Holyrood Palace. Wade alleged, when Milligan expressed pleasure at a disallowed England goal, 'Her Majesty had growled "One is not amused"'.[54] When challenged, in the oral testimony, about his source,[55] Wade said, 'That is true, that was in the *Evening News*'. The interviewer commented, 'that doesn't mean it's true', and Wade's response was laughter. This method of media dissemination was evident from the spread of reports about another alleged anti-English incident. On this occasion it was alleged that an English family were driven out of Brechin, in Angus. Again this story was remembered, this time by two contributors, and again four years after the event.[56] Elizabeth Bunting recalled:

> There were people in Angus who were driven out of their home while I was living there and there was an English couple who left and went back to England because their kids were getting threatened . . . it was in the papers.

Bunting admitted that this had made her feel uncomfortable living in Angus. Again, close inspection of the press coverage indicated that there may have been other factors involved. Under the headline 'Stop trying to send the Sassenachs homewards', Andrew Denholm of *The Scotsman* wrote that the community council had accused them of 'causing vandalism, crime and an influx of drugs'.[57] In another article, under the headline 'Families leave town after anti-English abuse claims', Councillor Audrey Mitchell was reported as alleging that 'they had increased the crime rate'.[58] From the small print of the articles there would certainly appear to have been other factors at play, yet the positioning and impact was one of anti-English behaviour. The press were surely hoist by their petard when another story admitted that one of the families originally came from Dundee and the mother was a Scot.[59]

– THE POLITICAL DIMENSION –

Another issue surrounding the alleged English families in Brechin were claims of 'inabootcomers'[60] jumping housing queues, although officials from the Angus Council denied this.[61] Interestingly, Dot Jessiman alleged that this type of reporting was part of a general media conspiracy against the SNP, and in this respect her complaint to the Press Complaints Commission (above) was consistent with her belief. She suggested that it was more than a coincidence that the BBC broadcast an anti-incomer interview with a Brechin councillor in the run-up to the Monklands by-election.[62] Jessiman argued that the media falsely painted a picture of the SNP being anti-English, and that this frequently occurred around the time of elections. One of a number of examples she cited was a by-election in 1998.

> There was the thing in the North East by-election when em *World in Action*[63] actually hired actors to wrap themselves in Union Jacks and stride round the streets and see if anybody picked on them. Nobody told them of course about what would happen to you if you sort of disappeared into a pile of Celtic supporters wrapped in the Union Jack. [Laughter.]

What was happening here was that television journalists were trying to get video footage of anti-English behaviour, in other words, trying to manufacture news. Whether there was a general conspiracy against the SNP is outwith the scope of this study, but there appears to be sufficient evidence to suggest that this might be a fruitful area for further research. Another contributor provided evidence of the press manipulating the facts to put over the story they wanted to tell. Ron Curran, then head of NUPE (National Union of Public Employees), alleged that the *Scottish Daily Express* deliberately misrepresented him during a Health Service strike in the early 1980s. He recalled the end of the interview:

> She [the journalist] says 'You know Mr Curran I don't think you are being perfectly honest with me. You know people will die, because of it.' And I blew me top. I said: 'Look we are talking about the Health Service. People die all the time in the Health Service. You know that and I know that.' But I says: 'It will not be as a result of my members' action.' She got up straight away said: 'I'll have to go. Can I use your phone?' I said: 'Yes.' So she came back crying, tears in her eyes. I said: 'What on earth's the matter?' She said: 'I'm sorry to have to do this to you Mr Curran. You've got to read the paper tomorrow morning.' I says: 'Tell me what are you trying to say?' She said: 'Well that was my editor I was talking to and he said that "did you get it out of him that people will die?" ' She said: 'Well he did say that but he said "that's all I want".' And the headlines the following day was *This man* [photograph of Curran] *said people will die.*

What this testimony demonstrates is that the *Scottish Daily Express* editor had a political point he wanted to put over and the techniques he employed to achieve it. Curran's testimony is believable as there is little reason to suspect that an experienced trade union official would admit to industrial action being responsible for the death of patients. Arguably, this is a classic example of the media in the guise of 'spin doctor'.

This example, along with the behaviour of *World In Action*, clearly demonstrates the lengths to which the media would go to put over a pre-configured point of view. This raises the question: was it common practice for the media to construct, or manipulate, stories about anti-Englishness and English-born migrants in Scotland, or did this just happen occasionally? This is an extremely difficult question to answer, and one that merits further research. Over the period under review there were certainly hundreds, if not thousands, of articles and programmes about Scottish feelings about England as the centre of governmental power, as well as English people in Scotland. A further complicating factor was the changing scale and scope of coverage over time, as well as differences in regional reporting, reflecting the regional structure of the press and broadcast media in Scotland.

One trend was readily discernible. This was that coverage of Scottish relationships with England the state, anti-Englishness and existence of English-born residents in Scotland was most widespread from the late 1980s. This was certainly evident from the testimonies, and was corroborated by David McCrone, who argued, 'the progress to a Scottish parliament generated press speculation that it was generating anti-English attitudes, and a more exclusive sense of Scottishness.'[64] In addition to the examples already cited in this chapter, there were two notable stories, excluding sport, which generated considerable English-themed press coverage in the mid-1990s. These were about the activities of Scottish Watch and Settler Watch and the film *Braveheart*. The Watch groups generated extensive and prolonged reporting and debate in the media.[65] In addition, Settler Watch, which was based in the north east, was heavily covered by the (Aberdeen) *Press and Journal*. Similarly, there was extensive and continued comment about *Braveheart*. Different sections of the press portrayed actor Mel Gibson's cries for 'Freedom' as anti-English, and when his picture appeared on an SNP recruitment leaflet the party was accused of being anti-English.[66] By associating with *Braveheart*, Ewan MacAskill of *The Scotsman* argued, 'Salmond [the SNP leader] would be among the first to deprecate any political movement based on anti-English sentiment, and yet that is what his party has signed up to'.[67] Stories about the film rumbled on for a few years, and, as was seen in two schoolgirls' testimonies, the film was capable of generating anti-English behaviour amongst their Scots-born classmates. Hannah

Green's worst memory of school was having to keep her head down after watching *Braveheart* in a history lesson.

Media coverage of English/Scottish issues was less common in the earlier part of the period under review, when it was sporadic and tended to be directed against England the state, or source of power, rather than English people. This was certainly the case when Tim Underwood recalled the extensive press coverage about the theft of the Stone of Destiny in 1950/51, and whether the Queen should be Elizabeth I or II in 1953.[68] Referring to the sixties and seventies Liz Potts recalled: 'When Brian Wilson started the *West Highland Free Press*, he went, he was, you felt he was very anti-English.' Potts did, however, struggle to remember precise details, but was clear about her perceived memory, and strong dislike of Wilson's anti-English position. The fact that these comments came immediately after she expressed approval of the anti-English elements in *The Cheviot, the Stag and the Black, Black Oil*,[69] tend to add credence to her comparative memory of the *West Highland Free Press*, and the impact of the press.

— Conclusion —

What was evident from Potts' testimony was that reporting in her regional newspaper created feelings of anxiety. As seen above, there was also evidence that other contributors, too, were made to feel uncomfortable by media reporting. In the middle of offering his personal testimony, Mike Hadrian stopped and brought out a press cutting from his wallet. It was a four-year-old letter to the *Ayrshire Post*. The letter read:

> I noticed Michael Heseltine's comments of optimism that Phil Gallie would hang on in the Ayr seat. The only way Gallie will hang on is when the thousands of English who have moved up here denying Scots jobs and houses panic vote for this southerner in disguise. Meanwhile the London Labour Party have found in Sandra Osborne the worst possible candidate that has ever been put forward in political history.

The following week there was a rebuttal from an anonymous English-born resident. When asked why he had kept these letters in his wallet, Hadrian answered,

> That's a good question. The answer is that at the time when I read them I was slightly incensed by the anti-English feeling expressed in the first letter which was not uncommon in the local paper for local people to write letters which were derogatory to the English people and I just decided on the spur of the moment to cut it out of the paper and put it in my wallet and there it remained ever since.

What was significant here was the long-term impact of published correspondence. Furthermore, the recall of Dot Jessiman, Elizabeth Bunting, Mike Wade and Liz Potts (above) belies the aphorism that today's newspapers are tomorrow's chip wrappings. Memory, and its impact, clearly had a bearing on the lives of English-born migrants.

There can be little doubt about the impact of the media upon both migrants and Scots. Reporting about sporting occasions and political change, especially from the Thatcher years, brought an increased intensity to the lives of English people living in Scotland. According to Benedict Anderson, the media played an important role in the construction of the 'imagined community that is the nation'.[70] He argued that newspapers were a cultural product, linked to their market, and that he was struck by their 'profound fictiveness'.[71] 'Fictiveness' is an interesting description, meaning, as it does, fictitious and imaginative. As such, it more than adequately describes the reporting in the Sunday Times, The Scotsman, the Spectator, World in Action and other sources mentioned above. Why the media should report in this way is far from clear, making this an important topic for further research. What this study demonstrates is that sporting occasions, political events and surrounding media reporting played a significant role in increasing awareness of competing national identities, a topic that will be discussed in the next chapter.

— Notes —

1. 'The media' refers to the press (tabloids and broadsheets), radio and television operating north and south of the Border.
2. Cited by Jarvie and Walker (eds), (1994), *Scottish Sport in the Making of a Nation: Ninety-Minute Patriots?*, p. 1.
3. Bairner, 'Football and the Idea of Scotland', in Jarvie and Walker (eds), *Scottish Sport in the Making of the Nation*, pp. 9–26.
4. Jarvie and Walker (eds), *Scottish Sport in the Making of the Nation*, p. 1.
5. Smout, (1994), 'Perspectives on Scottish Identity', pp. 101–13.
6. Blain, Boyle and O'Donnell, (1993), *Sport and National Identity in the European Media*, p. 237.
7. Bairner, 'Football and the Idea of Scotland', p. 25.
8. The Calcutta Cup is played for annually between England and Scotland. Crowd segregation was not introduced at Murrayfield, in Edinburgh, or Twickenham, in London.
9. David Hilton was born in Bristol, England. He, and the Scottish Rugby Union (SRU), believed he was qualified to play for Scotland on the grounds that his grandfather was born in Edinburgh. In 1999, however, press investigations into southern hemisphere players falsely declaring Welsh ancestry and playing for Wales (Grannygate) drew attention to checking Hilton's ancestry. It was discovered that Hilton's grandfather had been born in Bristol, and not Edinburgh. Hilton was dropped from the Scottish team. Hilton remained in Edinburgh, playing for Glasgow, and in 2002 was selected for the Scottish World Cup training squad and gained a further cap, on the basis of three years' residential qualification.

10. J. Connor, 'Part of Lewsey's heart beating on foreign field as he is cast into Dublin cauldron', *Scotland on Sunday*, 30/3/03, p. 14.
11. See Chapter 8.
12. Moorhouse, ' "We're off to Wembley!" The History of a Scottish Event and the Sociology of Football Hooliganism', in McCrone, Kendrick and Straw (eds), (1989), *The Making of Scotland: Nation Culture and Social Change*, pp. 207–27.
13. Blain et al., *Sport and National Identity*, p. 237.
14. Ibid.
15. Ibid., p. 194.
16. G. Jarvie and I. A. Reid, *Sport, Nationalism and Culture in Scotland*, web site accessed 5/11/01.
17. Ibid.
18. Anderson, (1992), *Imagined Communities: Reflections on the Origin and Spread of Nationalism*, p. 145.
19. Bairner, 'Football', in Jarvie and Burnett (eds), *Sport, Scotland and the Scots*, p. 89.
20. Cited by Jarvie and Walker, *Scottish Sport in the Making of a Nation*, p. 5.
21. See Moorhouse, ' "We're off to Wembley!" '.
22. Bill McLaren was known as the 'Voice of Rugby'.
23. Grant destroyed this threatening letter. He did not report it to the police. He was not attacked. From other comment in his testimony, although this was an unpleasant incident, at the time, he dismissed it as the actions of a crank. It did, however, stop him writing letters to the press.
24. Government of Scotland Forum, *The Role of the Media, Research Programme Interim Report January 2001*, web site accessed 7/2/02.
25. See Moorhouse, ' "We're off to Wembley!" '.
26. Smith, (1994), *Paper Lions The Scottish Press and National Identity*.
27. Blain, Boyle and O'Donnell, *Sport and National Identity in the European Media*.
28. Moorhouse, ' "We're off to Wembley!" '. Moorhouse's citations covered the press, north and south of the Border.
29. *Daily Express*, 17/4/67, cited in Moorhouse, ' "We're Off to Wembley!" '.
30. *Daily Express*, 6/6/77, cited in ibid. A photograph of members of the 'Tartan Army' sitting on a broken crossbar, after the 1977 game, was reprinted many times, and for years afterwards by the English press as visual evidence of Scottish football hooliganism.
31. See Smith, *Paper Lions*, pp. 25; 82, 136 and 140.
32. Blain and Boyle, 'Battling Along the Boundaries: The Marking of Scottish Identity in Sports Journalism', in Jarvie and Walker (eds), *Scottish Sport in the Making of the Nation*, p. 130.
33. Ibid., p. 130.
34. Freuchie CC won the English Village cricket competition at Lord's in 1985.
35. Blain and Boyle, 'Battling Along the Boundaries', p. 130.
36. J. Shields and R. Corbidge, 'Anti-English Feeling Grows in Scotland', *Sunday Times*, 28/6/98, p. 1.
37. R. Corbidge and J. Shields, 'It's All Over Now', *Sunday Times*, 28/6/98, p. 10.
38. Ibid., p. 10.
39. J. Shields and R. Corbidge, 'Anti-English Feeling Grows in Scotland', p. 1.
40. Also see below about an incident involving a Currie High School former pupil.
41. Letter from Dot Jessiman, to the editor, *Sunday Times*, 2/7/98 (Dot Jessiman's private papers).
42. M. Russell, 'Sunday Times Poll: "Headline Not Supported by Details" ', *SNP News Release*, 28/6/98.
43. On 18 July 1998 Jessiman received a two-line letter of acknowledgement from the *Sunday Times* letters editor, not the editor to whom she had written. Five days later she received a letter from Will Peakin, the Scottish editor, in Glasgow, saying her original letter was 'being

considered for publication', in spite of the fact that her original letter had in underlined capital letters 'Not for publication'. (Dot Jessiman's private papers.) There was no evidence that the *Sunday Times* published her letter or a retraction.

44. Letter from Dot Jessiman, to the Press Complaints Commission, 17/7/98 (Dot Jessiman's private papers).
45. Letter from the Press Complaints Commission, to Dot Jessiman, 17/8/98 (Dot Jessiman's private papers).
46. T. Thompson, 'Affluent Suburb Shattered by Killing', *Scotsman*, 24/11/97.
47. Cited by, Nairn, (2000), *After Britain: New Labour and the Return of Scotland*, pp. 204–5.
48. T. Thompson, 'Affluent Suburb Shattered by Killing'.
49. Ibid.
50. Nairn, *After Britain*, pp. 204–5.
51. Currie Community Council, Minutes, May 1998, web site accessed 29/10/02.
52. Dot Jessiman.
53. Nairn, *After Britain*, pp. 204–5.
54. M. Wade, 'Home Truths of Cross-Border Rivalry', *Scotsman*, 2/2/02.
55. I wrote to the Lord Provost, on 2/2/02, asking him to verify, or deny, this story. He did not reply.
56. Dot Jessiman and Elizabeth Bunting.
57. A. Denholm, 'Stop Trying to Send the Sassenachs Homewards', *Scotsman*, 21/10/97.
58. G. Currie, 'Families Leave Town After Anti-English Abuse Claims', *Scotsman*, 14/10/97.
59. S. O'Shea, 'Small Town Vents Fury Against Incomers', *Scotsman*, 27/8/97.
60. Ibid.
61. G. Currie, 'Families Leave Town'.
62. Email from Dot Jessiman to the author 17/2/96. The author was unable to see this BBC recording.
63. A popular weekly investigative journalism television programme, networked on Independent Television.
64. McCrone, (1999), 'Opinion Polls in Scotland', pp. 32–43.
65. See Chapter 2 and the work of Eric Zuelow; also see the testimonies of T. C. Smout and Emma Wood.
66. E. Quigley, 'Gibson Unaware of Star Role in SNP Drive', *Scotsman*, 1/9/95.
67. E. MacAskill, 'No Oscar for SNP over Braveheart', *Scotsman*, 12/9/95.
68. See Chapter 7.
69. See Chapter 2.
70. Anderson, *Imagined Communities*, p. 25.
71. Ibid., p. 33.

CHAPTER 10

National identities

Ogden Nash's pastiche, *England Expects*, in which Englishmen consider they belong to the most exclusive club there is, confirms many of the stereotypical images of Englishness, namely: certainty, confidence, exclusivity, superiority – arrogance! But how did this lie with English migrants in Scotland, and to what extent did these labels affect response from the host community? All bar 12 per cent of the contributors talked about their sense of identity, or more precisely their sense of identities, and their awareness of changing identities. Their discourses and narratives connected, in Foucauldian terms, through an interrelated sequence of life events and experiences, including sporting occasions, consciousness of accent, social interaction, bringing up children, and the like. They also talked about notions of Englishness, Scottishness, Britishness, and relationships and differences between England and Scotland. This chapter will explore these interfaces, and in so doing will seek to explain how English-born migrants rationalised their English identity, and to what degree they may have rejected it and replaced it with Scottish values. Malcolm Dickson's study suggested that 'the English population in Scotland has experienced some form of "Scottishing" effect'.[1] Could it be that this was validated by this study?

Before seeking answers to this question a point needs to be made about the testimonies quoted in this chapter. Many contain apparent contradictions, but, as will be explained, this is the norm when people seek to explain their sense of identity, or perhaps more accurately, their sense of identities. You will also notice that, in a number of the quoted extracts, some contributors are hesitant, as if searching for the right thing to say to express their feelings. And, compared to narratives about employment, or bringing up children, some contributors are less coherent, and less certain. This makes for tortuous reading, in some cases, but it does reflect the difficulties some contributors had in describing the complexities, and inherent contradictions, involved in the construction of identity.

— What is national identity? —

What we are talking about here is national identity, but what does this mean? This plunges us into a maelstrom of a global academic debate that intensified in the closing years of the twentieth century. The ideas surrounding nationalism incorporate competing theories that try to explain the paradoxical growth of nationalism at a time of emerging globalisation, and the development of supranational governmental organisations. It is outwith the scope of this study to consider these debates in depth. The main purpose is to explore and analyse what identity meant to English-born people living in Scotland, and to apply, when appropriate, theoretical explanations to assist understanding. This, in itself, is problematic, as perceptions of identity changed over time, influenced by social, economic and political change. Furthermore, as was evident from the testimonies, perceptions of identity were manifested in different ways in different contexts. In this respect the testimonies conformed to the findings of Frank Bechhofer and his team of sociologists:

> We are putting forward the argument that a complex process forms a person's national identity, whereby individuals make identity claims, be they explicit or very tentative, in differing contexts over time, and these claims are received in different ways, and in turn modified by their reception.[2]

Jonathan Hearn cut through the complexities of the theoretical perspectives of the perennialists, the modernists, neo-nationalists and Marxists, by adopting a pragmatic approach that catered for civic, cultural, political and ethnic forms of nationalism, in a Scottish context. He chose to adopt a middle path, one that is followed in this study: 'that nations are processes that are constantly made and remade, in some sense invented, but also the outcomes of very real histories, parts of which can reach back before the modern period'.[3] And there is a dialectical relationship here. While identities are formed by the making and remaking of nations, the changing nature of the perception of identities is contributing to the processes involved in the manufacture and reinvention of nations themselves. In the case of English migrants in Scotland, this relationship is further complicated by the fact that there are three nations involved: England, their place of birth; Scotland, their place of residence; and Great Britain, a political construct going back to 1707 and 1603.

As has been seen in earlier chapters, the experience of migration is a significant life event, a process that, in itself, challenges and re-forms individuals' personal perceptions of identity and sense of place in society. Over and above daily life experiences of earning a living, falling in and out of love, bringing up a family, illness and death, the migrants in this study were subjected to an unprecedented barrage of cultural, social, economic and political change, all of which had a bearing on the perception of identity. These external factors, some of which were specifically mentioned in the testimonies, cannot be ignored. Jeremy Paxman in his attempt to define Englishness[4], and Andrew Marr, in *The Day Britain Died*, both highlighted four key factors. These were the demise of Empire, the emergence of the European Community, the impact of a globalised economy, and the materialisation of Celtic nationalism and devolution.

Tom Devine and Paddy Logue in their anthology of personal reflections on Scottish identity offered a longer, and equally valid, list:

- The state of the Union.
- Devolution (a symptom of confident strength or of decline and fall?) in Wales and Northern Ireland as well as in Scotland, and tensions in all three countries between unionists/devolutionists and nationalists.
- The rise of English nationalism: the seeking of a devolved national assembly in London and regional assemblies, and the implications of all this for Scotland.
- The debate about the distribution of public spending in different parts of the UK and of the Barnett formula.
- Britain's membership of the European Union and the debate about future British political and economic sovereignty and its relevance to Scotland.
- The steamroller advance of USA-led global capitalism with important economic decisions for Scotland, often being taken elsewhere.
- The lingering after-effects of the loss of Empire with its resultant crisis of identity for Scotland, a nation which played a key role in the imperial project.
- The new global world order based on the USA-declared war against terrorism in the aftermath of the events of 11 September 2001.[5]

To these might be added a host of other influences including: the cold war, the fear of the bomb, weakening of territorial sovereignty, the loss of respect for the royal family, the influence of the mass media, the impact of the Internet, the secularisation of society, persistent relative economic decline, the roller-coaster progress of the SNP, so on and so on. All these factors had a bearing on how individuals – Scots, English, and other migrant groups – perceived, recast and re-formed their perceptions of national identity.

Out of this complexity it is possible to structure explanations about feelings of national identity of English people living in Scotland, based on close analysis of the testimonies. A number of the testimonies, however, appeared to lack internal consistency, with contributors, at first, seeming to make contradictory statements in different places, and in different contexts.

This, however, was not necessarily inconsistent, nor contradictory, but in line with Bechhofer and his team's observations about contextualisation, and the inherent complexity in constructing identity. T. C. Smout's testimony provided an example of this phenomenon. He variously said:

> I don't think I'm Scottish. That's quite clear to me. You cannot be Scottish including being brought up in Scotland unless you are Scottish so there is no point at all in pretending being Scottish. On the other hand em I would be appalled to go and live in England. I don't feel at home in England. I don't feel I like the place. It's overcrowded. Em I don't find the people *simpatico* as people up here.

He went on to say,

> ...so in a way I feel kind of British. That's a sort of old-fashioned label. I am quite comfortable being British. Because it expresses to me a kind of cross-border loyalty which I feel quite pleased with.

Later on he said that his interest in cricket made him feel English. Interestingly, in this complex self-examination of national identity, Smout said that when it came to football, he could never make up his mind whether to support Scotland or England. On reviewing this testimony Smout observed:

> Funnily enough, I don't find this contradictory! I am not Scottish because that is a matter of roots and upbringing, so I cannot be, but I like being here. I am an Englishman who no longer wishes to live in England: again roots and upbringing make me English. I am British: both Scotsmen and Englishmen can claim British nationality, just as all Brits can claim European identity and all Europeans human identity. It is a nest of Russian dolls.[6]

Bearing in mind this tendency for apparent contradiction, a number of themes emerged from analysis of the testimonies. These are shown in table 10.1. Before attempting to draw conclusions, however, it is important to bear in mind two factors. First, the testimonies were essentially spontaneous. The nature of this study's approach to oral history minimised the likelihood of contributors providing answers they may have felt the interviewer wanted to hear. This contributes to the credibility and validity of the evidence. Secondly, the timing of the interviews, taking place a couple of years after the formation of the new Scottish parliament, may have created an unnaturally exaggerated interest in national identity, but it is no less valid for that. Nevertheless, proximity to the 1997 referendum, and the introduction of the new parliament, may have coloured earlier memories about identity.

Table 10.1 Guide to testimony topics surrounding national identity

Theme or issue
Positive feelings of Englishness
Negative feelings of Englishness
Feelings of Britishness
Feelings of Scottishness
Consciousness about the role of Scottish history
Recognition of 'civic' society
Scotland is a separate country from England
Interest in devolution and Scottish nationalism
North/south divide and English nationalism

Source: The oral testimonies gathered for this study.[7]

— ASSESSING NATIONAL IDENTITY —

Within this theoretical complexity there are a number of useful tools that can be employed to assess the extent of national identity at a personal, community and national level. Significantly, given the degree of ambivalence expressed by a number of the contributors, these tools can also be used to gauge processes of change in personal expressions of national identity. This section will set out, and evaluate, these tools, which will be used to analyse the national identity themes that emerged from the testimonies (see table 10.1).

Anthony Smith provided a useful model in defining what he called *ethnie*, in which he identified five elements: (i) a common name; (ii) a shared myth of descent; (iii) a common history; (iv) a distinctive shared culture; and (v) links to common territory.[8] Applying this model to English migrants in Scotland immediately introduces degrees of ambiguity. In terms of sharing a common name, English and Scottish, and England and Scotland, are different names. They also refer to different territories. Furthermore, these two elements are confused by the notion of Britain and Britishness. Sarah Thomas observed, 'I don't feel Scotland is a separate country. I never have done ... To me you can look at it on the map, it's one island there's no reason to have any break in it.' But hers was an exceptional view. Most contributors either identified Scotland as a separate country, or came to see it as one. A shared myth of descent, a shared culture and a common history are also confused by the notion of Britishness. Sarah Thomas referred to her Scottish ancestry: 'My mother came from somewhere near Blairgowrie ... However,

I never felt particularly Scottish, considering em I have a middle name Rattray which is a Scottish town.'[9] Others such as Ron Curran, Patricia Yeaman, Peter Crown, Ian McGeechan, David Hilton, Mike Russell and Janice Grant all referred to their Scots ancestry, with some amongst them being conscious of returning to 'their roots'. The sense of shared history was more complex, and will be discussed below. The most common observation, however, was admission of an initial ignorance about Scottish history, and an emerging awareness of its importance within Scottish politics, society and culture.

Benedict Anderson introduced the useful concept of imagination in his definition of a nation as 'an imagined political community'.[10] It was imagined because people did not know everyone in the nation, or community, and this produced deep horizontal comradeship. Referring to the work of Tom Nairn,[11] he suggested that:

It is useful to remind ourselves that nations inspire love, and often profoundly self-sacrificing love. The cultural products of nationalism – poetry, prose, fiction, music, [and] plastic arts – show this love in thousands of different forms and styles. On the other hand, how truly rare it is to find analogous nationalist products expressing fear and loathing.[12]

What he was talking about here was patriotism. George Orwell made an important distinction between patriotism and nationalism, where patriotism was for the love of your surroundings, its culture and its environment, whereas nationalism was actually saying that your country was superior. Bernard Crick, who is also a distinguished Orwellian scholar, concurred with this distinction in oral testimony. Asking a rhetorical question Crick mused:

Could I say I was a Scottish patriot? No, a patriot for Scotland, an enthusiast for Scotland um but I didn't feel that one could hope to be regarded as Scottish in one's lifetime coming in from England. If I'd been young enough, and my partner was young enough to have had children in Scotland they would have grown up considering themselves Scottish and being accepted as Scottish without any doubt.

Further analysis (below) will provide additional evidence of this sense of patriotism amongst English migrants.

One of the more useful tools is the sense of 'other'. Linda Colley argued that national, ethnic and communal identity was conditional and relational, and that this was defined by social and territorial boundaries.[13] In other words, we usually decide who we are by reference to who, and what, we are not. An example she supplied was that, during the eighteenth and early nineteenth centuries, the English used the French as the 'other' to define themselves. The same conditions apply for Canadians and Americans, Catalans and Spaniards, and Scots and English. Referring to the latter pairing, Jonathan Hearn defined the English as the 'significant other'[14] – raising an intriguing corollary, that the Scots were essentially the 'insignificant other'. Furthermore, for the English in Scotland, what role did the Scots play as their 'other', and did this influence the definition of the elusive concept of Englishness? This is a particularly interesting question, as the contributors, many of whom progressively perceived themselves as Scottish, corroborated evidence from elsewhere that the English were becoming increasingly perplexed about their own sense of identity (this will be discussed below[15]).

Colley also recognised the holding of multiple identities, referred to by David McCrone as 'pick 'n' mix identities'.[16] Colley wrote, 'It was quite possible for an individual to see himself as being, at one and the same time, a citizen of Edinburgh, a Lowlander, a Scot and a Briton.'[17] Colley's application of the concept of 'other' was not restricted to national boundaries. They applied at smaller community or social levels. Intriguingly, in this context, at least two of the contributors were not recognised as Englishmen, but as locals. Neil Bayfield recalled:

> There are problems of acceptance at every level of society. It is interesting that at one point when my first wife was alive we were thinking of writing a history of Banchory and I remember . . . I visited one of the local postmen who was a great authority and he said: 'ah you must go and see Mr So and So who lives just down the road and of course he's nae from Banchory ye ken he's nae a local he comes from Strachan'. Strachan is about two miles away just outside the [town]. So it just shows that you know a stranger is anyone who lives at the bottom of the garden really or just a little bit further away. It's all a matter of scale and the same prejudices apply throughout society I believe.

Mike Waters shared a similar experience. He applied for a job with the Forestry Commission, and did not get the job. Shortly afterwards he recalled, 'I heard the locals grumbling in the street that they had given the job to a foreigner from Struy [a neighbouring village] when Mike Waters who was local was turned down'.

Another interpretation of the concept of 'other' was revealed by Simon Frith, an English-born sociologist, who came to Scotland in 1987. Writing in *Critical Quarterly*, he argued that to know what it was to be Scottish was to understand what it meant to be non-Scottish. He remembered when he used to take the train back to England every weekend:

Increasingly, though, I found the journey south – through damp mountains to the industrial Midlands – depressing. By the time my job was done I wanted to stay. Scotland's immediate appeal was aesthetic. I grew up in the north of England and first thought of Scotland as further north. Living here I began to realise that Scotland's beauty is qualitatively different. Scottish nature is just there in a way I never felt in England.[18]

He went on to describe other features of Scottish life 'with more of a sociologist's eye'. In addition to his growing appreciation of Scotland as a sense of place, his observations resonated with comment after comment throughout the testimonies – frustration with the media, sectarianism, football, voting in favour of devolution, adverse reactions to English life, and the nature of 'civic society' in Scotland. His article made frequent comparisons with England, as the 'other' in a way that was not always the case in the testimonies, but which was left unsaid, and understood.

Frith was one of a group of visible English migrants who were accused of contributing to the 'Englishing of Scotland'. English academics and students were routinely accused of coming in such numbers as to be a threat to Scottish values and cultural traditions. (This subject was discussed in Chapter 2.) It was symptomatic, however, of accusations, from groups such as Siol nan Gaidheal, that Scotland was a colonised country, with English migrants as the colonisers.[19] This is an example of the English being seen as the 'aggressive other', and was seen by certain Nationalists, with a capital 'N', as a threat to Scotland's culture, economy and political structure.

The idea of Scotland as an internal colony was developed in Hechter's thesis in which the Celtic peripheries were dominated by the Westminster core.[20] Hechter's hypothesis has been rigorously appraised elsewhere, and need take no further space here.[21] But what is significant, for this analysis, is that the idea of Scotland as a colonised country was relatively widely held, albeit, according to Angus Calder, by 'ignorant people'.[22] Nevertheless, aspects of Hechter's theory lay submerged in a number of the testimonies, especially in comments about devolution and the north/south divide (see below).

Related to the idea of Scotland as a colonised nation, was Beveridge and Turnbull's construct of Scottish inferiorism a negative conceptualisation of 'other' where inferiorism is the internalisation of the values of the 'other', over the values of oneself?[23] And of course inferiorism is not simply a resentment of the 'other', indeed it can manifest itself as a welcoming of the 'other'. Tom Nairn also felt that there was a Scottish inferiority complex, and that in spite of a fiercely Scottish identity there was an awareness of the country's dependency, and that a form of Caledonian Antisyzygy[24] concealed assertions of deep-seated beliefs of inferiority.[25] Linda Cusick was attracted to these theories, but was 'irritated' by the lack of empirical evidence. This led her to conduct an experiment, and she was surprised that its outcome 'showed that the phenomenon of Scottish inferiorism could be empirically demonstrated and statistically supported.'[26] On her own admission there were some question marks about her methodological approach, but it seems reasonable to suggest that Scottish inferiorism was positioned in opposition to a perceived significant or superior 'other' – in this case the English. There was no empirical evidence, however, in the testimonies gathered for this study, to corroborate Cusick's findings, in so far as the contributors did not see themselves as inherently superior to the Scots. Conversely, forms of deferential behaviour were not reported to have either eased, or hindered, assimilation. There was, however, anecdotal evidence that some English migrants did perceive themselves to be superior.[27]

One of the problems for national identity theorists was the fact that after 1707 Scotland was not a sovereign nation, and that this led to uniquely Scottish manifestations of national consciousness. This brings us to the final tool for assessing aspects of national identity amongst English-born migrants: the concept of 'civil society',[28] or 'principled society'.[29] Tom Nairn saw this as a distinct heterogeneous social culture, combining the institutions of the Church, law and local authorities, which developed into a distinct separate identity.[30] Jonathan Hearn took this further, suggesting that this aspect of Scottish identity was inexorably linked to a culture of dependency and paternalism.[31] This, he argued, was largely responsible for the 'political and ideological polarization' with the Thatcher governments and the UK core of London and the south east.[32] The sense of 'civil society' was manifested in different ways, but was distinctly Scottish. We have already seen (in Chapter 7) how English-born migrants, some originally Tory supporters, adopted anti-Thatcher positions once settled in Scotland. To what extent other aspects of 'civil society' influenced the contributors' senses of identity will be considered below.

– SCOTTISHNESS, ENGLISHNESS AND BRITISHNESS –

When it came to admitting feelings of national identity there was a wide range of responses, including dual and multiple senses of identity. This very much conforms to the Bechhofer group's conclusions that identity claims vary in different contexts. This can be seen in table 10.2. There were two difficulties, however, in interpreting this data. First, because of the free-flowing and open-ended nature of the testimonies, no specific questions were asked about how each contributor perceived their identity. This meant that only 43 per cent of the sample commented on whether they thought themselves English, Scottish or British.[33]

Secondly, because of differences in linguistic expression, precise comparative interpretation was difficult. In spite of these methodological difficulties, the table provides a useful guide, and goes some way to corroborating Malcolm Dickson's findings about the Scottification of English migrants.

Table 10.2 Expressed feelings about national identity

Perception of identity[a]	Percentage of cohort
English only	3.8
Scottish only	34.6
British only	7.7
Not English only	23.1
English and British	3.8
English and Scottish	11.5
British and Scottish	11.5
British, Scottish, and not English	3.8

Source: The oral history testimonies gathered for this study.
a. NB this represents only the 43% of the sample who chose to talk about these aspects of national identity.

The largest category was those who claimed Scottish national identity, with just over a third declaring single Scottish identity and the rest claiming dual nationality, either English/Scottish or British/Scottish. Nearly a quarter said they did not feel English, without necessarily saying why they felt that way. Close inspection of these testimonies, however, indicated they tended towards feelings of Scottishness or Britishness. This means that 84.6 per cent of these migrants no longer felt English. Because of the difficulties of interpreting the data, however, these findings need to be treated with caution.

These perceptions of identity were expressed in different ways. For example, Liz Potts' sense of Scottishness was reinforced and confirmed by other people:

People have said they don't think I'm English, which might sound smug, but I've been with people for so long that you know they know me and maybe that's the lucky part of it. I've been able to meet people individually and know them well.

Isobel Murray defined her identity through support of the Scottish rugby team, and June Williams by becoming a member of the Church of Scotland. Agnes Swift described herself as a 'Scottish granny', but also saw herself as British:

> I never felt foreign and I've been up here longer now than I was in Lincolnshire and yet there was a lorry driver stopped [in Ayr] once and I was chatting to somebody I'd met going down town and asked the way and I started to tell him and he said: 'Oh it's no use asking you', meaning that he probably thought I was on holiday and I probably knew better than the person I was chatting to because I'd lived here so long. Something was said once something about England English and I said: 'To tell the truth I just feel British.'

It was difficult to find common factors that might have explained this relatively widespread sense of Scottishness. Of those who claimed to be wholly Scottish, the average length of residence was twenty-three years, compared with an average of twenty-two years for the sample as a whole. Looking at partners, 31 per cent were married to Scots compared to 24 per cent of the whole sample, so this was hardly significant either. There were further similarities with the sample as a whole, in terms of gender, location of residence, and occupational background. What is significant was that more than three quarters of those expressing views about national identity found themselves to have feelings of Scottishness.

Less than one in five of the contributors admitted to feelings of English-ness, and of those, three quarters also admitted to feelings of Scottishness. For example, in the cases of Patricia Yeaman and Elizabeth Bunting. Patricia Yeaman commented, 'I was always very conscious of the fact that I was English and privileged to be here'. She also observed, 'people say "do you come from England?" I always say Scotland and then I feel such a hypocrite. I want Scotland to be recognised in its own right and myself as an accepted resident of here'. She also added that she did not want to leave Dundee. Elizabeth Bunting, having said she was an 'English woolly liberal', qualified this with the following observation:

> My friend Christine who is very Scottish and very patriotic about being Scottish turns round and says: 'You're more Scottish than Gordon Brown' [the Scots-born Chancellor of the Exchequer]. And I just sort of looked at her and she said: 'At least you bloody live here and work here and pay taxes [adopts Scottish accent]. He doesn't. He spends his entire life down south'. So her attitude is that if you live in Scotland you are Scottish and I think that's probably quite a reasonable approach. I mean I have been here for fifteen years now I mean as well as the four years I was here as a student so it's about half my life almost I've been in Scotland.

Only one contributor admitted, unequivocally, to being English. This was Margaret Cox, who said:

> I still feel really English. It's funny. I feel really English. And particularly when I've mixed with these quite, it's funny isn't it, when I've mixed with these quite

normal people. You know, working-class people. They're not, you know, people who've just gone out to work and, and that when I mix I realise their culture's so diff, you know, their culture is very different from mine. Where I might be a reserved English girl that, that the type of people I'm coming into contact with here in the Borders, I'm just so unlike. But the, you know, the male or the female equivalent. So I don't know that I'd ever feel Scottish. Think I will always, and maybe even [the] longer I'm here, [the] more English I feel.[34]

The cultural difference Margaret Cox was referring to was almost certainly based on class, as she was middle class. There was also another significant factor, which will be discussed below, and this was her awareness of 'civic society'.

A quarter of these contributors expressed feelings of Britishness, and this too revealed feelings of multiple identities. Charlotte Howe, who had earlier differentiated between Mulleachs and Scots, was clear about her sense of identity:

I just consider myself British I don't consider myself, I consider this as the British Isles, I don't consider myself English or Scottish or anything, I just happen to be somebody who was born in England living in Scotland and I love the country for what it is, I love the way of life for what it is and I love the people for what they are, the majority of them.

Leeds-born Ian McGeechan provided an example of dual nationality, claiming to be both British and Scottish. This is perhaps not surprising for someone who has both played for, and coached, the British Lions and Scotland rugby teams.

Peter Crown discussed national identity at length, and his self-examination clearly made him feel uncomfortable. The recording session in his dental surgery 'opened up a Pandora's box of feelings'. His thoughts are worth exploring in some depth:

I think the Scottish have a much clearer identity of being Scottish. And Scotland has less divisions in Scotland, all behind one flag whereas being English is more basically, not because I'm from the north, but northern English is very much different than being from the south. You notice there are actually divisions in actually being English. Much more so than I get the impression from being Scottish or Welsh or Irish. And that being English you are also aware that eh that England is the biggest part of the United Kingdom, with the highest population and that Scotland is much smaller and Wales is smaller still and Northern Ireland is smaller still. And so that you almost had to em deny your nationalistic fervour of being English to be polite and caring and be aware that other smaller nations can get trampled under you know what is good for England is good for, good for the rest of the British Isles . . . you can't be too English because you know it will just echo and steamroller the smaller countries that we want to be seen as British. I think most, or a lot of English people, see themselves as being British before they see themselves being English. And I certainly do get that impression that since devolution and all the fuss that was made about that that Scotland wants to have some room for itself is that, I think, time is turned a little bit and a lot of English are saying: 'Well hang on a minute then what about English rule for England?' So in many ways I think it is quite backward. It's stirred up, you know, some bad feeling where . . . being English is different from being Scottish.

There are many issues, apparent contradictions, and paradoxes in this short extract. It displays a certainty and confidence about being English deriving from England's dominant role in the Union. Yet there is uncertainty about what it means to be English compared to the certainty of the Celtic fringe. He continued on this theme:

I think the English see the bigger picture, in that yes being English is important, but also being British is important as well that you have to take account of other nations and sometimes the Scottish see the picture purely from a Scottish point of view. And OK yes they probably have to do that because they are a small nation and, they have got to bat for their wicket much harder or else they will get trampled on. But sometimes it would be nice to see the English respected sometimes as well. Smaller country, another country not purely jump up and down as Scottish. But I certainly wouldn't say that that's in yer face all the time. That sort of attitude. But it is there from time to time. And a lot of it is whipped up by the media.

What we are seeing here is possible adoption of British identity by default, and arguably out of a sense of guilt for the evil that England had done to Scotland in the past and, as the following extract implies, perhaps for peace of mind:

It's almost like being English is being a second-class citizen [in Scotland] . . . I mean not by individuals but as a nation as a whole that somehow em we are, or I personally, am responsible for evil that was done in the past, years ago. We are still being held responsible for those things that were done to Scotland as a nation.

Crown also worked in England. When he was living and working in the Borders he had a spell practising as an industrial dentist in London for two days a week. This created further ambivalence as the following extract demonstrates:

> I felt more Scottish when I lived in England because again eh you were in a minority so you were defending...I think I am just a natural defender of the underdog and that in Scotland, in England I'm quite happy to be as Scottish as I wanted to be and I was happy to defend the Scottish nation.

Continuing this theme of pro-Scottishness, Crown was scathing about an English prop (an international rugby player) who was critical about Scotland. He could not remember his name, but he recalled that he had front teeth missing:

> Occasionally I have been annoyed by sometimes what the English have said about the Scottish eh particularly there was one English rugby player and again he was so fervently English . . . em, partly because what he was saying was a load of rubbish, but also that I knew very well that that would actually just stir up more em more bad feeling and that somebody in that sort of position says things that are so outrageous would then just tar you know all of us English living in Scotland with the same brush. We'd then be portrayed as arrogant English people, because I think that's the way that we are, or have been seen.

These extracts are only a fraction of what Crown had to say on the subject of national identity. What is evident is that, for many individuals, constructs of national identity were extremely complex, and frequently in conflict.

— UNDERSTANDING THE SCOTTISHING EFFECT —

A number of topics emerged from the testimonies that help to explain this drift towards adopting a Scottish identity. These were, first, a sense of the importance of, or interest in, Scottish history, second, recognition of 'civic society', third, interest in Scottish nationalism and devolution, and finally, comments about the north/south divide.

According to most theorists a precondition for shared national identity is the existence of some form of collective history.[35] A third of the contributors recognised the importance of the legacy of history in Scotland and how this contributed to a strong sense of Scottish identity. Earlier discussions about accent, social networks, Anglophobia, sport, politics and the media, as well as testimony extracts in this chapter, all showed the importance of history, and in particular England's dominant role in relations between the two countries. In Foucauldian terms, 'history' kept on recurring and provided connections between different genealogies or life events.

Over a fifth of the contributors became conscious of Scotland's sense of 'civic society' compared with England. Many of the anti-Thatcher reactions, described earlier, arose out of a growing appreciation of the values of 'civic society'. Interestingly, this awareness of 'civic society' also came from contributors who did not make claims about Scottish identity. Margaret Cox, the only contributor who said the 'longer I'm here, [the] more English I feel', saw Scottish society as being different from that in England:

> [Referring to her neighbours] it was actually quite a nice being brought into the, into the community. So it didn't happen overnight but that's perhaps more a reflection of me rather than them. Particularly in that row of cottages. Everybody, we all looked out but it was quite conscious that we all looked out for each other but actually without being nosey and interfering with each other. So, for me that was actually quite reassuring...I can identify in that, the, the idea about community and working together that actually brought me here on an instinct and on a gut feeling, which now I can see that I was right to have.

This appreciation of a Scottish, as opposed to English, sense of community was also commented on by the Dowlings, Roger Smith, Patricia Yeaman and Elizabeth Bunting, amongst others.[36] Emma Wood, who was motivated by her move north to write a book about the history of the English and the Scots,[37] also commented at length about community, but added a cultural dimension:

> One of the things I liked most about Scotland...I just had this really strong feeling that Scottish culture was just infinitely more vibrant and even though there were plenty of folks in Scotland who didn't give a toss about it there were also a big big hunk of Scottish people who did. I don't know things like Highland dress which we all know is a nonsense on one level it's not you know its an anachronism and it does make folk look a bit phoney but that doesn't matter, people believe it to be symbolic of Scotland and there is absolutely no English equivalent. That's just one thing, there's a lot of other things like that, music, traditional music, there is absolutely nothing like a sort of culture-wide sense of English traditional music or poetry or you know, just not the same, with no. Yeah, and I really like that about Scotland there's something sort of civil society-ish.

Other contributors also commented on cultural aspects of Scottish society, notably Neil Bayfield, Amanda Green, Mary MacLeod, Liz Potts and Sarah

Brown. Another feature of observations about the concept of 'civic society' in Scotland was its comparative inclusiveness. Dot Jessiman explained this in the following terms:

> I suppose I'm unfashionable in that sense [in her understanding of social class], perhaps it's my age but I do, certainly I think one of the things that England, England is classmatic in England I think. It's part of its culture. In fact I would say that England is two cultures, where I was brought up we, one set of values and attitudes and language and expectations and all the rest of it amongst working-class people and I don't mean Marxist sense of working class I mean, I mean it is a cultural thing I think in England. And it's, it's, you only have to open your mouth and you pinpoint yourself. I don't think Scots have that kind of class. It's not a question of em who you are? in Scotland so much but I do think that they're frightful snobs about what you do. I mean, do you know what I mean? I've had people try and clinch an argument with me by by saying: 'I've got a degree.' [Laughs.] And I think, I think it's a, it's much more like, I think Scotland's much closer to the Continent in that obviously you get real, you get differences very serious differences between people in terms of wealth and expectations in terms of what you can expect and certainly you still get a strong sense of rich people exploiting poorer people. But what you don't get in Scotland, I don't think, is the sense that people from a different background are a different species whereas in England I think you do.

There were other interpretations of 'civic society'. One of these was Paul Adams' commenting about Scotland being a more honest society:

> I have to say there is a big huge difference, another huge difference between London and North Berwick and that is that, I think my philosophy is that in London, on a person-to-person basis people believe you're dishonest and you have to prove that you are honest and certainly in our experience in North Berwick people believe that you are honest until proved dishonest which is a huge difference in standards and we've had some very very pleasant experiences. [He and his wife then proceeded to provide a number of examples.]

An underlying feature behind these examples was the tendency to explain 'civic society' in terms of an 'other' – Linda Colley's concept of relative and conditional circumstances, where people create their identity in terms of 'who we are and what we are not'. In all cases of discussion about 'civic society' the 'other' was England, so demonstrating contributors' appreciation of differences in Scotland. There was strong evidence that a very significant proportion of the contributors aligned themselves with this form of

Scottishness. These patterns of behaviour were corroborated in Jonathan Hearn's anthropological study, in which he found that a number of his English informants held similar views to Scots on egalitarian myths, and that this seemed to indicate a process of going native – 'acquiring the perspective of one's adoptive country'.[38]

From the election of Robert McIntyre as the first Scottish Nationalist MP in 1945[39] to the creation of the Scottish Parliament in 1999, political nationalism was rarely out of the news. Here, England, or the status of the Union, was the 'other'. Not surprisingly, this was commented on by around a third of the contributors. As has already been seen[40] some of the migrants adopted Scottish nationalist values. Related to this was recognition of the north/south divide, where, interestingly, the south tended to be defined as London and the south east. Mary Mulligan MSP talked about the similarities between the north of England and Scotland:

> [There] was a time [during the Thatcher years] when you did feel quite awkward about being Scottish, about being English in Scotland because she [Margaret Thatcher] was seen as very much representative of an English characteristic that was all about an individual in England with no recognition of the differences that there are within Great Britain. However, what I felt I had to often remind people was that people in my own area around Liverpool and the north west of England felt just as cut off as somebody maybe in Scotland and also, where my husband was from, in the north east [England] felt equally disengaged from what was actually going on at that time and it wasn't just about being English versus Scottish but was quite clearly about being Conservative and taking forward Conservative ideas which were about the individual and about um you know supporting a certain business structure over the things that I felt that the Labour Party stood for. So, you know, I'm not nationalist in that sense but recognise that it was, it was a political thing as much as anything and that people in the north of England, and in fact people probably in the south west of England, felt equally cut off from the decision-making that was taking place.

All the MSP contributors mentioned the north/south divide, but in different ways. Mike Russell, of the SNP, talked about being prepared to negotiate with Carlisle and Berwick-upon-Tweed to become part of Scotland, and, as already seen, Nick Johnston was dismissive of his compatriot English Tories who patronised Scots as colonials. Liberal Democrat Euan Robson, a Northumbrian, also recognised the existence of a north/south divide, aligning Scotland with the north of England:

> As far as England goes, I think England is, particularly the further south you go, less aware of itself than the Scots are. It's not the case in northern England. In northern

England there is an awakening of the northern spirit. I used to see the same problems that the Scots were having when I sat on the [Northumberland] County Council. In fact some of them were even worse in the north of England. London was seen as just as remote from Newcastle and Northumberland as Scotland felt it was remote from them...I don't see that the development of Englishness as such, happening quite as quickly as has happened in Scotland.

Here he also raised the issue of English nationalism. One thing that was apparent from the majority of the testimonies was that, until coming to Scotland, most English migrants had not really thought deeply about issues of national identity. Coming to Scotland introduced the migrants to cultural differences, and a strongly manifested sense of Scottish identity, which made them question their own identity.

The advent of devolution in the Celtic nations, preceded by a decade of intensifying public debate, made the English in England contemplate their own sense of identity, and led John Prescott, in 2002, to consider the prospect of regional assemblies south of the Border. Living in Scotland, a number of the contributors talked about a growing sense of English identity. Peter Crown suggested that England was getting a 'rum deal', and Elizabeth Bunting mentioned that the English were beginning to get angry with the Scots. In talking about this Bunting referred to connecting issues of culture, history, sport, economics and politics.

I'd had a slight argument with Dougie MacLean in a pub one night. He was singing anti-English songs and I actually challenged him afterwards and said: 'you have to [unclear]' and I had a long discussion about that with Dick McGaughin one night at a folk festival as well because his attitude was well you know all this bad feeling between the Scots and the English stems from history about two or three hundred years ago and it's really past the point of making any sense any more. You know if the Scots want to be independent go on and do it. I mean every time you've had a vote you've just fluffed it which seems to be what they do all the time you know they sort of 'oh we're gonna do this' and then they always fluff it. It's the same with the football team. Everything they set out to do they fluff so nobody's stopping them. If they really feel that badly about it they should just get on with it. They've had plenty of chances. I think what is interesting now is about nationality in England. The English now are becoming extremely patriotic about being English; the bloody Scots are being so horrible to them. They are starting to get angry about it now and they have put up with for two hundred and fifty or three hundred years they have taken no bloody notice but now they are now getting quite cross. And that bodes ill in some ways for Scotland because if you think how much they take out of the UK purse just purely in Health Service terms. The spend on health in Scotland is much higher than it is in England, much much higher. And if that you know I mean Scotland may feel that they can continue to spend that but the latest economic forecast suggests not so. I think that they talk of the [unclear]. It's like doing the MEd and Scottish education tells a story about how wonderful the education system is in Scotland and just how long can they go on living on memory because a lot of what they are fantasising about how good it is is you know thirty forty fifty years ago. It is not what's happening now. Is it that much better really? So I don't know. But yeah I still like living here. I just sometimes get a bit cross with the jingoistic.

Mike Russell MSP commented about growing English nationalism and how this was manifested by the increasing sightings of the cross of St George at football matches:

If you go to football matches the St George's cross is much more in evidence than it has ever been. I suspect a crude Union Jack count at an England game over the last twenty years would show a considerable rise in the St George's cross and the Lions and a considerable fall in the Union Jacks. I think it's a very very long-term project to convert what has been the, using Britain as a synonym for England into an understanding of England's place and England's role. But I think it's a process underway. It's a very uncomfortable process for the English, you can see that, very uncomfortable indeed and it leads, you know, if not directly there are elements of within the Euro-scepticism with fear of the Euro, with you know, with the 'Save the pound' campaign. These are all symbols of a nervousness about identity. Just as the Scots you know, have gone through that. I think the Scots are much more comfortable with identity now. The polls that you undoubtedly see show that over 70 per cent of people regard themselves as Scottish first and not even some British second. And I think that's a process that will continue whereas most English people, they may call themselves English but they have this mixed-up notion of England and Britain and it would be good to shear that off and get people to face the reality of the situation.

As was seen in Chapter 2, Bernard Crick indicated the English were insecure about their identity, and this was corroborated by a series of books by the likes of Tom Nairn, Jeremy Paxman, Andrew Marr and Simon Heffer.[41] What the testimonies told us was that, until they came to Scotland, most of the contributors had not thought about issues of national identity. Tom Bond's comments were typical:

When we were in England you didn't think Scottish were different from English or Irish, or Welsh. I worked with them at Fawley, Englishmen, Scottish, Irish, Welsh and there was never polarisation down there. Now this is at least twenty-four, twenty-five years ago so maybe it's changed but there wasn't the same sort of polarisation that you get up here.

Arrival in Scotland introduced English-born migrants to this relatively alien concept, that of national identity, and its inherent conflicts and complexities. Awareness was manifested in a kaleidoscope of nation, history, accent, sport, community, politics, landscape, environment and belonging. For all, this was a complex and shifting process; and for many, an uncomfortable one.

— CONCLUSION —

Any analysis of national identity, especially using the concept of 'other', will tend to emphasise differences, but, as David McCrone found, 'Scotland has far more similarities than differences with its southern neighbour.'[42] This was a view shared by a number of the contributors. Mike Wade was typical when he commented:

> I feel completely at home in Scotland . . . I regard myself, not as Scottish but I feel completely at home here . . . I think there's a great deal in common between the upbringing I've had on both sides of the Border and all the people that I regard as friends in Scotland. I can see no distinction between my friends in Scotland and my friends in England.

Here, Wade was referring to forms of behaviour in both the private and public spheres. Jürgen Habermas made this distinction when he defined the public sphere as a 'domain of social life', where public opinion can be formed.[43] He was referring to the mechanisms of the state, and 'institutional conditions conducive to the relatively unconstrained production of ideas'. Coincidentally, Jonathan Hearn argued that Scotland's 'civic society' facilitated this process of communication.[44] This distinction between public and private spheres is an important one when trying to assess the impact of national identity upon the lives of English-born migrants in Scotland.

Having read this, and the preceding chapters, you might be left with the impression that ideas of national identity – Scottishness, Englishness, Britishness and their surrounding complexities – were dominating features in the lives of the English in Scotland. But this would be a misleading impression. The bulk of the testimonies were concerned with the day-to-day realities of life – having sex, getting married, bringing up children, earning a living, enjoying leisure, dealing with illness, coping with death, so on and so forth. In this respect the migrants were no different from their Scots neighbours. In terms of the multi-layered complexities of national identity, as the testimonies demonstrate, the majority of English migrants came to adopt many of the values and perspectives of their host communities and country of adoption. In this sense there was a discernible Scottishing effect.

– NOTES –

1. Dickson, 'Should Auld Acquaintance Be Forgot?', p. 131.
2. Bechhofer et al., 'Constructing National Identity: Arts and Landed Elites in Scotland', *Sociology*, vol. 33, no. 3, August 1999, p. 527.
3. Hearn, *Claiming Scotland*, p. 7.
4. Paxman, *The English*.
5. Devine and Logue, (2002), *Being Scottish*, p. x.
6. Correspondence with T. C. Smout 10/12/02.
7. Given different linguistic expressions used by the contributors, these general headings are for guide purposes only.
8. Smith, *National Identity*. See also Chapter 2.
9. Ibid.
10. Anderson, *Imagined Communities*, p. 5.
11. Nairn, *The Break Up of Britain*, pp. 14–15.
12. Anderson, *Imagined Communities*, pp. 141–2.
13. L. Colley, 'Britishness and Otherness: An Argument', *Journal of British Studies*, vol. 31, 1992, pp. 309–29.
14. Hearn, *Claiming Scotland*, p. 11.
15. See also Chapter 2.
16. McCrone, (1992), *Understanding Scotland: The Sociology of a Stateless Nation*, p. 195.
17. Colley, 'Britishness and Otherness: An Argument', p. 315.
18. Frith, 'On Not Being Scottish', *Critical Quarterly*, vol. 42, no. 4, pp. 1–6.
19. See Chapter 2.
20. Hechter, (1975), *Internal Colonialism: The Celtic Fringe in British National Development, 1536–1966*.
21. See, amongst others, Nairn, *The Break Up of Britain*, p. 202.
22. Calder, (2002), *Scotlands of the Mind*, p. 176.
23. Beveridge and Turnbull, (1989), *The Eclipse of Scottish Culture: Inferiorism and the Intellectuals*.
24. Antisyzygy refers to a conflicting sense of identity, the existence of many.
25. Nairn, *The Break Up of Britain*.
26. Cusick, 'Scottish Inferiority', *Scottish Affairs*, no. 9, Autumn 1994, pp. 143–50.
27. See Chapter 4, and Dot Jessiman, Tape MW0036, 9/7/01.
28. Smout, 'Union of the Parliaments', in Menzies (ed.), (1972), *The Scottish Nation: A History of the Scots from Independent Union*, pp. 158–9.
29. Foster, 'The Twentieth Century, 1914–1979', in Houston and Knox, *New Penguin History of Scotland*, p. 454.
30. Nairn, *The Break Up of Britain*, p. 135.
31. Hearn, *Claiming Scotland*, pp. 38–9
32. Ibid., p. 130.
33. This meant that where contributors did discuss these aspects of national identity they considered it important, as they were selecting the agenda. Conversely, from the 57 per cent who did not raise these issues, it could be argued that matters relating to national identity were not considered important in their lives, especially as all the contributors were aware that the recordings were for a study into English migration into Scotland. All the proportional figures in this section relate to the 43 per cent cohort.
34. Just before publication of this book Margaret Cox emailed the author to say she was returning to work in England and that she planned to keep her cottage for weekends.
35. See, amongst others, Smith, *National Identity*. See also Chapter 2.
36. See earlier chapters, especially Chapter 7.
37. Wood, *Notes from the North*. See also Chapter 1.
38. Hearn, *Claiming Scotland*, p. 153.

39. Harvie and Jones, (2000), *The Road to Home Rule: Images of Scotland's Cause*, p. 57.
40. See earlier chapters, especially Chapters 7 and 9.
41. See Chapter 2.
42. McCrone, *Understanding Scotland*, pp. 197–8.
43. Habermas, 'The Public Sphere', in Seideman (ed.), (1989), *Jürgen Habermas on Society and Politics: A Reader*, (Boston, 1989), p. 231.
44. Hearn, Claiming Scotland, p. 77.

CHAPTER 11

Conclusion

This book set out with the objective of filling an inexplicable gap in Scottish, English and British history. Arguably this has been achieved, proving beyond any reasonable doubt that English-born settlers have formed Scotland's most significant migrant group in modern times. The analysis, especially that in Chapter 3, dispelled many of the myths about the English in Scotland. As a group they were by no means exclusively 'superior', middle class, retired people, benefiting from expensive property sales in the south east of England, nor were they taking Scots' jobs. As a whole, the English in Scotland were a heterogeneous group, differing in many respects from Scotland's other migrant communities. In terms of assimilation, the vast majority of the English merged into Scottish society, effectively making them invisible. Contributing to their invisibility was the extent to which a significant proportion perceived themselves as adopting a sense of Scottish national identity, particularly in terms of their appreciation of the Scottish sense of civic society. Malcolm Dickson's 1993 findings that English migrants in Scotland had experienced some form of 'Scottishing effect' were certainly validated.[1]

This study benefited hugely from the life history testimonies of English-born migrants living in Scotland. The rigorous structure of the sample and the methods involved in data collection, verification and interpretation provided a dependable source from which to draw relatively reliable conclusions, in line with Gordon's 'principle of intelligibility'.[2] Furthermore, the testimonies provided a revealing insight into the lived-in life experiences of this migrant group, disclosing a wealth of data about the aspirations, fears, highs and lows associated with the process of migration. In addition, the testimonies penetrated the *mentalité* of the contributors, indicating what they were thinking and why they were thinking about what they were thinking. Bringing added validity to our conclusions was the fact that there was no attempt, in the interview methods, to lead the contributors. They set the agenda and they incorporated the events they perceived to be of significance in telling their life stories. This approach facilitated levels of understanding that were not apparent in the majority of documentary sources and led, in Chapter 5, to the proposition that traditional historical models for explaining migration (push and pull, and cause and effect) could result in misleadingly simplistic explanations of the process and impact of migration.

The life history approach also satisfied the need to view migration as a longitudinal process – from understanding pre-migration motivation through to individual lifetime experiences in the host communities, be they local, regional, national, workplace, familial or any number of social scenarios. What emerged was a wide range of issues and themes, usually inter-related, and sometimes incorporating apparent contradictions. Put simply, the life experiences of this group of migrants were complex and multi-faceted. Foucault argued that the world as we know it was a tangled profusion of events, and this was evidently reflected in the contributors' life stories. Indeed, in a wide ranging review of oral history studies of migration, Al Thomson observed that 'most migration oral history recognises the complex inter-connections between migration and the formation and development of migrant communities and ethnic identities'.[3] The English in Scotland certainly conformed to these patterns of complexity in terms of their motivations for migrating, but not necessarily in the formation of a migrant community or construction of a distinctly English ethnic group. On the contrary, the English merged into Scottish society and tended to adopt Scottish identities and values, although this was not always the case.

To make sense of this complexity, Foucault's genealogical approach suggested seeking out 'the appearance of recurrences, regularities, proximities and symmetries'.[4] These existed in profusion throughout the testimonies and other source material. Connectivity featured both at micro and macro levels, though not always in a teleological or structured way. Foucault resisted historiographical traditions of seeking continuities and postulated that connections between events were unlikely to be hierarchical or linear. For example, in the case of Patricia Yeaman, it was possible to identify a number of disparate factors, experiences and events in her assessment of personal acceptance in Scotland (see Chapters 6, 7, 8 and 10). These included: accent, class, work, loneliness, exclusion from tight-knit local family networks, gender, one experience of anti-English prejudice, love of Scotland, and homophobia. This diverse pattern was mirrored in all the testimonies, over a wide range of subjects and issues.

At a macro level, the sum of these events and life experiences combined to form a general explanation of aspects of the impact of the migratory experience. One of the best examples of this was the recognition that, as a group, English migrants began to consider questions of national identity, many for the first time, when stimulated by sports events involving England and Scotland, as well as at times of political elections. Reporting in the media acted as a catalyst, occasionally generating passionate responses, and frequently causing frustration from perceived bias in reporting. The role played by the media in the construction of national identities, the difficulties this created for incoming migrants, and the extent to which 'fictiveness'[5] was common practice, is certainly an area that merits further research.

One of the symmetries that emerged was the role played by Scottish history. Most of the contributors had little idea of Scottish history before they came, but quickly realised its importance in Scottish society and culture. This ranged from the function it performed in the formation of communities and social groups, the construction of identity, iconography, cultural valorisation, and political relationships with Westminster, amongst other things. In sport, this was explained by the Bill McLaren hypothesis. This was evident on the terraces, in the pubs and in the media where the use of military metaphors and the general tone of reporting sometimes verged on the xenophobic. More than half of the contributors came to appreciate the significance of the legacy of history and the consequences for Scotland arising from living in the shadow of her larger neighbour to the south. Around a third consciously sought to enhance their knowledge in a variety of ways. These included conversations with their friends and participation in uniquely Scottish events like common ridings, hogmanay, Burns suppers and the Mod. A small number actively participated in history societies and Emma Wood even wrote a book about it, targeted at English incomers.

Generally, throughout the period under review, the media painted a picture of a climate of anti-English feeling. This was not the general experience of the contributors, nor was it evident from other sources. Studies from a number of social scientists, albeit they were mostly restricted to peripheral areas, essentially corroborated the findings of this study. That was not to say that tensions did not exist. There were low levels of anti-English feeling and exceptional extremist activity, but the latter was largely directed against England, the state, and not English people. Compared with prejudicial reactions to other migrant communities, the English were largely welcomed into Scottish society, and this is certainly borne out by the constant growth of English migrants settling in Scotland.

This expansion in numbers came at a time of decline and stagnation in Scotland's population. At the outset of the twenty-first century civil servants and politicians have been calling for immigration policies to arrest the downturn. And as the nationalist MSP, English-born Mike Russell, put it, 'Scotland is not full up'. Throughout the second half of the twentieth century and in the early twenty-first century the English, an invisible diaspora, have played a significant role in Scotland's demography, society, culture, economy and politics. Why they remained absent from the historiography for so long remains a mystery. At least (or should that be at last?) this book corrects this omission.

– NOTES –

1. M. Dickson, 'Should Auld Acquaintance Be Forgot?'
2. See Chapter 1.
3. Thomson, 'Moving Stories: Oral History and Migration Studies', *Oral History*, Spring 1999, p. 25.
4. Foucault, *The Archaeology of Knowledge*, p. 124.
5. See Benedict Anderson, chap. 9.

Bibliography

— ORAL TESTIMONIES —

Contributor's name	Tape number
Isobel Murray[ab]	MW0001
Christine Kirkton[ab]	MW0002
Jimmy Smith[ab]	MW0006
Jack Brown[ab]	MW0004
Charlotte Roberton[ab]	MW0005
Jennifer Roberton[ab]	MW0005
Hannah Green[ab]	MW0008
Mary Duncan[ab]	MW0009
Margaret Cox[ab]	MW0003
Euan Robson MSP[b]	MW0007
Nick Johnston MSP	MW0012
Tim David[ab]	MW0011
T. C. Smout	MW0013
Stuart Brook	MW0015
Peter Crown[a]	MW0014
Mary Mulligan MSP	MW0017
Rob Nicholson	MW0018
Roger Smith	MW0019
Paul Armstrong[a]	MW0016
Bernard Crick	MW0020
Ron Curran	MW0021
David Hilton	MW0023
Tom Bond[a]	MW0024
Mike Russell MSP	MW0025
Liz Potts[a]	MW0026
Mike Waters[a]	MW0027
Pat Waters[a]	MW0027
James Dowling[a]	MW0030

Lucy Dowling[a]	MW0030
Peter Goodfellow[a]	MW0028
Emma Wood	MW0029
Neil Bayfield	MW0031
Mary MacLeod[a]	MW0032
Revd Brian Woodcock	MW0033
Tim Underwood[a]	MW0034
Sarah Thomas[a]	MW0035
Dot Jessiman	MW0036
Ian McGeechan	MW0037
Jim Grant[a]	MW0038
Janice Grant[a]	MW0038
Trevor Steven	MW0039
Paul Adams[a]	MW0040
Amanda Adams[a]	MW0040
Elizabeth Bunting[a]	MW0041
Sarah Brown[a]	MW0042
Amanda Green[a]	MW0043
Martin Robson[a]	MW0044
Patricia Yeaman[a]	MW0045
Patricia Yeaman[a]	MW0045A
June Williams[a]	MW0046
Sarah Andrews[a]	MW0047
Mike Hadrian[a]	MW0048
Agnes Swift[a]	MW0049
Eileen MacDonald[a]	MW0050
Pauline McLaren[a]	MW0051
Charlotte Howe[a]	MW0052
Catherine Parr[a]	MW0053
Pheona Sinclair[a]	MW0054
Mike Wade	MW0056
Bill McLaren	MW0022S
Fiona Langford	MW0055S
Malcolm Dickson	MW0057S
Murdo MacLeod	MW0058S
Ronnie Mitchell	MW001S

a. To protect confidentiality for these contributors, use is made of a pseudonym.
b. Indicates interviews conducted as part of the pilot programme, and as part of the Scottish Borders Memory Bank Millennium project.

Tapes and transcripts will be available for researchers in the Archives at the School of Scottish Studies, Edinburgh. Tapes are cited as follows: name [pseud. if applied], tape number, date of recording. All recordings are with English migrants unless the number has the suffix S, which indicates Scots. Unless they are public figures, contributors were given pseudonyms to guarantee anonymity.

— Documentary primary sources —

Barron, H (ed.), *The Third Statistical Account of Scotland, The County of Inverness,* (Edinburgh, 1985).

Bulloch, J. P. B. and Urquhart, J. M. (eds), *The Third Statistical Account of Scotland, The Counties of Peebles and Selkirkshire,* (Glasgow, 1964).

Campaign for a Scottish Assembly, *Claim of Right for Scotland,* (Edinburgh, 1989).

Correspondence from Ron Curran.

Correspondence from Christine Grahame MSP.

Correspondence from Mairi MacArthur.

Correspondence from Carol Riddell.

Correspondence from George Rosie.

Correspondence from Kenneth G. Silver.

Correspondence from T. C. Smout.

Correspondence from Brian Wilson MP.

Coull, J. R. (ed.), *The Third Statistical Account of Scotland, The County of Shetland,* (Edinburgh, 1985).

Crouther, G. T. (ed.), *The Third Statistical Account of Scotland, The County of Clackmannan,* (Glasgow, 1966).

Cunnison, J. and Gilfillan, J. B. S. (eds), *The Third Statistical Account of Scotland, The City of Glasgow,* (Glasgow, 1958).

Dilke, M. S. and Templeton, A. A. (eds), *The Third Statistical Account of Scotland, The County of Dunbarton,* (Glasgow, 1959).

Hamilton, D. (ed.), *The Third Statistical Account of Scotland, The County of Banff,* (Glasgow, 1960).

Hamilton, H. (ed.), *The Third Statistical Account of Scotland, The County of Aberdeen,* (Glasgow, 1960).

Hamilton, H. (ed.), *The Third Statistical Account of Scotland, The County of Moray and Nairn,* (Glasgow, 1965).

Herdman, J. (ed.), *The Third Statistical Account of Scotland, The County of Berwick,* (Edinburgh, 1992).

Herdman, J. (ed.), *The Third Statistical Account of Scotland, The County of Roxburgh,* (Edinburgh, 1992).

Houston, G. (ed.), *The Third Statistical Account of Scotland, The County of Dumfries,* (Glasgow, 1962).

Illsley, W. A. (ed.), *The Third Statistical Account of Scotland, The County of Angus,* (Arbroath, 1977).

Jackson, J. M. (ed.), *The Third Statistical Account of Scotland, The City of Dundee,* (Arbroath, 1979).

Keir, D. (ed.), *The Third Statistical Account of Scotland, The City of Edinburgh,* (Glasgow, 1966).

Kirkland, H. (ed.), *The Third Statistical Account of Scotland, The County of Midlothian*, (Edinburgh, 1985).

Laird, J. and Ramsay, D. G. (eds), *The Third Statistical Account of Scotland, The Stewartry of Kirkcudbright*, (Glasgow, 1965).

MacDonald, C. M. (ed.), *The Third Statistical Account of Scotland, The County of Argyll*, (Glasgow, 1961).

Mackenzie, H. (ed.), *The Third Statistical Account of Scotland, The City of Aberdeen*, (Edinburgh, 1953).

Mather, A. S. (ed.), *The Third Statistical Account of Scotland, The County of Ross and Cromarty*, (Edinburgh, 1987).

Miller, R. (ed.), *The Third Statistical Account of Scotland, The County of Orkney*, (Edinburgh, 1985).

Moisley, H. A. and Thain, A. G. (eds), *The Third Statistical Account of Scotland, The County of Renfrew*, (Glasgow, 1962).

Private papers belonging to Dot Jessiman, Convenor, New Scots for Independence.

Rennie, R. C. (ed.), *The Third Statistical Account of Scotland, The County of Stirling*, (Glasgow, 1966).

Smith, A. (ed.), *The Third Statistical Account of Scotland, The County of Fife*, (Edinburgh, 1952).

Smith, D. (ed.), *The Third Statistical Account of Scotland, The County of Kincardine*, (Edinburgh, 1988).

Smith, J. S. (ed.), *The Third Statistical Account of Scotland, The County of Caithness*, (Edinburgh, 1988).

Smith, J. S. (ed.), *The Third Statistical Account of Scotland, The County of Sutherland*, (Edinburgh, 1988).

Snodgrass, C. P. (ed.), *The Third Statistical Account of Scotland, The County of East Lothian*, (Edinburgh, 1953).

SNP News Release, 28 June 1998.

Somerville, A. C. and Stevenson, W. (eds), *The Third Statistical Account of Scotland, The County of Bute*, (Glasgow, 1962).

Strawhorn, J. and Boyd, W. (eds), *The Third Statistical Account of Scotland, The County of Ayrshire*, (Edinburgh, 1951).

Taylor, D. B. (ed.), *The Third Statistical Account of Scotland, The Counties of Perth and Kinross*, (Coupar Angus, 1979).

Thomson, G. (ed.), *The Third Statistical Account of Scotland, The County of Lanark*, (Glasgow, 1960).

— PERIODICALS —

Am Mulleach
Ayrshire Post
Border Telegraph
Courier and Advertiser (Dundee)
Daily Record

Evening Telegraph (Dundee)
Glasgow Herald
Guardian Unlimited Special Reports
Ross-shire Journal
Round About
Scotland on Sunday
Sunday Times
The [Glasgow] Herald
The Scotsman
The Southern Reporter
The Sun

— MEDIA BROADCASTS —

The Day That Britain Died, BBC2, 31/1/00, 1/2/00, and 2/2/00.
McLaren, W. P., *Scotland's Grand Slam*, BBC video, (BBC Enterprises Ltd, 1990).
You the Jury, Grampian TV, tape supplied by SMG. Date not confirmed but in the mid 1990s.

— WORLD WIDE WEB —

Bean, F. D., Corona, R., Tuirán, R., Woodrow-Lafield, K. A. and Hook, V., *Circular, Invisible and Ambiguous Migrants, Components of Differences in Estimates of Unauthorised Mexican Migrants in the United States*, (http://www.migracioninternacional.com/docum/recom.html, web site accessed 29/7/02).
Census Data Unit, *The Census Datasets*, (http://www.census.ac.uk/cdu/datasets/, web site accessed 2/6/00).
Currie Community Council, *Minutes, May 1998*, (http://www.ma.hw.ac.uk/ccc/reports/may98.html, web site accessed 29/10/02).
Fonte, J., *Hudson Institute*, (http://www.nationalreview.com/comment/coment-fonte, web site accessed 28/8/02).
Guide to the River Affric, (http://www.guidebook.free-online.co.uk/affric.htm, web site accessed 9/12/02).
Government of Scotland Forum, *The Role of the Media, Research Programme Interim Report January 2001*, (http://www.ed.ac.uk/usgs/forum/Leverhulme, web site accessed 7/2/02).
Holomek, K., *Roma in the Former Czechoslovakia*, (http://www.czechia.com/hcaroma/newspage31.htm, web site accessed 28/8/02).
Jarvie, G. and Reid, I. A., *Sport, Nationalism and Culture in Scotland*, (http://www.umist.ac.uk/sport/Jarvreid/%20May/%2099.htm, web site accessed 7/2/02).
Joint Declaration by the Russian Maoist Party and the Scottish Separatist Group, (http://www.rmp.Maoism.ru/English/internati/rmp-ssg.htm, web site accessed 15/10/02).
Kagyu Samye Ling, (http://www.samyeling.org, web site accessed 17/1/02).

Mather, S., *The Settler Problem; Cause & Effect*, (http://srsm.port.com/srsm/settler.html, web site accessed 29/1/02).

McIntosh, A., *Cultural Reflections at the Hub*, (http://www.AlistairMcIntosh.com, web site accessed 9/8/99).

Racism in Scotland, *Electronic Herald*, (http://members.ncbi.com_XMCM/iansmith_/mirror/29Aug97e.htm, web site accessed 22/2/01).

Re: Relocation, (http://www.standrews.co.uk/Bb/messages/151.html, [February 18 2000], web site accessed 22/2/01).

Responding to Migrant Workers' Needs in Asia, [Hong Kong, June 1992], (http://www.daga.org/urm/up9v/v92-3-29.htm, web site accessed 28/7/02).

Scots Law News, (http://www.law.ed.ac.uk/sln/index.htm, web site accessed 14/8/02).

Scottish Executive, *Audit of Research on Minority Ethnic Issues in Scotland from a Race Perspective*, (http://www.scotland.gov.uk/cru/kd01/red/auditethnic-16.asp, web site accessed 13/5/02).

Siol nan Gaidheal, *Demography: The White Settler Phenomenon*, (http://www.siol-nangaidheal.com.demog.htm, web site accessed 27/4/00).

Siol nan Gaidheal, *Devolution in Scotland and Nationalism in England*, (http://www.siol-nangaidheal.com.national.htm, web site accessed 3/4/01).

The Community Work Training Company, *About Racism in Scotland: A Case Study*, (http://www.community-work-training.org.uk/multic/ris.htm, web site accessed 23/2/01).

The Findhorn Foundation, *Who Are We?*, (http://findhorn.org/about_us/display.html, web site accessed 11/01/01).

Wood, W., *Patriot and Nationalist*, (http://www.siol-nangaidheal.com/wendy.htm, web site accessed 18/3/02).

Wood, W., *Scottish Patriot*, (http://www.altculture.org.ccult/ccult52.html, web site accessed 18/3/02).

Zuelow, E., *Nationalism in a Global Age: The Case for Scotland's Three Nationalisms*, (http://www.sit.wisc.edu/~egzuelow/Acad/, web site accessed 23/2/01).

– GOVERNMENT DOCUMENTS –

Annual Reports, Commission for Racial Equality in Scotland, 1997, 1998, 2000 and 2001.

The Censuses of Scotland, 1951–2001.

– BOOKS –

Anderson, B., *Imagined Communities: Reflections on the Origins and Spread of Nationalism*, (London, 1992).

Anderson, M., 'Population and Family Life', in Dickson, A. and Treble, J. H., *People and Society in Scotland*, vol. III, (Edinburgh, 1992).

Armstrong, B., *A People without Prejudice? The Experience of Racism in Scotland*, (London, 1989).

Baker, R., *The Terror of Tobermory: An Informal Biography of Vice-Admiral Sir Gilbert Stevenson, KBE, CB, CMG,* (Edinburgh, 1999).

Baldwin, J. R. (ed.), *Peoples and Settlement in North-West Ross,* (Edinburgh, 1994).

Bertaux, D., *Biography and Society,* (London, 1981).

Beveridge, C. and Turnbull, R., *The Eclipse of Scottish Culture: Inferiorism and the Intellectuals,* (Edinburgh, 1989).

Blain, N., Boyle, R. and O'Donnell, H., *Sport and National Identity in the European Media,* (Leicester, 1993).

Bogle, K. and Smith, R., *The Green Machine: 125 Years of Hawick Rugby,* (Hawick, 1998).

Boyle, P. and Halfacree, K. (eds), *Migration into Rural Areas: Theories and Issues,* (Chichester, 1998).

Boyle, S., Burns, M. et al., *Scotland's Economy: Claiming the Future,* (London, 1989).

Brierley, P. and MacDonald, F., *Prospects for Scotland 2000,* (Glasgow, 1995).

Brown, C., *A Social History of Religion in Scotland since 1730,* (London, 1987).

Bruley, S., *Women in Britain since 1900,* (Basingstoke, 1999).

Budge, I. and Urwin, D. W., *Scottish Political Behaviour: A Case Study in British Homogeneity,* (Longmans Green, 1966).

Calder, A., *Scotlands of the Mind,* (Edinburgh, 2002).

Cohen, R. (ed.), *The Cambridge Survey of World Migration,* (Cambridge, 1995).

Coleman, D. and Salt, J., *The British Population: Patterns, Trends and Processes,* (Oxford, 1992).

Colpi, T., *Italian Migration to Scotland: Settlement, Employment and the Key Role of the Padrone,* (Glasgow, 1986).

Colpi, T., *Italians Forward: A Visual History of the Italian Community in Great Britain,* (Edinburgh, 1991).

Cooke, A. et al., *Modern Scottish History 1707 to the Present Vol. 2: The Modernisation of Scotland 1850 to the Present,* (East Linton, 1998).

Costello, J., *Love Sex and War: Changing Values 1939–45,* (London, 1985).

Currie, R., Gilbert, A. and Horsley, L., *Churches and Churchgoers: Patterns of Church Growth in the British Isles Since 1700,* (Oxford, 1977).

Davie, G. E., *The Democratic Intellect,* (Edinburgh, 1961).

Davie, G. E., *The Crisis of the Democratic Intellect: The Problem of Generalism and Specialisation in Twentieth Century Scotland,* (Edinburgh, 1986).

Devine, T. M., *The Scottish Nation 1700–2000,* (London, 1999).

Devine, T. M., and Finlay, R., *Scotland in the Twentieth Century,* (Edinburgh, 1996).

Devine, T. and Logue, P., *Being Scottish: Personal Reflections on Scottish Identity Today,* (Edinburgh, 2002).

Ennew, J., 'Gaelic and the Language of Industrial Relations', in Parsler, R. and Shapiro, D., *The Social Impact of Oil in Scotland: A Contribution to the Sociology of Oil,* (London, 1980).

Ferguson, R., *George Macleod: Founder of the Iona Community,* (London, 1990).

Ferguson, W., *Scotland: 1689 to the Present,* (Edinburgh, 1994).

Finlay, C. K., *Mull the Isle the Fairest,* (Kippielaw, 1987).

Flinn, M. et al., *Scottish Population History from the 17th Century to the 1930s*, (Cambridge, 1977).

Forsythe, D., 'Urban-Rural Migration and the Pastoral Ideal: An Orkney Case Study', in Jackson, A., *A Way of Life: Integration and Immigration*, (London, 1980).

Foucault, M., *The Archaeology of Knowledge and the Discourse on Language*, (New York, 1972).

Foucault, M., *Power Knowledge*, (Brighton, 1980).

Giddens, A., *A Contemporary Critique of Historical Materialism*, (London, 1981).

Glasser, R., *Scenes from a Highland Life*, (London, 1981).

Glock, C. and Bellah, R., *The New Religious Consciousness*, (Berkeley, 1976).

Harvie, C., *No Gods and Precious Few Heroes*, (Edinburgh, 1993).

Harvie, C., *Scotland and Nationalism: Scottish Society and Politics 1707–1994*, (London, 1997).

Harvie, C., *Travelling Scot: Essays on the History, Politics and Future of the Scots*, (Glendaruel, 1999).

Harvie, C. and Jones, P., *The Road to Home Rule: Images of Scotland's Cause*, (Edinburgh, 2000).

Hearn, J., *Claiming Scotland: National Identity and Liberal Culture*, (Edinburgh, 2000).

Hechter, M., *Internal Colonialism: The Celtic Fringe in British National Development*, (London, 1975).

House, J. D., 'Oil Companies in Aberdeen: The Strategy of Incorporation', in Parsler, R. and Shapiro, D., *The Social Impact of Oil in Scotland: A Contribution to the Sociology of Oil*, (London, 1980).

Houston, R. A. and Knox, W. W. (eds), *The New Penguin History of Scotland: From the Earliest Times to the Present Day*, (London, 2001).

Hutching, M., *Long Journey for Sevenpence: Assisted Immigration to New Zealand from the United Kingdom 1947–1975*, (Wellington, 1999).

Jackson, A., *Way of Life: Integration and Immigration*, (London, 1980).

Jackson, P., *Race and Racism: Essays in Social Geography*, (London, 1982).

Jarvie, G. and Burnett, J. (eds), *Sport, Scotland and the Scots*, (East Linton, 2000).

Jarvie, G. and Walker, G. (eds), *Scottish Sport in the Making of the Nation: Ninety-Minute Patriots?*, (Leicester, 1994).

Jedrej, C. and Nuttall, M., *White Settlers: The Impact of Rural Repopulation in Scotland*, (Luxembourg, 1996).

Jenkins, K., *Rethinking History*, (Trowbridge, 1991).

Johnston, T. L., Buxton, N. K. and Mair, D., *Structure and Growth of the Scottish Economy*, (London, 1971).

Jones, H., *Recent Migration in Northern Scotland: Pattern, Process, and Impact*, (London, 1982).

Kay, B., *The Complete Odyssey: Voices from Scotland's Recent Past*, (Edinburgh, 1980).

Kellas, J. G., *Modern Scotland: The Nation Since 1870*, (London, 1968).

Kenefick, W., *Rebellious and Contrary: the Glasgow Dockers 1853–1932*, (East Linton, 2000).

Kennedy, L., *In Bed with an Elephant: A Journey through Scotland's Past and Present*, (London, 1995).

Knox, W. W., *Industrial Nation: Work, Culture and Society in Scotland 1800–Present*, (Edinburgh, 1999).

Lumb, R., 'Integration and Immigration: Some Demographic Aspects of Highland Communities', in Jackson, A., *Way of Life: Integration and Immigration*, (London, 1980).

Maan, B., *The New Scots: The Story of Asians in Scotland*, (Edinburgh, 1992).

MacLeod, I. et al. (eds), *The Pocket Scots Dictionary*, (Edinburgh, 1988).

Marr, A., *The Day That Britain Died*, (London, 2000).

Mayhew, S., *A Dictionary of Geography*, (Oxford, 1992).

McCrone, D., *Understanding Scotland: The Sociology of a Stateless Nation*, (London, 1992).

McCrone, D., Kendrick, S. and Straw, P. (eds), *The Making of Scotland: Nation, Culture and Social Change*, (Edinburgh, 1989).

McGrath, J., *The Cheviot, The Stag and the Black, Black Oil*, (London, 1994).

Menzies, G. (ed.), *The Scottish Nation: A History of the Scots from Independent Union*, (London, 1972).

Millar, J., *The Lithuanians in Scotland*, (Isle of Colonsay, 1998).

Mitchison, R., *A History of Scotland: Second Edition*, (London, 1993).

Moore, R., *Labour Migration and Oil*, (London, 1980).

Mugglestone, L., *'Talking Proper': The Rise of Accent as a Social Symbol*, (Oxford, 1995).

Muir, E., *Scottish Journey*, (London, 1935).

Murray, J. and Stockdale, D., *The Miles Tae Dundee: Stories of a City and Its People*, (Dundee, 1990).

Nairn, T., *The Break Up of Britain: Crisis and Neo-Nationalism*, (London, 1977).

Nairn, T., *After Britain: New Labour and the Return of Scotland*, (London, 2000).

Ollila, A. (ed.), *Historical Perspectives on Memory*, (Helsinki, 1999).

Orwell, S. and Angus, I., *The Collected Essays, Journalism and Letters of George Orwell, Vol. IV, In Front of Your Nose*, (London, 1968).

Parsler, R. and Shapiro, D., *The Social Impact of Oil in Scotland: A Contribution to the Sociology of Oil*, (London, 1980).

Paxman, J., *The English: A Portrait of a People*, (London, 1999).

Payne, P. L., *Growth and Contraction: Scottish Industry c1860–1990*, (Glasgow, 1992).

Philip, G., Taylor, P. and Hutton, A., 'Oil-Related Construction Workers: Travelling and Migration', in Jones, H. (ed.), *Recent Migration in Northern Scotland: Patterns, Processes and Impact*, (London, 1982).

Pooley, C. G., and Whyte, I. D., *Migrants, Emigrants and Immigrants: A Social History of Migration*, (London, 1991).

Rabinow, P. (ed.), *The Foucault Reader: An Introduction to Foucault's Thought*, (London, 1991).

Ratcliffe, P., *Ethnicity in the 1991 Census*, (London, 1996).

Riddell, C., *The Findhorn Community: Creating a Human Identity for the 21st Century*, (Findhorn, 1990).

Schacter, D. L. (ed.), *Memory Distortion: How Minds, Brains, and Societies Reconstruct the Past*, (Cambridge, MA, 1997).

Scott, A. M. and Macleay, I., *Britain's Secret War: Tartan Terrorism and the Anglo-American State*, (Edinburgh, 1990).

Scott, J. and Hughes, M., *The Anatomy of Scottish Capital*, (London, 1980).

Seideman, S. (ed.), *Jürgen Habermas on Society and Politics: A Reader*, (Boston, 1989).

Shucksmith, M., Chapman, P. and Clark, G. M., *Rural Scotland Today: The Best of Both Worlds?*, (Aldershot, 1996).

Smith, A. D., *National Identity*, (London, 1991).

Smith, M., *Paper Lions: The Scottish Press and National Identity*, (Edinburgh, 1988).

Smout, T. C., *A Century of the Scottish People, 1830–1950*, (London, 1986).

Solomos, J., *Race and Racism in Britain*, (Basingstoke, 1993).

Stephenson, J. B., *Ford: A Village in the West Highlands of Scotland*, (Lexington, KY, 1984).

Stillwell, J., Rees, P. and Boden, P., *Migration: Processes and Patterns Vol. II: Population Redistribution in the UK*, (London, 1992).

Sweet, H., *The Sounds of English*, (Oxford, 1908).

Trouillot, M.-R., *Silencing the Past: Power and the Production of History*, (Boston, 1995).

Walker, A. L., *The Revival of the Democratic Intellect*, (Edinburgh, 1994).

Watts, H. D., *The Branch Plant Economy: A Study of External Control*, (Harlow, 1981).

Wells, F. A., *The British Hosiery and Knitwear Industry: Its History and Organisation*, (Newton Abbot, 1972).

Welsh, I., *Trainspotting*, (London, 1994).

Whatley, C. A., *Scottish Society 1707–1830: Beyond Jacobitism Towards Industrialisation*, (Manchester, 2000).

Wood, E., *Notes from the North: Incorporating a Brief History of the Scots and the English*, (Edinburgh, 1998).

– JOURNALS –

Bauer, L., 'Tracing Phonetic Change in the Received Pronunciation of British English', *Journal of Phonetics*, no. 13, 1985.

Bechhofer, F., McCrone, D., Keily, R. and Stewart, R., 'Constructing National Identity: Arts and Landed Elites in Scotland', *Sociology*, vol. 33, no. 3, August 1999.

Boyle, P., 'Modelling Population Movement into the Scottish Highlands and Islands from the Remainder of Britain, 1990–1991', *Scottish Geographical Magazine*, vol. 111, no. 1, 1994.

Cant, B. and Kelly, E., 'Why Is There a Need for Racial Equality Activity in Scotland?', *Scottish Affairs*, no. 12, Summer 1995.

Colley, L., 'Britishness and Otherness: An Argument', *Journal of British Studies*, vol. 31, 1992.

Crick, B., 'Essay on Britishness', *Scottish Affairs*, no. 2, Winter 1993.

Cusick, L., 'Scottish Inferiority', *Scottish Affairs*, no. 9, autumn 1994.

Dickson, M. B., 'Should Auld Acquaintance Be Forgot? A Comparison of the Scots and English in Scotland', *Scottish Affairs*, no. 7, Spring 1994.

Firn, J., 'External Control and Regional Development: the Case of Scotland', *Environment and Planning* A, 7 (1975).

Forsythe, D. E., 'Urban Incomers and Rural Change: The Impact of Migrants from the City on Life in an Orkney Community', *Sociologia Ruralis*, 20, 1980.

Frith, S., 'On Not Being Scottish', *Critical Quarterly*, vol. 42, no. 4.

Gallagher, T., 'Protestant Extremism in Urban Scotland 1930–1939: Its Growth and Contraction', *The Scottish Historical Review*, vol. 64, 1985.

Hood, A. et al.,'Foreign Direct Investment in Scotland: The European Dimension', *Scottish Journal of Political Economy*, vol. 28, no. 2, 1981.

Jedrej, M. C. and Nuttall, M., 'Incomers and Locals: Metaphors and Reality in the Repopulation of Rural Scotland', *Scottish Affairs*, no. 10, Winter 1995.

Jones, H., Ford, N., Caird, J. and Berry, W., 'Counter-urbanization in Societal Context: Long-distance Migration to the Highlands and Islands of Scotland', *Professional Geographer*, vol. 36, no. 4.

Kelly, E., 'Racism, Police and Courts in Scotland', *Scottish Affairs*, no. 30, Winter 2000.

Lindsay, I., 'The Uses and Abuses of National Stereotypes', *Scottish Affairs*, no. 20, Summer 1997.

Lumb, R., 'A Community-based Approach to the Analysis of Migration in the Highlands', *Sociological Review*, vol. 28, no. 3, August 1980.

McCrone, D., 'Who Do We Think We Are?', *Scottish Affairs*, no. 6, Winter 1994.

McCrone, D., 'Opinion Polls in Scotland: July 1998–June 1999', *Scottish Affairs*, no. 28, Summer 1999.

Nairn, T., 'Tartan and Blue', *Marxism Today*, June 1988.

Short, D. and Stockdale, A., 'English Migrants in the Scottish Countryside: Opportunities for Rural Scotland?', *Scottish Geographical Journal*, vol. 115, no. 3, 1999.

Smout, T. C., 'Perspectives on the Scottish Identity', *Scottish Affairs*, no. 6, Winter 1994.

Stockdale, A., Findlay, A., Short, D., 'The Repopulation of Rural Scotland: Opportunity and Threat', *Journal of Rural Studies*, no. 16, 2000.

Thomson, A., Frisch, M. and Hamilton, P., 'The Memory and History Debates: Some International Perspectives', *Oral History*, Autumn 1994.

Thomson, A., 'Moving Stories: Oral History and Migration Studies', *Oral History*, Spring 1999.

— CONFERENCE PAPERS, LECTURES AND THESES —

Devine, T. M., 'Strangers in a Strange Land? Two Centuries of the Irish in Scotland', *Royal Society of Edinburgh Lecture*, (Dundee, 21/11/01).

Houston, R. A., 'The State of Scottish History', *Edinburgh International Book Festival*, (Edinburgh, 17/8/02).

Lackenbauer, H., *VIth European Conference of the International Federation of Red Cross and Red Crescent Societies*, (Berlin, 19/4/02).

Smith, A., 'Europe's "Invisible" Migrants', *Europe's 'Invisible Migrants': Consequences of the Colonists' 'Return'*, (New York, 9/4/99).

Watson, M., *The Invisible Diaspora: The English in Scotland 1945–2000*, unpublished Ph.D. thesis, (University of Dundee, 2003).

Williams, W., 'No Homecoming: The Repatriation of the Dutch from the Indies', *Europe's 'Invisible Migrants': Consequences of the Colonists' 'Return'*, (New York, 9/4/99).

Williams, W., 'The Invisible Dutch: A Reconstruction of Academic Involvement', *Europe's 'Invisible Migrants': Consequences of the Colonists' 'Return'*, (New York, 9/4/99).

Index

Aberdeen, 16, 42, 68, 112, 119, 130
Aberdeenshire, 52
Abergavenny, 75
Abernelty, 50
Africans, 86
Americans, 59, 170
Andrew, Rob, 149
Angus, 41, 157
Angus Council, 158
Annan, 140
Anstruther, 17, 110
Archer, Lord, 155
Argyll and Bute, 56
Arm nan Gaidheal, 13
Army for Freeing Scotland, 13
Arthur's Seat, 74
Asian community, 90
Asians, 1, 32, 81, 83, 91–2, 126, 129, 138
asylum seekers, 65
ATS, 48
Auchtermuchty, 134, 137
Austrians, 59
Ayr, 119, 174

Baker, Richard, 48
Balerno, 156
Banchory, 31, 42, 71, 170
Bannockburn, Battle, 1, 9, 150–3
Barnett formula, 166
Belgians, 59
Berwick-upon-Tweed, 180
Berwick, Roxburgh and Selkirk constabulary,
    66, 128
Beshara School, 75
Buccleuch Estate, 75
bigotry, 89–90
Blair, Tony, 114

Blairgowrie, 109, 168
Blunkett, David, 106
Bonnie Prince Charlie, 9
Bradford, 87
'branch plant economy', 14, 33
Braveheart, 159–60
Brechin, 156–7
Brent, 139
Brick Lane, 139
British Aluminium Co., 53
British European Airways, 52–3
British Lions, 175
Brixton, 107
Brown, Gordon, 174
Broxburn, 132
Butcher Cumberland, 121

Caddy, Eileen and Peter, 75
Caithness, 41
Calcutta Cup, 147–9
Cambridge, 12
Cambridgeshire, 79
Cameron, Sonja, 16; *see also* Vathjunker,
    Sonja
Campaign for Nuclear Disarmament, 116
Canvey Island, 67
Cardiff, 77–8
Cardiff Arms Park, 149
Caribbean, 85
Carling, Will, 148
Carlisle, 147, 180
Catalans, 170
Cawdor Church, 88
Celtic FC, 150, 158
Chertsey, 73
Cheviot, the Stag and the Black, Black Oil, The,
    7, 160

Chinese, 86, 99
Church of England, 87–8
Church of Latter-Day Saints, 87
Church of Scotland, 16, 76, 87–90, 112, 119, 173
Churchill, Winston, 114
Citizens' Advice Bureau, 117
Clackmannan, 42
Clan Chisholme, 75
Clause 28, 139
Claymore, oilfield, 68
clearances, 9, 15, 121
Clifford, Timothy, 155
Coatbridge, 53
Coigach, 20
Coldstream, 110
Commission for Racial Equality, 17–18, 130, 141
Common Riding, 104, 120
Commonwealth immigrants, 127
Confederation of British Industry, 1
Conservative election victory in 1992, 16
Conservatives, 88, 115, 180
Cornwall, 73
Corries, 114
counterurbanisation, 18–20, 29–30
cricket, 167
Culloden, Battle, 15, 153
Currie, 156
Currie Community Council, 156
Currie High School, 155–6
Czech government, 106

Danes, 59
Dawson Group, 104
Declaration of Arbroath, 132
Deeside, 66
democratic deficit, 116
Devizes, 109
Dingwall, 17
displaced persons, 47
Dixons, postcard manufacturer, 53
Douglas, Jill, 95
Dounreay, 58
Dounreay Atomic Energy plant, 56
Dublin, 141
Duffus, 56
Dundee, 42, 59, 98, 111–12, 137, 139, 157, 174
Dundee University, 112
Dunkeld, 107
Dutch, 59
Dutch colonists, 84

East European Jews, 1, 9, 65; see also Jews
Easter Ross, 39
Eastern Europe, 92
Eden Court Theatre, 114
Edinburgh, 9, 11, 30, 50, 53, 59, 66, 72, 74, 77, 79, 80, 91, 92, 109, 111, 119, 123–4, 131–2, 139, 142
Edinburgh University, 80
Edward I, King, 15, 121
11 September 2001, 166
Elgin, 119
Elizabeth I of Scotland, Queen, 121, 160
Elizabeth II, Queen, 121, 160
Empire, 166
'Englishing of Scotland', 171
Englishing of Scotland, The, 135
'Englishing' of Scottish universities, 80
Episcopalians, 57, 90
Errol, 141
Eskdalemuir, 76
Essex, 136, 155
Esso, 67
ethnie, 168
European Community, 166
European Union, 166
Euro-scepticism, 182
Eyemouth, 50, 55, 110

Fawley, 67
Fife, 40–1, 96
Findhorn, 74–5
Finnie, Ross, 1
Finns, 59
Firinn Albanach, 13
Five Nations championship, 148, 150
'Flame', 141
Flodden, 9
Flower of Scotland, 119, 149
Flying Piemen, ceilidh band, 120
Ford, 20
Forestry Commission, 170
Forfar, 50, 56
Fort William, 52
Foucauldian terms, 146, 164, 178
Foucault, Michel, 4, 62, 74, 80, 84, 113, 121, 187
French, 59, 170
Freuchie, 154
Freud, Sigmund, 48
Frosinone, 98

Gaelic, 56–7, 93, 105, 118
Gairloch, 46

Galashiels, 13
Galashiels Rotary Club, 117
Gallie, Phil, 160
Germans, 59
Gillette, 74
Glasgow, 9, 14, 59, 66, 79, 92, 132
Glassford, 46
God Save the Queen, 149
Gollanfield, 88
Gorbals, 90
Gorman, Theresa, 155
graffiti, 132
Grampian, 40
Greeks, 59
Green Belt, 73
Greenock, 11
grey settlers, 39
Grieve, Dominic, 115
Gruline, 73
Guide Association, 117
Guiding, 108

Hampden Park, 147, 149
Harrogate, 71
Hastings, Gavin, 148
Hawick, 10, 14, 49, 70, 92, 104, 108, 120
Headingley RFC, 136
Health Service, 158, 181–2
Heath, Ted, 114, 116
Henry VIII, King, 5
Heseltine, Michael, 160
Heysel disaster, 138
Hindu temples, 90
Holyrood Palace, 157
Holyrood Park, 74
Home Counties, 75, 95
homesickness, 113
House of Lords, 85
Houston, 14
Hungarians, 59

Ibrox, 138, 147
Icelanders, 59
ICI, 50
'illegal border crossers', 82
Inch Kenneth, 72
Indian settlers, 98
Indians, 38, 59, 86, 135
Indonesia, 84
Inner Hebrides, 73
International Labor Organization, 83
Inverness, 41, 49, 53, 110, 122, 141
Iona Community, 75

Iona, 72
Ireland, 89
Irish, 10, 19, 37, 59, 64–5, 70, 81, 83, 86,
    90–2, 99–100, 107, 126, 135, 138, 143, 175,
    182
Irish republicanism, 141
Islam, 87
Islamic mosques, 90
Isle of Wight, 53
Italians, 38, 59, 65, 90–1, 98
Italy, 92

Jedburgh, 58, 147
Jedburgh Grammar School, 96
Jehovah's Witnesses, 87
Jews, 59, 81, 83, 90; see also East European
    Jews

Kagyu Samye Ling, 75–6
Kilmonivaig, 52
Kincardine, 50, 52
Kincardineshire, 42
Kinlochbervie, 55
Kinloss, 31, 49
Kinross, 104
Kirkcaldy, 96
Knox, John, 119

Labour, 115, 138, 160, 180
Lanarkshire, 53
Lancashire, 96
Land Commission, 95
landgirls, 50
Latvian Club, 101
Lawson, Nigel, 153
Leeds, 136, 175
Leicestershire, 53, 107, 128
Leith, 142
Lewis Keep NATO Out group, 117
Lewis, 21, 71, 91, 107, 135
Liberal Democrat, 180
Liberal Party, 11–12
Lincolnshire, 174
Lithuania, 89
Lithuanian Club, 101
Lithuanians, 1, 9, 37, 65, 81, 83, 90–1,
    99
Liverpool, 66, 180
Livingston, 147
Loch na Keal, 72
Lochbroom, 59
Lockerbie, 54
London, 14, 72–3, 75, 77, 176, 179

Lowestoft, 50
Lucca, 98

McGauchin, Dick, 181
McIntyre, Robert, 180
McLaren, Bill, 148–50, 154, 188
MacLean, Dougie, 181
Macleod, George, 76
Maidenhead, 107
Marseille, 66
Mary Queen of Scots, 9
Menstrie, 53, 56
mentalité, 81, 113, 186
Mexico, 83
Middle East, 68
Milligan, Eric, 157
Mod, 105, 188
Monklands by-election, 158
Moray, 41
morris-dancing, 119
Mothers' Union, 88
Motherwell, 14
Muckairn, 57
Mull, 11, 29–30, 42, 67, 72–3, 132–4, 148
Mull Historical Society, 121
multinational enterprises, 14
Murrayfield, 119, 149

Nash, Ogden, 164
National Museum of Scotland, 117
National Trust for Scotland, 117
Neilston, 53
New Age, 75–6, 90
New Club, 101
New Mills Cloth Manufactory, 9
New Scots for Independence, 117, 154
New Zealand, 71, 106
Newbattle Abbey College, 67
Newcastle, 72, 74
Newcastle University, 70
Nigerians, 59
North Ayrshire, 19–20
North Berwick, 109, 179
North Sea oil, 20–1, 31, 41, 52
Northern Ireland, 175
Northumberland County Council, 181
North-West Ross, 108
Northwood, 72
Norwegians, 59
Notting Hill, 139
nuclear energy, 52
NUPE, 67, 158

'Oath of Renunciation and Allegiance', 105
Oban, 105
Occidental, 67–8
'Officers' Club', 42
'old enemy', 149
oral history, 3–4, 16, 62–3, 105, 124, 164, 186–7
Orange march, 89–90
Orkney, 17, 19, 40, 55–8, 68
Orrs Thread Mill, 53
Orwell, George, 7, 9, 21, 169
Osborne, Sandra, 160
Oxford, 12

padrone, 65, 91
Paisley, 11
Pakistanis, 59, 86, 135
Partridge Williams & Co., 53
patriotism, 169
peat-cutting, 107
Peebles 104, 110
Perth, 79, 109
Perthshire, 46
Peterhead, 71, 92
Petroleum Club, 68
'phonetic propriety' 92–3
Piper, oilfield, 68
Pleasant Sunday Afternoon choir, 117
Poles, 1, 59, 83, 86
Polish soldiers, 47
poll tax, 114, 150
Portsmouth, 122
Portuguese, 59
Prescott, John, 181
Press Complaints Commission, 156, 158
Prestonpans, 96
Pringle, knitwear company, 104
prisoners of war, 47
Probus, 109
Punjabi, 87

quangos, 94

Race Relations Act (1976), 85, 127–8, 136
Race Relations Board, 134
RAF, 31, 71, 77
Raigmore Hospital, Inverness, 122
Rangers FC, 66, 95, 119, 138, 147, 150, 156
Rattray, 169
Rauf, Bulent, 75
Red Clydeside, 9
Red Cross, 83
Robert the Bruce, 154

Rolls-Royce, 52–3
Roma, 106
Roman Catholic Church, 87
Ross and Cromarty, 41, 56
Royal Marines, 49
Royal Northern University Club, 117
Rugby Special, 95
Russian Maoist Party, 132

St Andrews, 140
St Andrews University, 77, 94, 126
St George's cross, 182
Salmond, Alex, 97, 154, 159
Sanday, 50, 58
Scenes from a Highland Life, 8
Scotland's oil, 153
Scottish Citizens' Army, 13
Scottish Episcopal Church, 87–8
Scottish Executive, 130
Scottish Football Association, 149
Scottish Gas Consumers' Council, 99
Scottish Journey, 107
Scottish Life, 66
Scottish National Liberation Army, 13, 141
Scottish Natural Heritage, 117
Scottish Parliament, 1, 12, 74, 138–9, 159, 167–8, 180
Scottish Republican Army, 13
Scottish Rugby Union, 149
Scottish Separatist Group, 132, 140–41
Scottish Trade Union Congress, 14
Scottish Watch, 11, 16–17, 33, 84, 132, 140, 159
Scottish Wild Land Group, 117
Scottish Women's Rural Institute, 109
Scourie, 107
sectarianism, 88–90, 121, 138, 150, 156
Settler Watch, 11, 16–17, 19, 33, 140, 159
7:84 Theatre Company, 7, 118
Shetland, 40–1, 55–6, 71, 93, 110, 131
Sillars, Jim, 146
Silver, Kenneth, 58, 96–7
Sinclair, Sir John, 45
Siol nan Gaidheal, 7, 9, 18, 21, 33, 36, 84, 132, 171
Six Nations championship, 148
Skye, 11, 29, 56
Small Isles, 56
SNP, 21, 94, 132, 153–5, 158, 166, 180
Somerset, 126
Souness, Graeme, 147
Souster, Mark, 95

South America, 68
Spaniards, 59, 170
spirituality, 75–6
Stanfield, Sir James, 9
Stirling Bridge, Battle, 154
Stobs Camp, 49
Stone of Destiny, 121, 160
Stormay (pseud.), 17, 57
Strachan, 170
Stranraer, 48
Strathclyde, 42–3
Struy, 170
Surbiton, 107
Surrey, 78
Sutherland, 72
Sutherland, Donald, 16
Swedes, 59
Swiss, 59
SWRI, 117

Tartan Army, 13, 154
Tayport, 130
Thatcher, Margaret, 13, 113–15, 150, 153, 172, 178, 180
Thurso, 56, 79
Tibet, 75
Tighnabruaich, 107
Tobermory, 48
Tokyo, 14
Tongue, 55, 58
Tootal-Broadhurst-Lee, 66
Tories, 115, 180
Tory, 12, 172
Town and Kirk Yetholm, 59
Trainspotting, 8
Treaty of Union, 1, 14–15
Trefoil Guild, 109
Troon, 97
Tunbridge Wells, 107

Ukrainians, 59
Ullapool, 107
Union Jack, 182
universities, 12, 80; *see also universities by name*
USA, 68, 83, 106, 166

Vathjunker, Sonja, 16; *see also* Cameron, Sonja

WAAF, 48
Wales, 96, 105, 175
Wallace, William, 154

Walters, Mark, 138
Watch groups, 132
Welsh, 175, 182
Wembley, 149, 152–4
West Kilbride, 50, 58
West Lothian, 41
West Riding, 92
Western Isles, 29, 40, 55

Westminster, 114–15, 171
Westminster Abbey, 121
'white settlers', 1, 11, 20, 29, 39, 41, 55–6
Wilkins, Ray, 147
Wilson, Brian, 56, 160
Worsthorne, Peregrine, 157

Yorkshire, 92, 137

Discover Your Scottish Ancestry

Internet and Traditional Resources

Graham S. Holton, Librarian at the University of Strathclyde and
Jack Winch, Senior Lecturer in Educational Computing at the
University of Strathclyde

June 2003   216pp   Paperback   0 7486 1864 3   £7.99

The perfect guide to tracing your Scottish ancestors. Combining the traditional methods of researching family history with new methods offered by information technology and the internet, this book is an essential resource.

Examples of family history research, lists of useful web sites and names and addresses of relevant offices, organisations and societies are provided. And a detailed bibliography is included for those who want to take their research further.

The most up-to-date book on the subject, *Discover Your Scottish Ancestry* is the ideal tool both for those starting out and for the more experienced family history researcher, whether living in Scotland or overseas.

- Find out how to build your family tree
- Use the power of the Internet in your research
- Understand the importance of traditional sources
- Explore the useful case studies
- Contact helpful organisations and societies
- Take your research further with the detailed bibliography
- Learn how to store and present your research using modern technology
- Ideal for the beginner or experienced family historian